"BLOOD IN THE WATER"

NAILBITER

VOLUME THREE

Story by
JOSHUA WILLIAMSON

Art by
MIKE HENDERSON
w/ADAM MARKIEWICZ, issue 12

Colors by
ADAM GUZOWSKI

Letters & Book Design by
JOHN J. HILL

Edited by
ROB LEVIN

NAILBITER Created by
**JOSHUA WILLIAMSON &
MIKE HENDERSON**

NAILBITER
VOL. 3: BLOOD IN THE WATER.
First printing. SEPTEMBER 2015. Copyright ©
2015 Joshua Williamson and Mike Henderson.
All rights reserved. Published by Image Comics,
Inc. Office of publication: 2001 Center Street, Sixth
Floor, Berkeley, CA 94704. Originally published
in single magazine form as NAILBITER #11-15,
by Image Comics. "Nailbiter," its logos, and the
likenesses of all characters herein are trademarks
of Joshua Williamson and Mike Henderson,
unless otherwise noted. "Image" and the Image
Comics logos are registered trademarks of Image
Comics, Inc. No part of this publication may be
reproduced or transmitted, in any form or by any
means (except for short excerpts for journalistic
or review purposes), without the express written
permission of Joshua Williamson, Mike Henderson
or Image Comics, Inc. All names, characters,
events, and locales in this publication are entirely
fictional. Any resemblance to actual persons
(living or dead), events, or places, without satiric
intent, is coincidental. Printed in the USA. For
information regarding the CPSIA on this printed
material call: 203-595-3636 and provide reference
#RICH–633516. For international rights, contact:
foreignlicensing@imagecomics.com.
ISBN: 978-1-63215-485-9

ISSUE ELEVEN

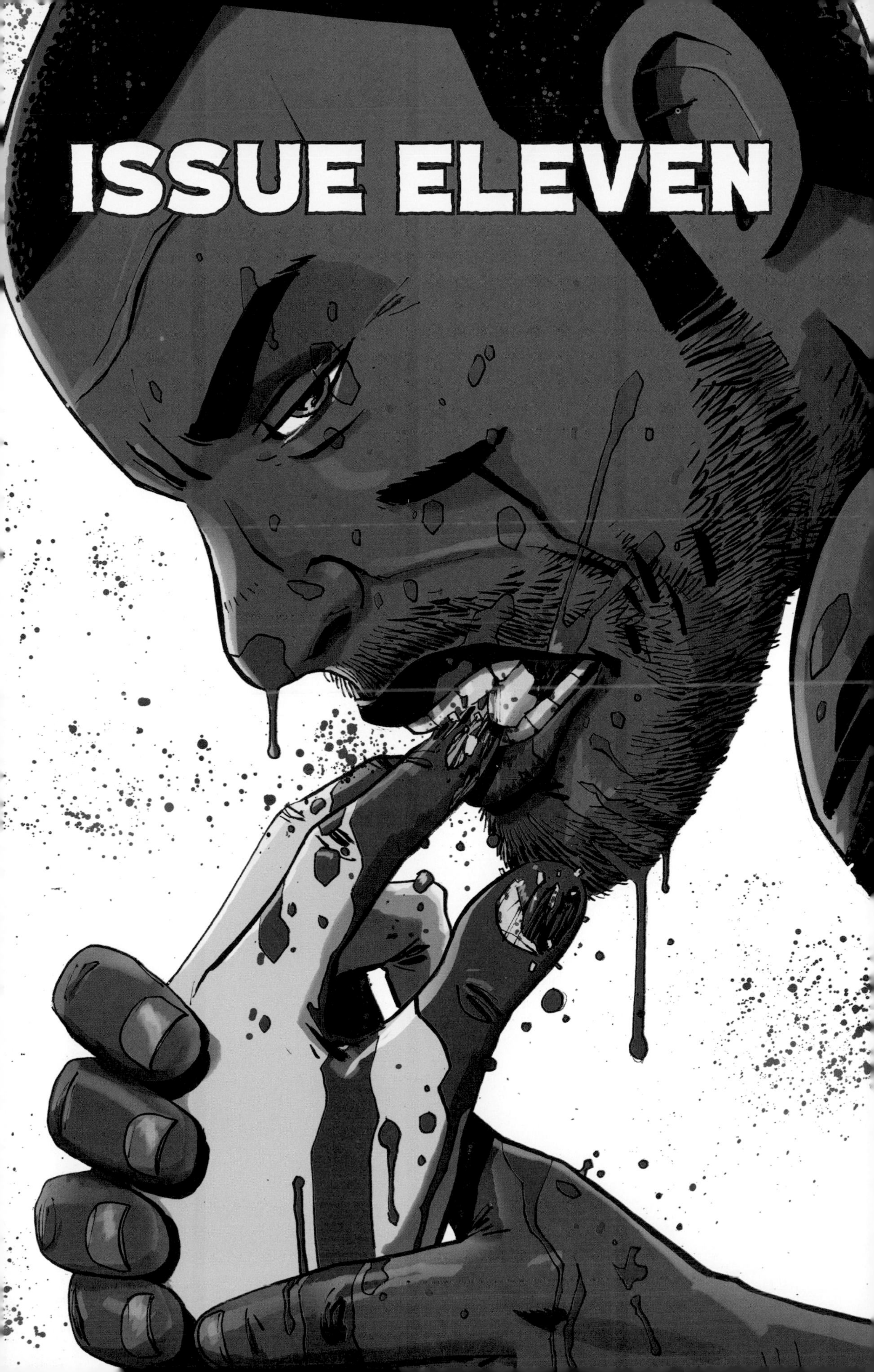

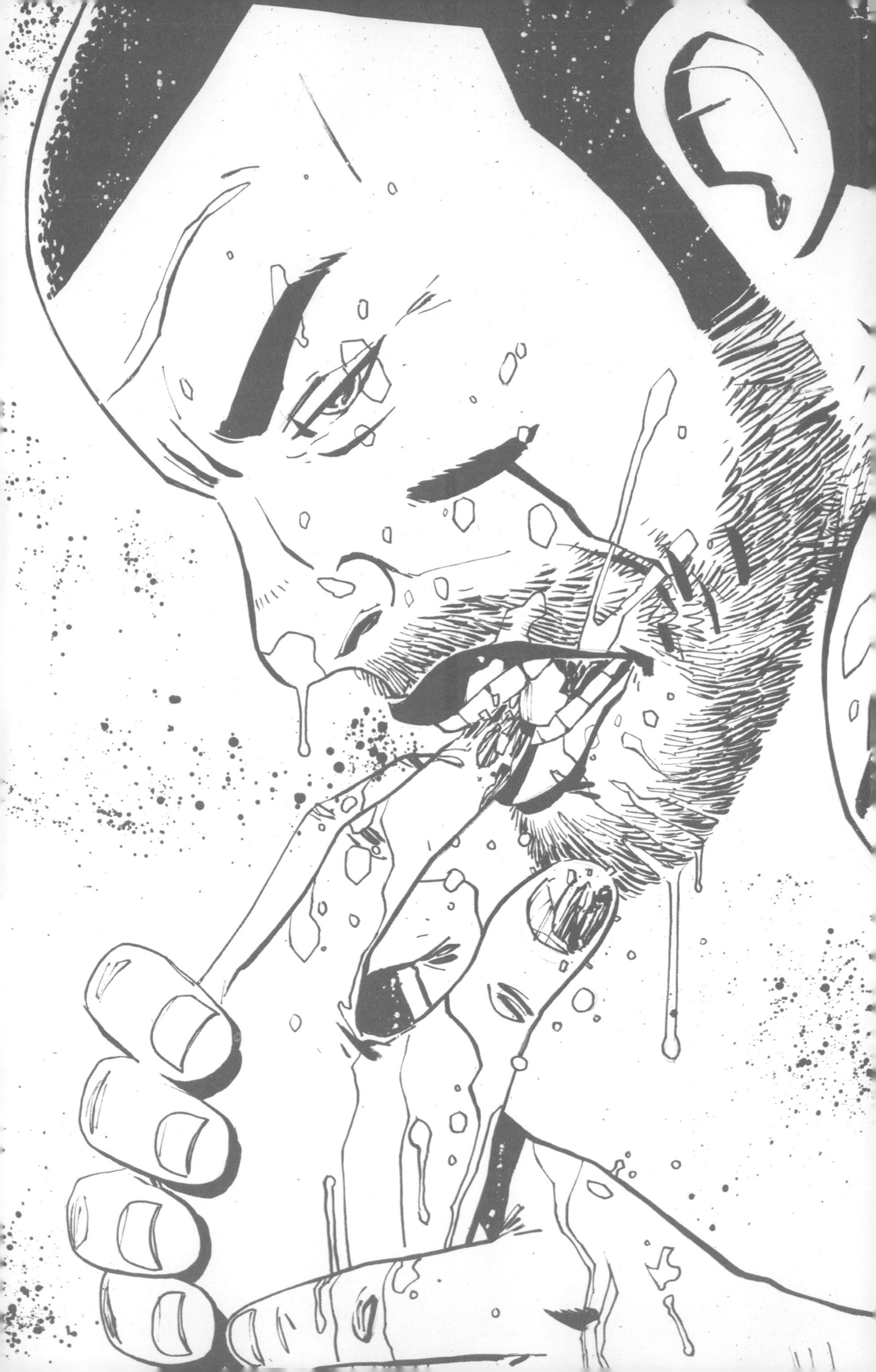

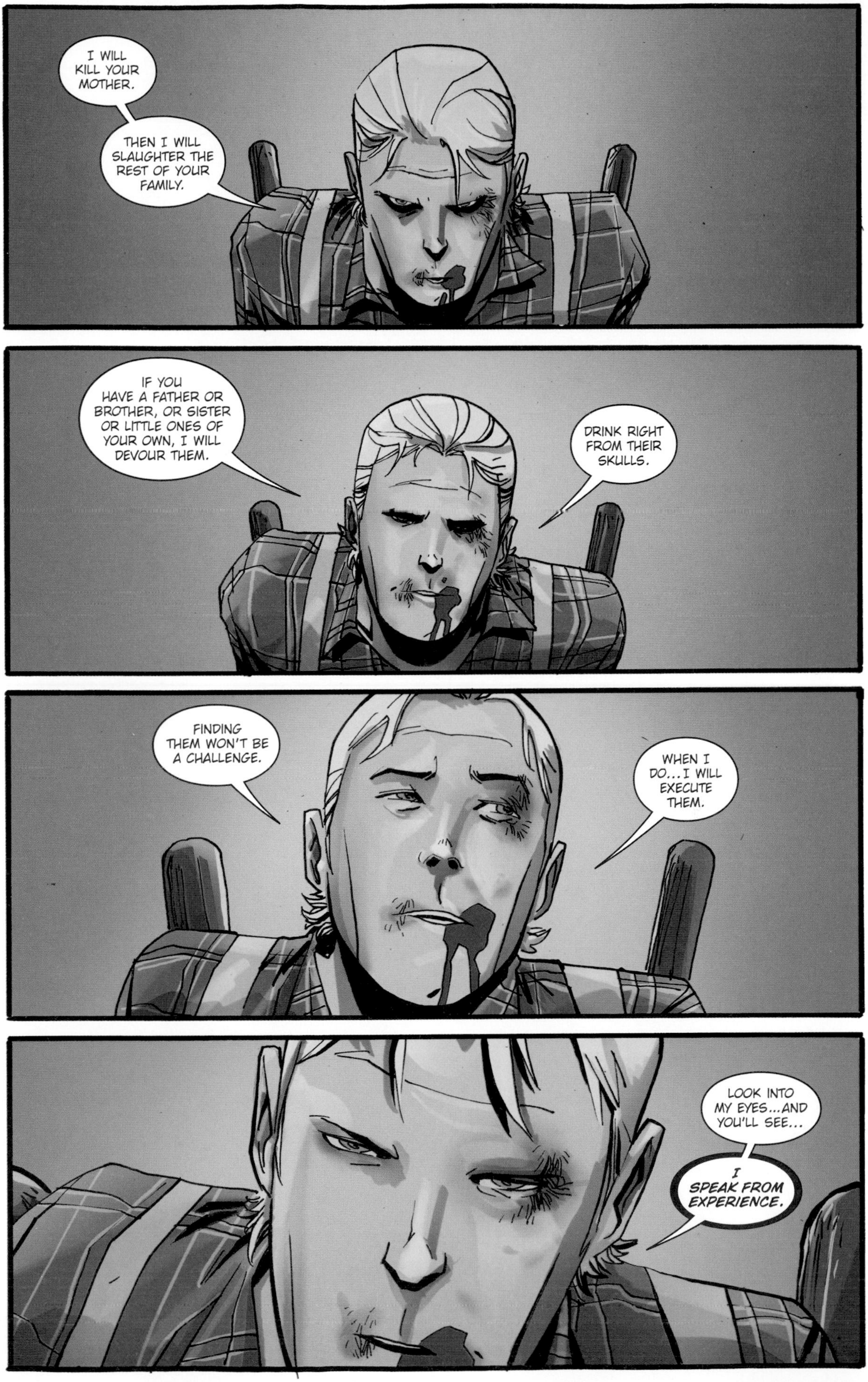
I WILL KILL YOUR MOTHER.
THEN I WILL SLAUGHTER THE REST OF YOUR FAMILY.
IF YOU HAVE A FATHER OR BROTHER, OR SISTER OR LITTLE ONES OF YOUR OWN, I WILL DEVOUR THEM.
DRINK RIGHT FROM THEIR SKULLS.
FINDING THEM WON'T BE A CHALLENGE.
WHEN I DO...I WILL EXECUTE THEM.
LOOK INTO MY EYES...AND YOU'LL SEE...
I SPEAK FROM EXPERIENCE.

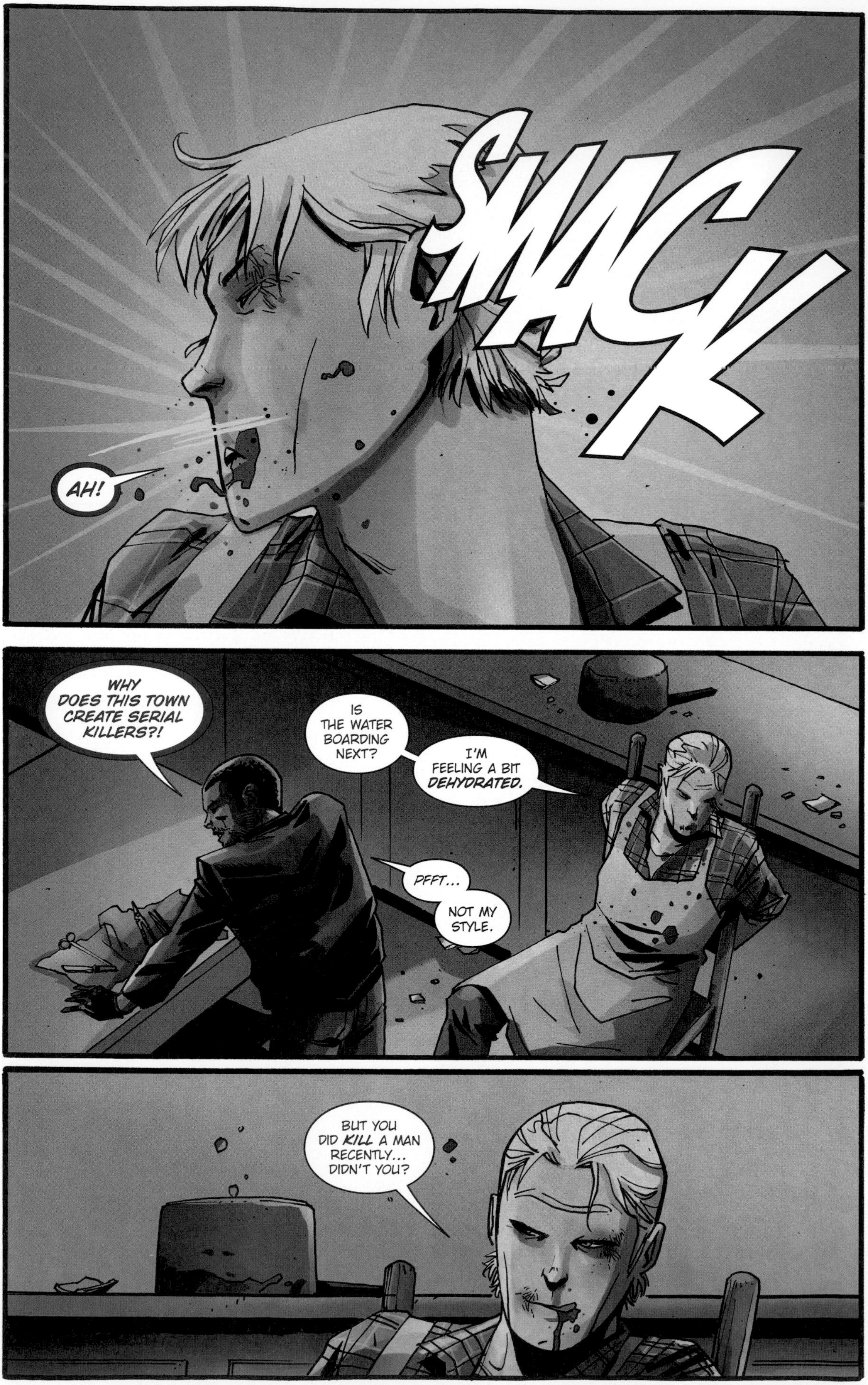
SMACK
AH!
WHY DOES THIS TOWN CREATE SERIAL KILLERS?!
IS THE WATER BOARDING NEXT?
I'M FEELING A BIT DEHYDRATED.
PFFT...
NOT MY STYLE.
BUT YOU DID KILL A MAN RECENTLY... DIDN'T YOU?

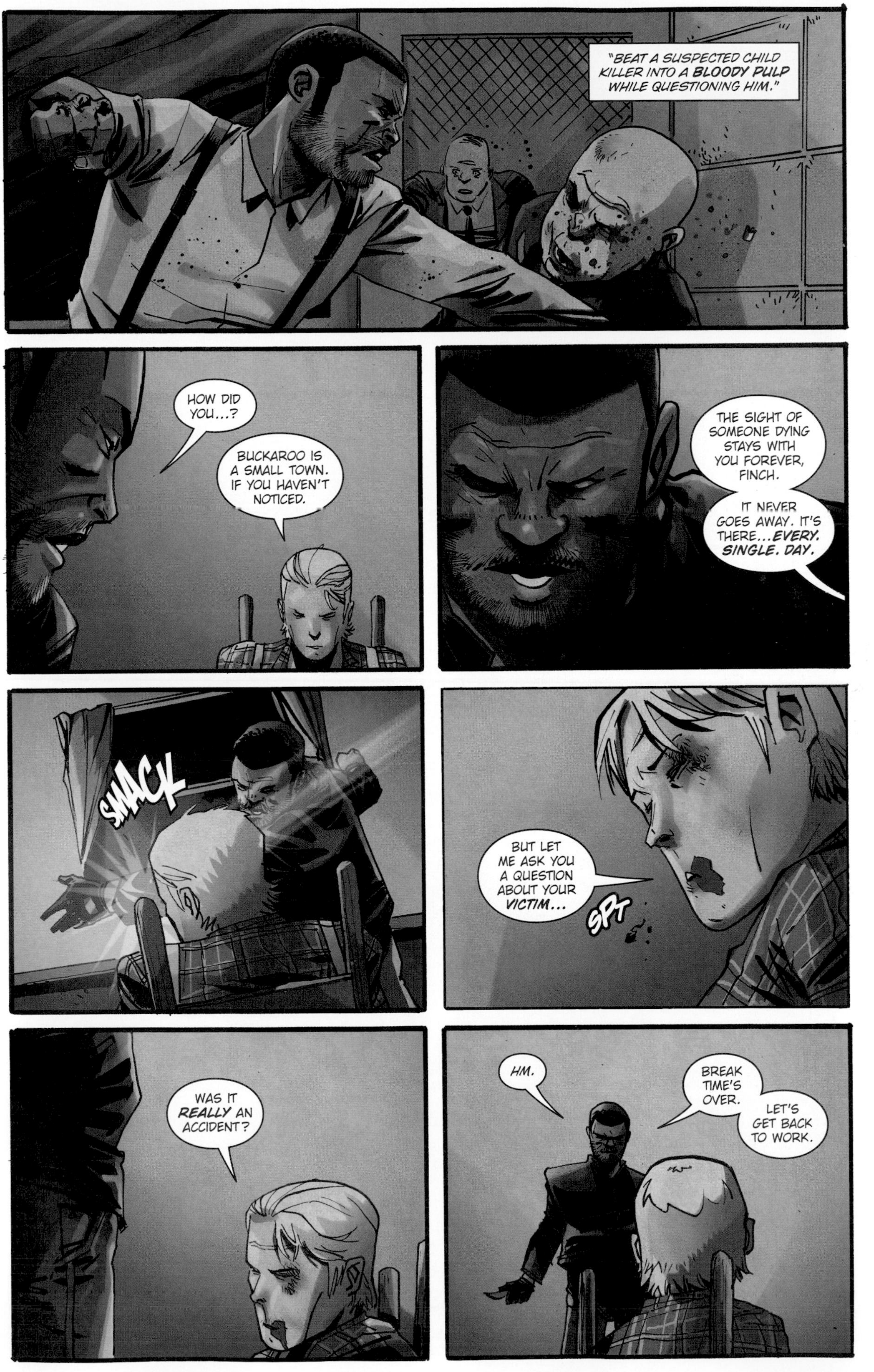
"BEAT A SUSPECTED CHILD KILLER INTO A BLOODY PULP WHILE QUESTIONING HIM."
HOW DID YOU...?
BUCKAROO IS A SMALL TOWN. IF YOU HAVEN'T NOTICED.
THE SIGHT OF SOMEONE DYING STAYS WITH YOU FOREVER, FINCH.
IT NEVER GOES AWAY. IT'S THERE...EVERY. SINGLE. DAY.
SMACK
BUT LET ME ASK YOU A QUESTION ABOUT YOUR VICTIM...
SPT
WAS IT REALLY AN ACCIDENT?
HM.
BREAK TIME'S OVER.
LET'S GET BACK TO WORK.

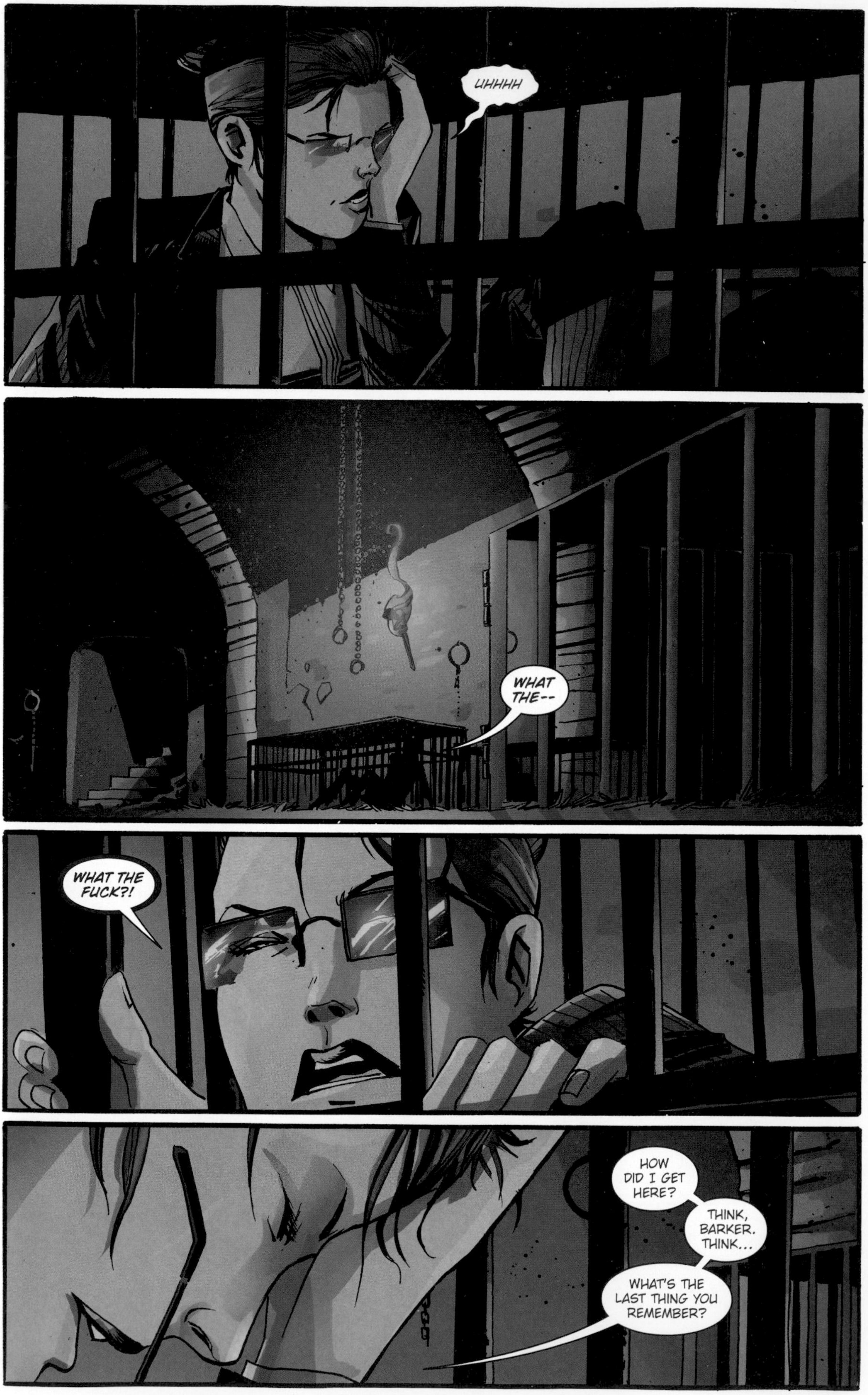
UHHHH
WHAT THE--
WHAT THE FUCK?!
HOW DID I GET HERE?
THINK, BARKER. THINK...
WHAT'S THE LAST THING YOU REMEMBER?

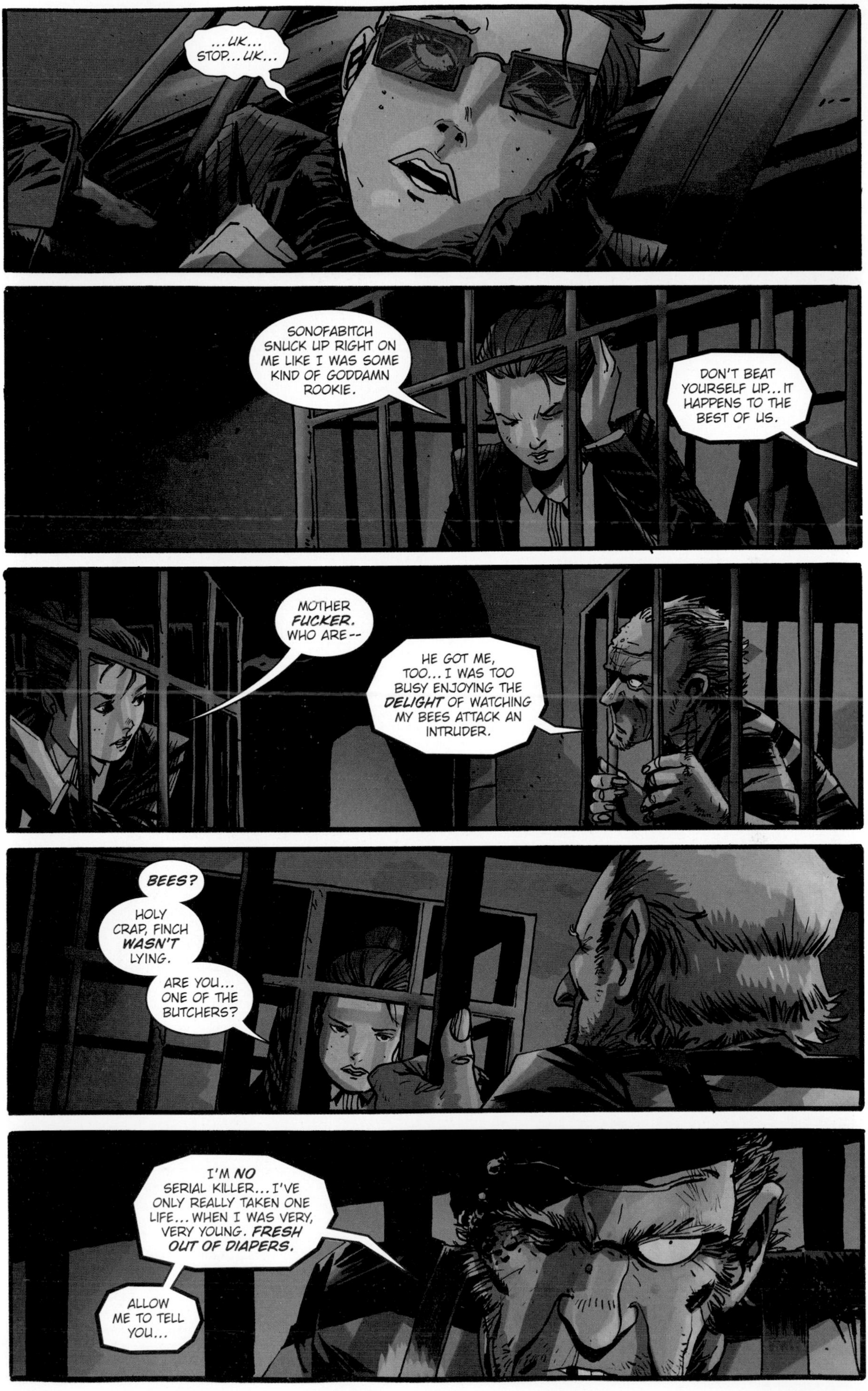
...UK... STOP...UK...
SONOFABITCH SNUCK UP RIGHT ON ME LIKE I WAS SOME KIND OF GODDAMN ROOKIE.
DON'T BEAT YOURSELF UP...IT HAPPENS TO THE BEST OF US.
MOTHER **FUCKER.** WHO ARE--
HE GOT ME, TOO...I WAS TOO BUSY ENJOYING THE **DELIGHT** OF WATCHING MY BEES ATTACK AN INTRUDER.
BEES?
HOLY CRAP, FINCH **WASN'T** LYING.
ARE YOU... ONE OF THE BUTCHERS?
I'M **NO** SERIAL KILLER...I'VE ONLY REALLY TAKEN ONE LIFE...WHEN I WAS VERY, VERY YOUNG. **FRESH OUT OF DIAPERS.**
ALLOW ME TO TELL YOU...

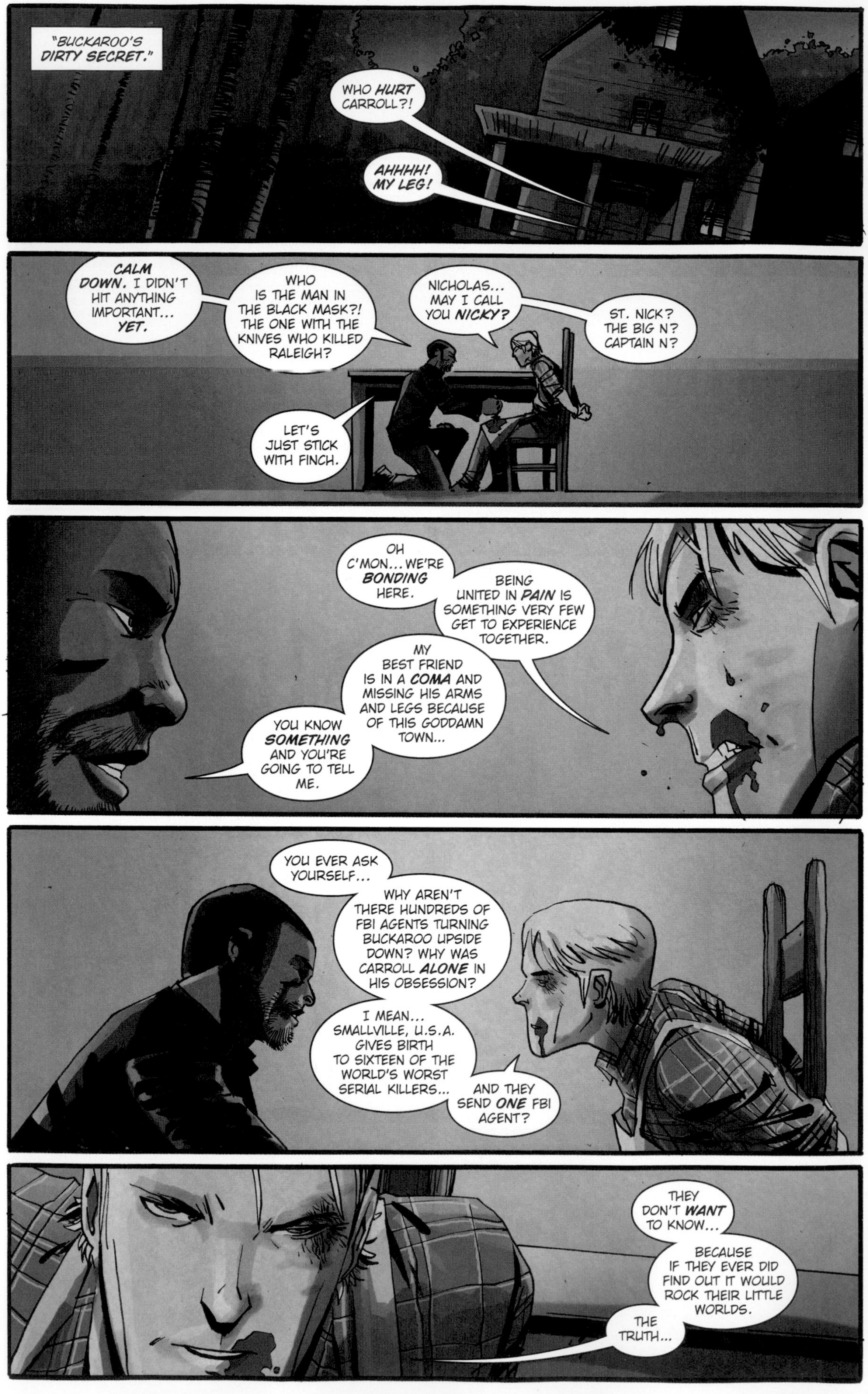
"BUCKAROO'S DIRTY SECRET."
WHO HURT CARROLL?!
AHHHH! MY LEG!
CALM DOWN. I DIDN'T HIT ANYTHING IMPORTANT... YET.
WHO IS THE MAN IN THE BLACK MASK?! THE ONE WITH THE KNIVES WHO KILLED RALEIGH?
NICHOLAS... MAY I CALL YOU NICKY?
ST. NICK? THE BIG N? CAPTAIN N?
LET'S JUST STICK WITH FINCH.
OH C'MON... WE'RE BONDING HERE.
BEING UNITED IN PAIN IS SOMETHING VERY FEW GET TO EXPERIENCE TOGETHER.
MY BEST FRIEND IS IN A COMA AND MISSING HIS ARMS AND LEGS BECAUSE OF THIS GODDAMN TOWN...
YOU KNOW SOMETHING AND YOU'RE GOING TO TELL ME.
YOU EVER ASK YOURSELF...
WHY AREN'T THERE HUNDREDS OF FBI AGENTS TURNING BUCKAROO UPSIDE DOWN? WHY WAS CARROLL ALONE IN HIS OBSESSION?
I MEAN... SMALLVILLE, U.S.A. GIVES BIRTH TO SIXTEEN OF THE WORLD'S WORST SERIAL KILLERS...
AND THEY SEND ONE FBI AGENT?
THEY DON'T WANT TO KNOW...
BECAUSE IF THEY EVER DID FIND OUT IT WOULD ROCK THEIR LITTLE WORLDS.
THE TRUTH...

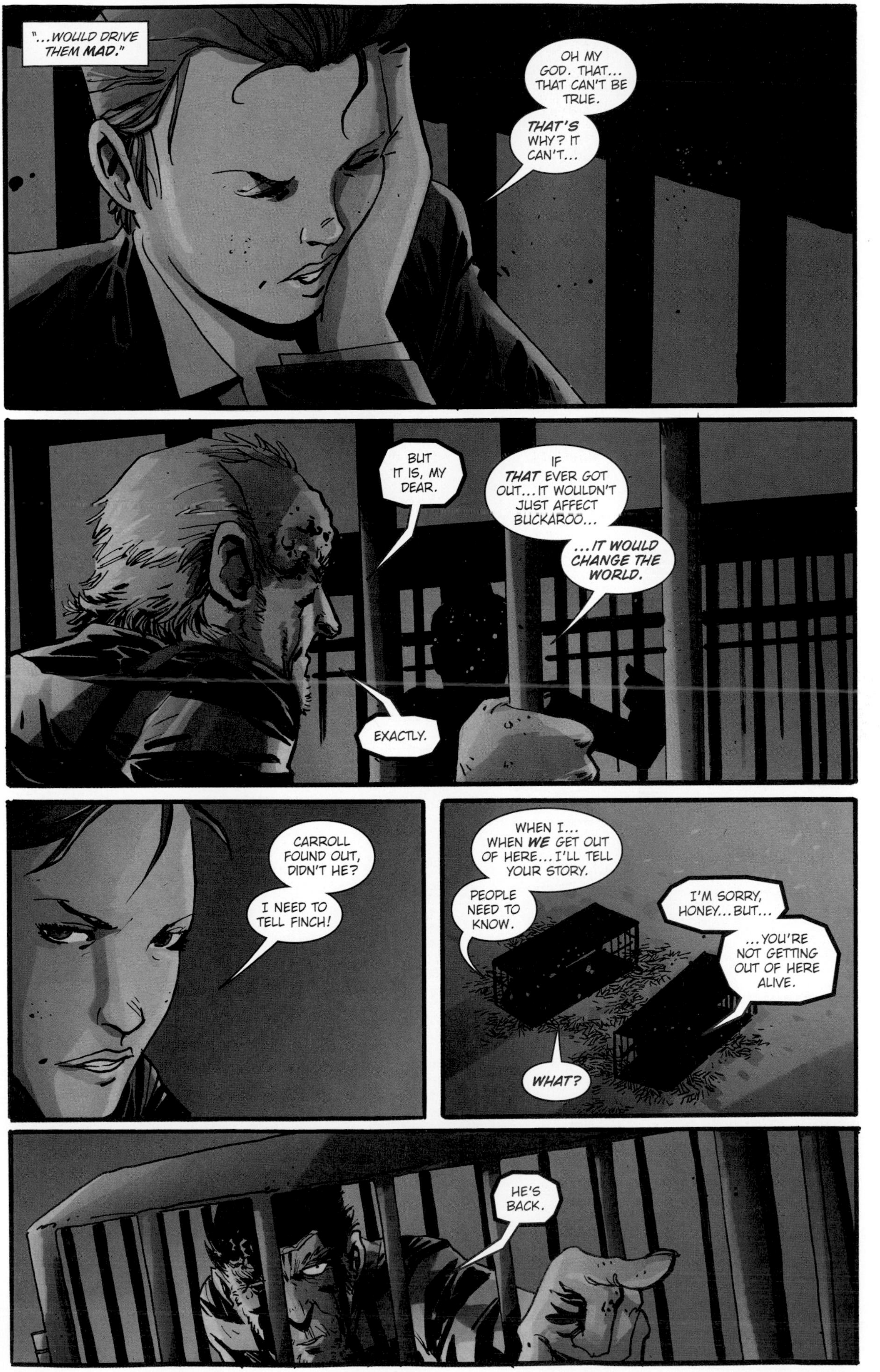
"...WOULD DRIVE THEM MAD."
OH MY GOD. THAT... THAT CAN'T BE TRUE.
THAT'S WHY? IT CAN'T...
BUT IT IS, MY DEAR.
IF THAT EVER GOT OUT... IT WOULDN'T JUST AFFECT BUCKAROO...
...IT WOULD CHANGE THE WORLD.
EXACTLY.
CARROLL FOUND OUT, DIDN'T HE?
I NEED TO TELL FINCH!
WHEN I... WHEN WE GET OUT OF HERE... I'LL TELL YOUR STORY.
PEOPLE NEED TO KNOW.
I'M SORRY, HONEY... BUT...
...YOU'RE NOT GETTING OUT OF HERE ALIVE.
WHAT?
HE'S BACK.

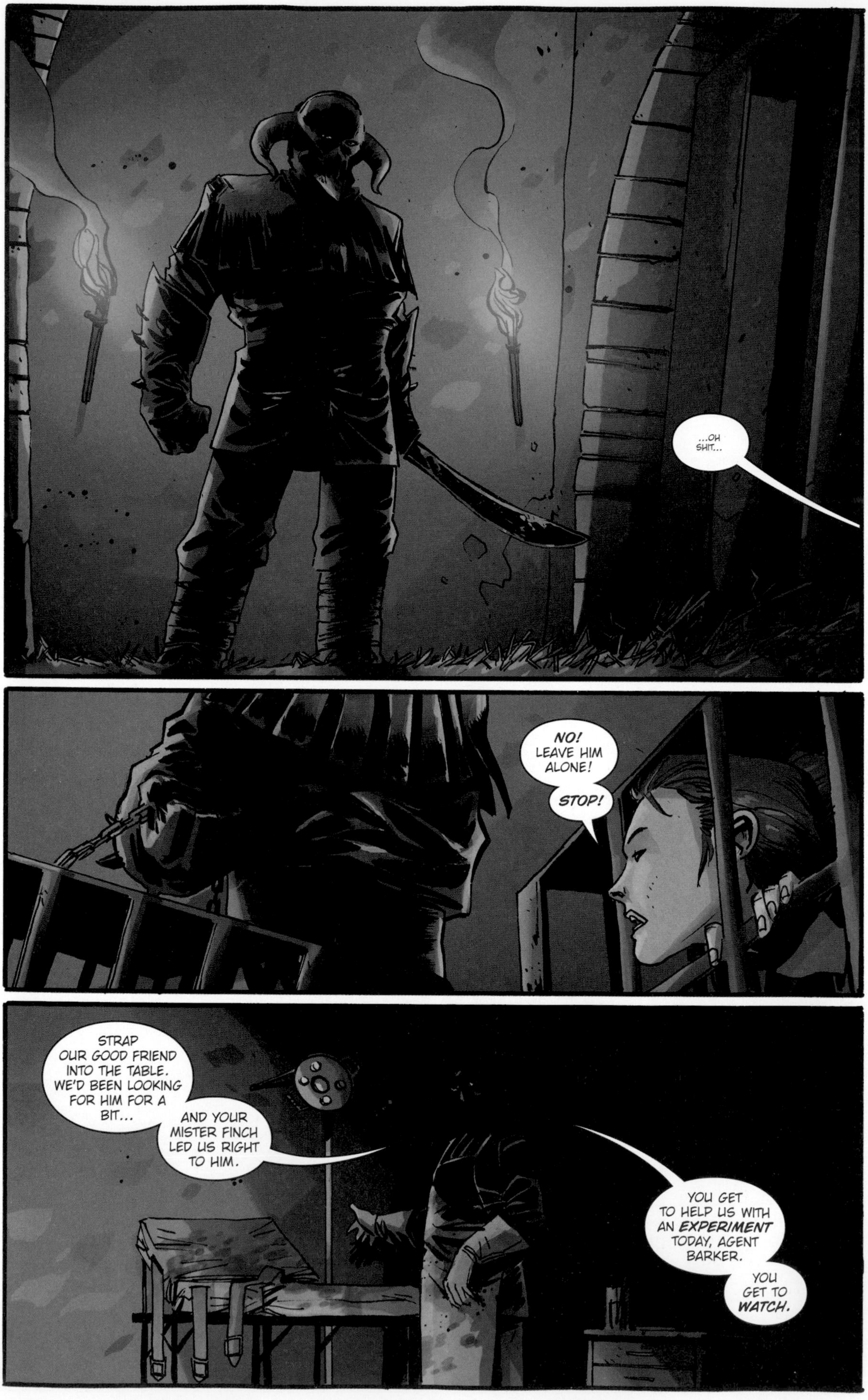
...OH SHIT...
NO! LEAVE HIM ALONE!
STOP!
STRAP OUR GOOD FRIEND INTO THE TABLE. WE'D BEEN LOOKING FOR HIM FOR A BIT...
AND YOUR MISTER FINCH LED US RIGHT TO HIM.
YOU GET TO HELP US WITH AN EXPERIMENT TODAY, AGENT BARKER.
YOU GET TO WATCH.

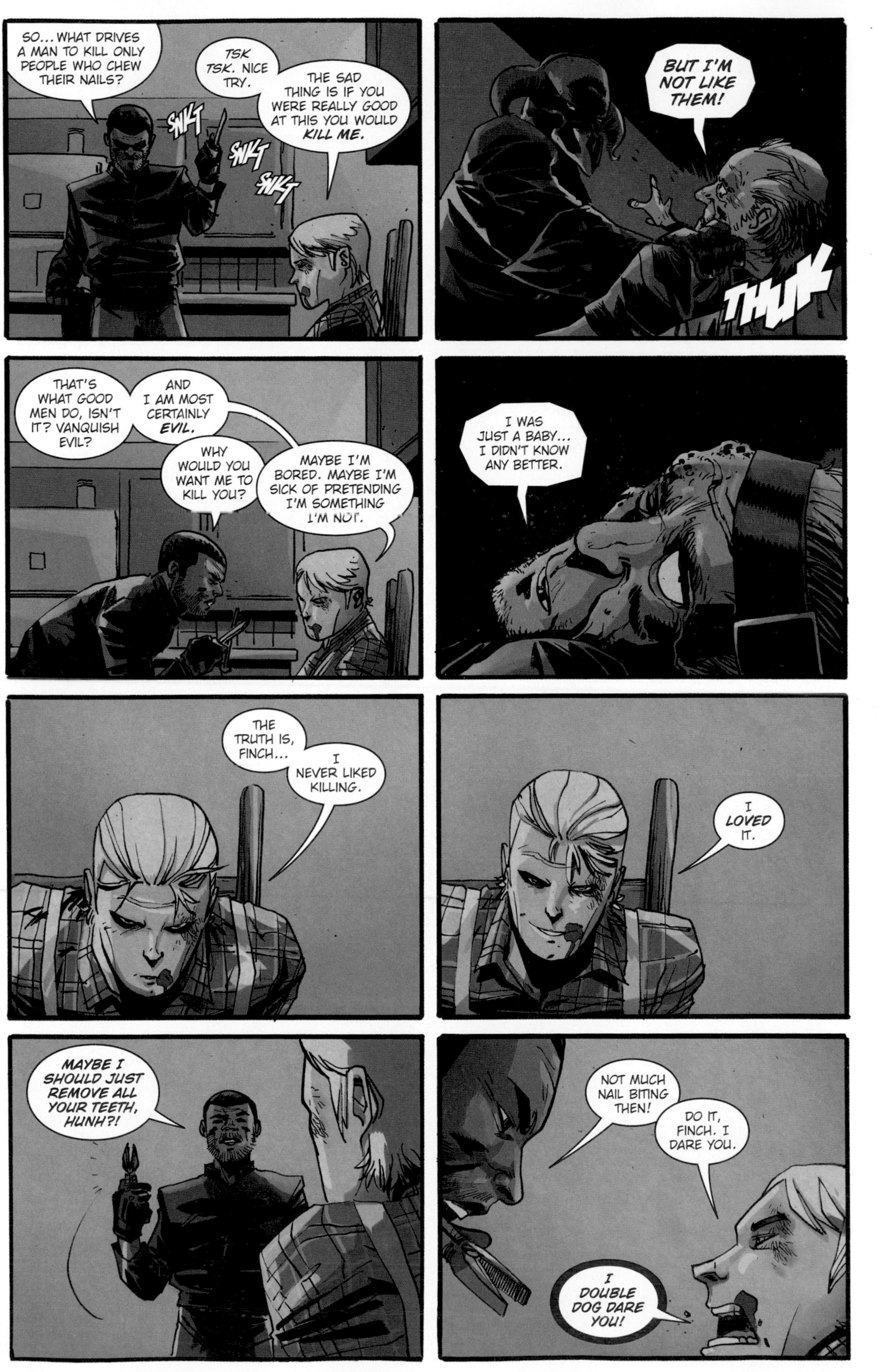
SO... WHAT DRIVES A MAN TO KILL ONLY PEOPLE WHO CHEW THEIR NAILS?
SNKT
SNKT
SNKT
TSK TSK. NICE TRY.
THE SAD THING IS IF YOU WERE REALLY GOOD AT THIS YOU WOULD KILL ME.
BUT I'M NOT LIKE THEM!
THUNK
THAT'S WHAT GOOD MEN DO, ISN'T IT? VANQUISH EVIL?
AND I AM MOST CERTAINLY EVIL.
WHY WOULD YOU WANT ME TO KILL YOU?
MAYBE I'M BORED. MAYBE I'M SICK OF PRETENDING I'M SOMETHING I'M NOT.
I WAS JUST A BABY... I DIDN'T KNOW ANY BETTER.
THE TRUTH IS, FINCH...
I NEVER LIKED KILLING.
I LOVED IT.
MAYBE I SHOULD JUST REMOVE ALL YOUR TEETH, HUNH?!
NOT MUCH NAIL BITING THEN!
DO IT, FINCH. I DARE YOU.
I DOUBLE DOG DARE YOU!

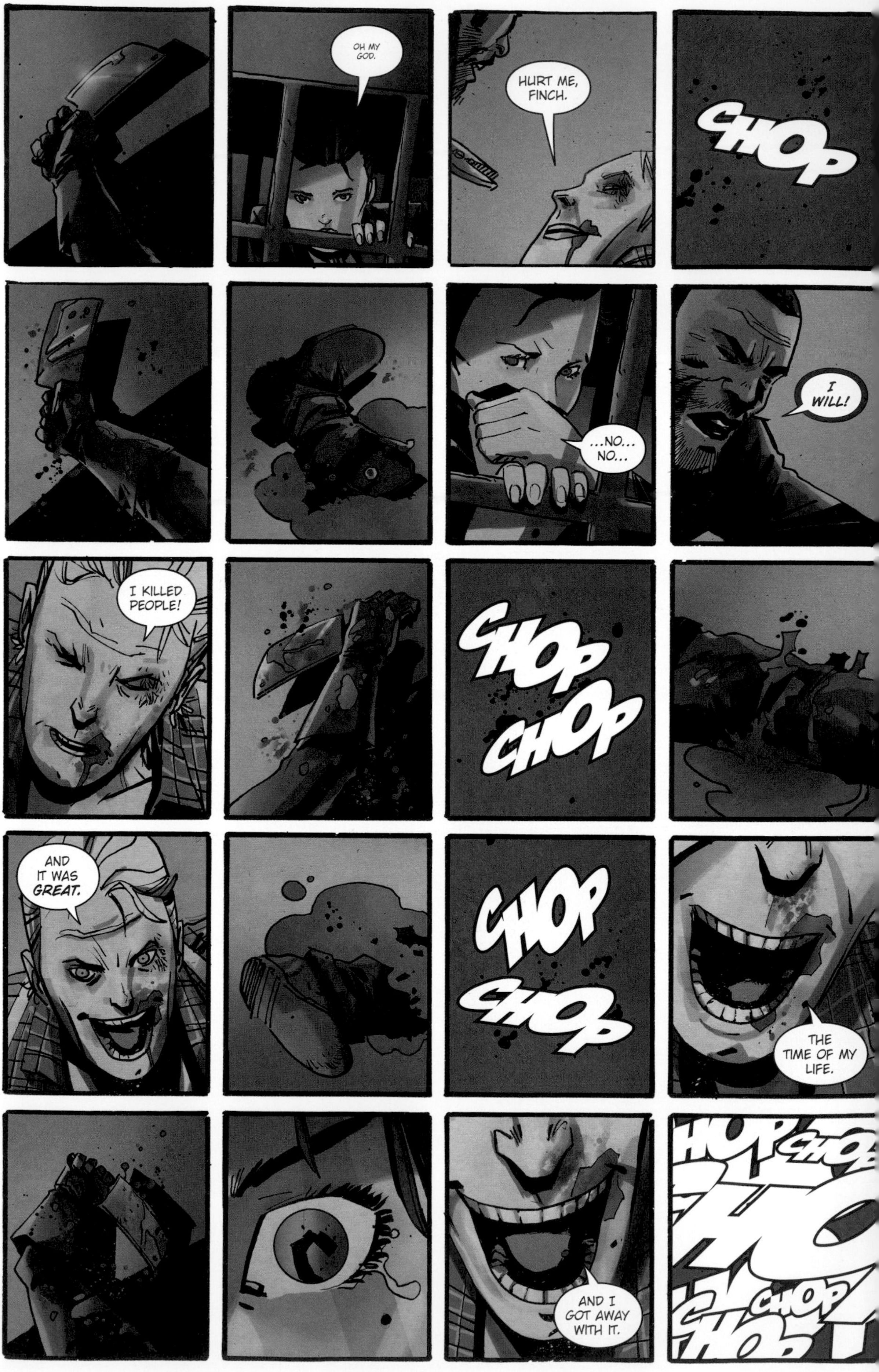
OH MY GOD.
HURT ME, FINCH.
CHOP
...NO... NO...
I WILL!
I KILLED PEOPLE!
CHOP CHOP
AND IT WAS GREAT.
CHOP CHOP
THE TIME OF MY LIFE.
AND I GOT AWAY WITH IT.
CHOP

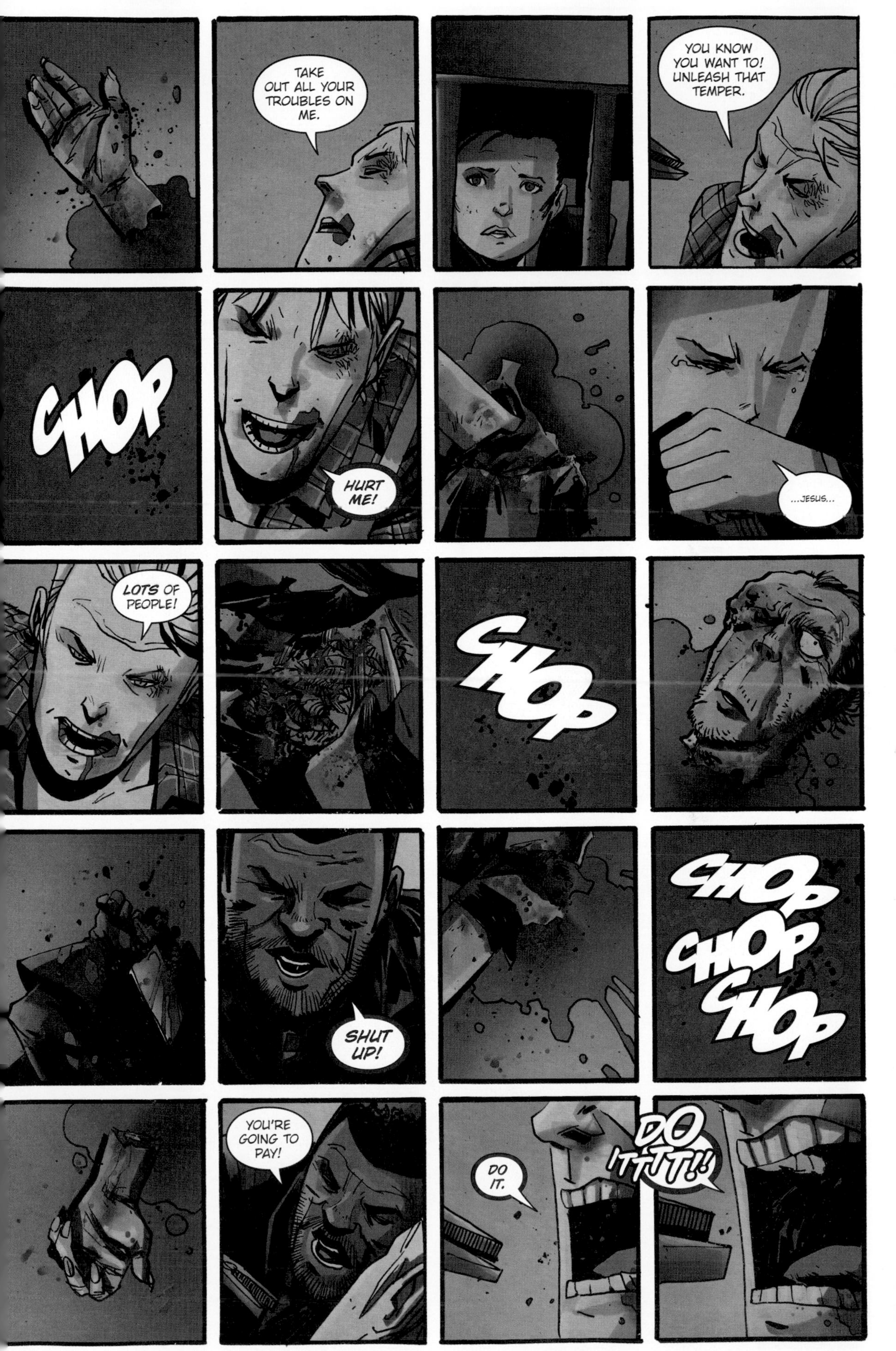
TAKE OUT ALL YOUR TROUBLES ON ME.
YOU KNOW YOU WANT TO! UNLEASH THAT TEMPER.
CHOP
HURT ME!
...JESUS...
LOTS OF PEOPLE!
CHOP
SHUT UP!
CHOP CHOP CHOP
YOU'RE GOING TO PAY!
DO IT.
DO ITTTTT!!

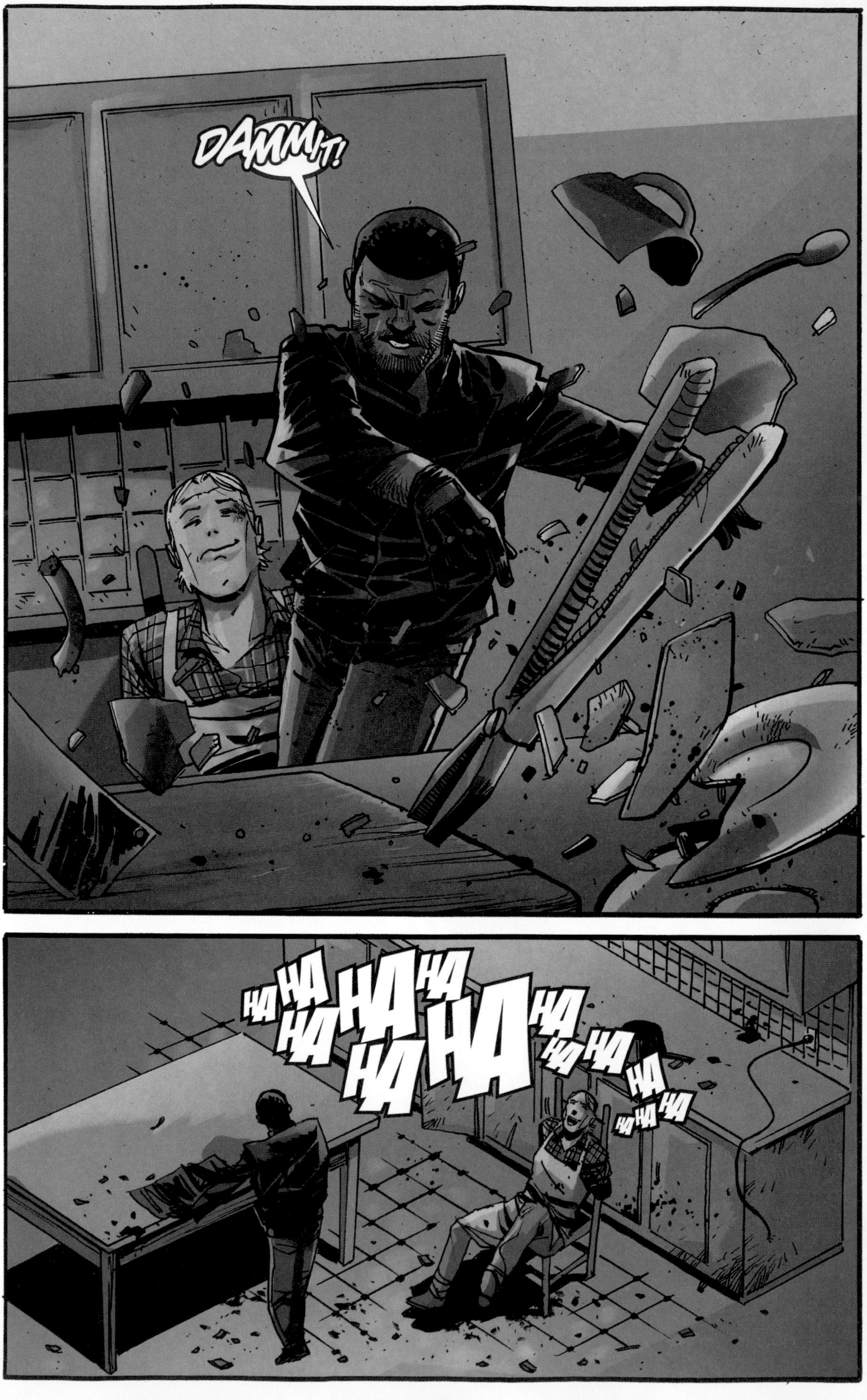
DAMMIT!
HA HA HA HA HA HA HA HA HA HA HA HA HA HA HA HA

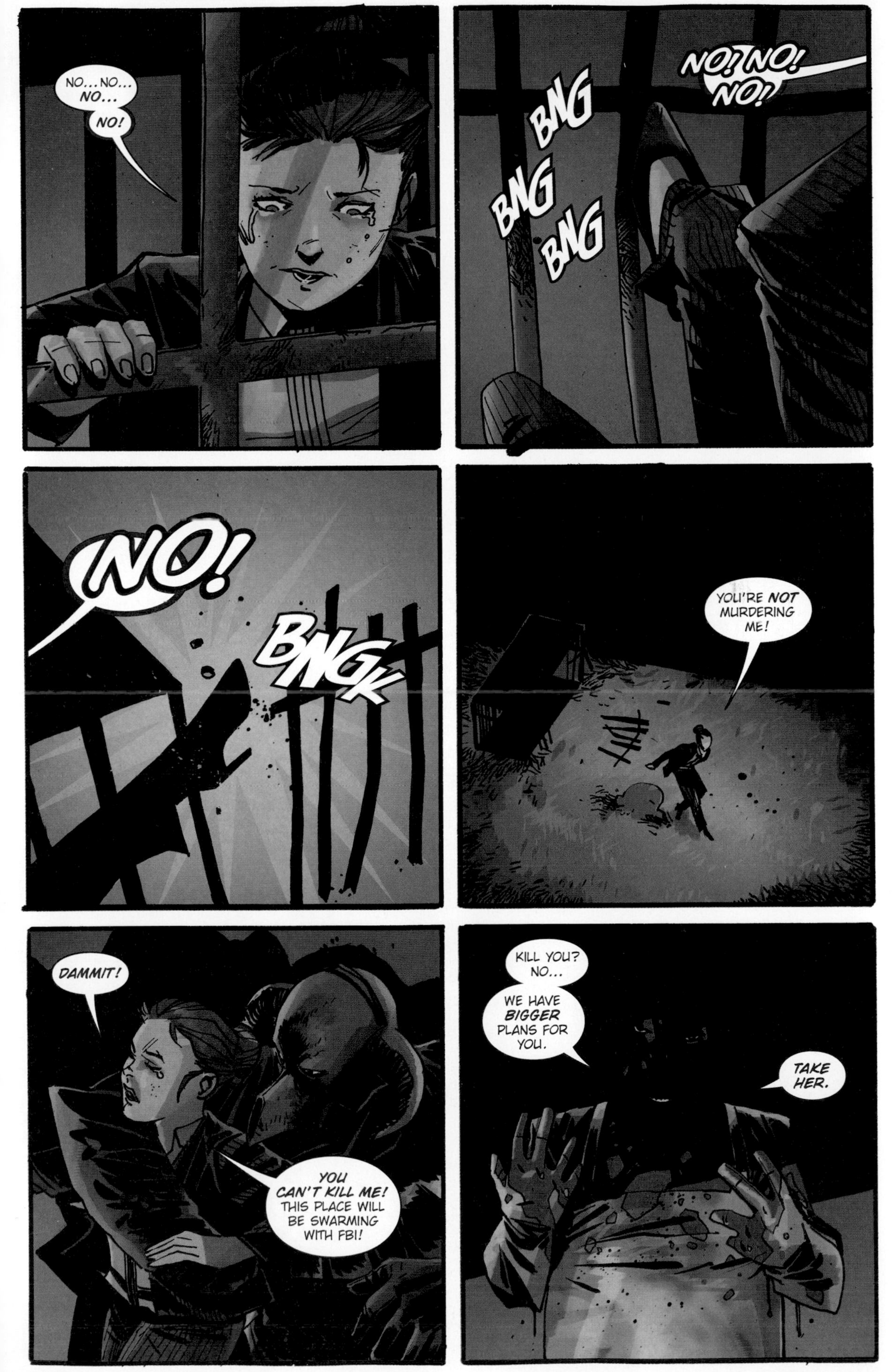
NO... NO...
NO...
NO!
BNG
BNG
BNG
NO! NO!
NO!
NO!
BNGK
YOU'RE NOT MURDERING ME!
DAMMIT!
YOU CAN'T KILL ME! THIS PLACE WILL BE SWARMING WITH FBI!
KILL YOU? NO...
WE HAVE BIGGER PLANS FOR YOU.
TAKE HER.

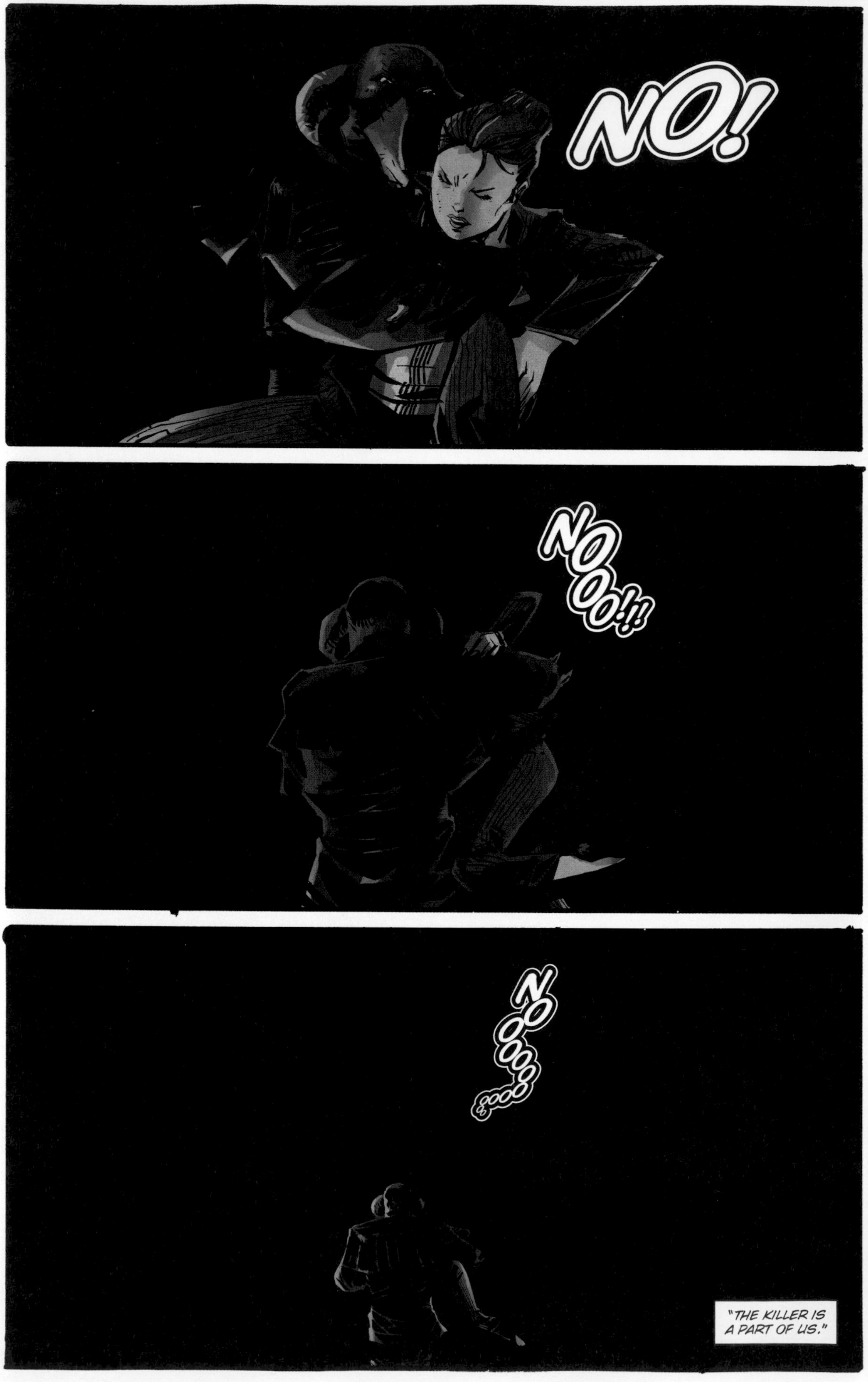
NO!
NOOO!!
NOOOOOOOOO...
"THE KILLER IS A PART OF US."

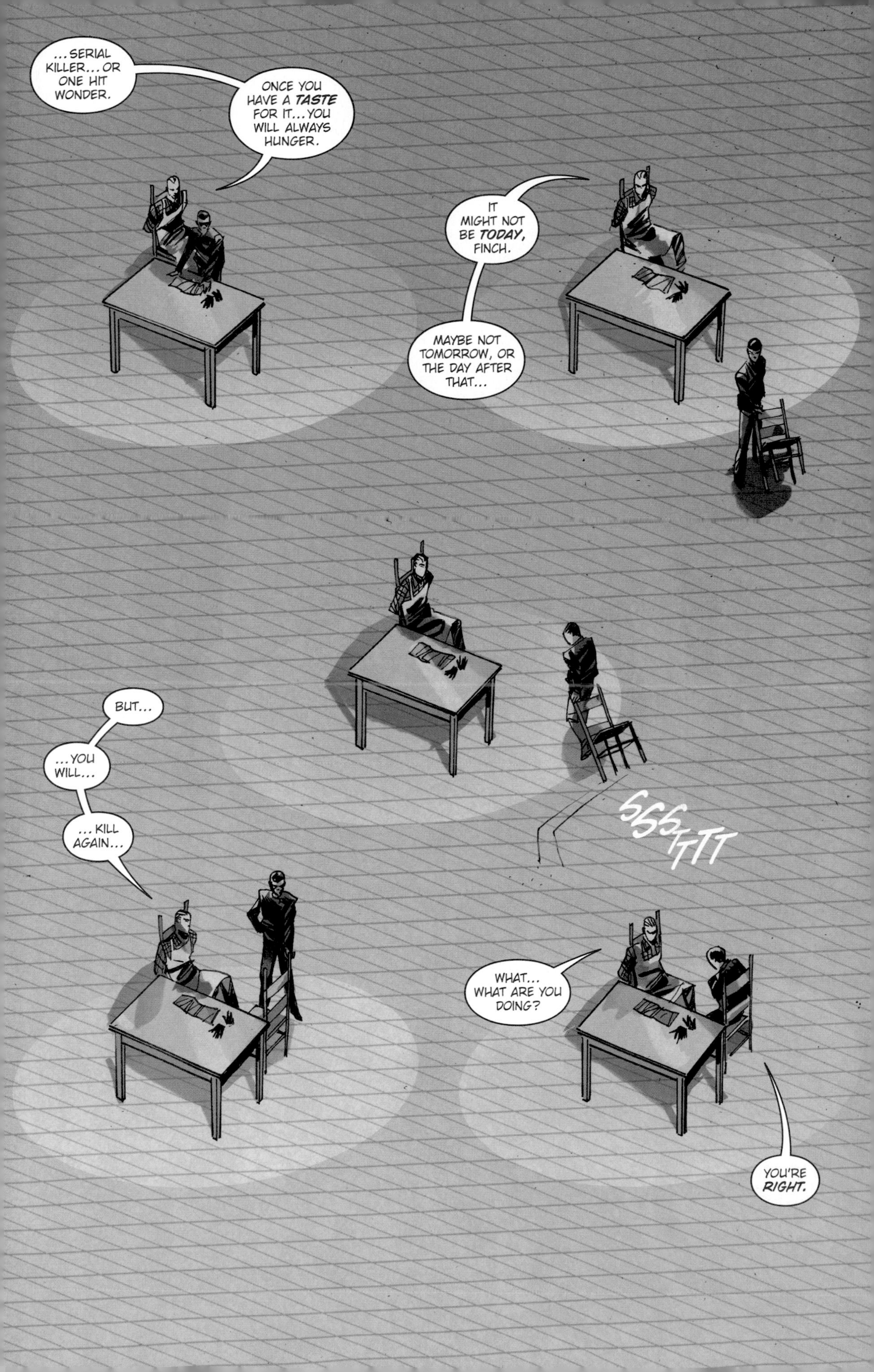
...SERIAL KILLER...OR ONE HIT WONDER.
ONCE YOU HAVE A *TASTE* FOR IT...YOU WILL ALWAYS HUNGER.
IT MIGHT NOT BE *TODAY,* FINCH.
MAYBE NOT TOMORROW, OR THE DAY AFTER THAT...
SSSTTTT
BUT...
...YOU WILL...
...KILL AGAIN...
WHAT... WHAT ARE YOU DOING?
YOU'RE *RIGHT.*

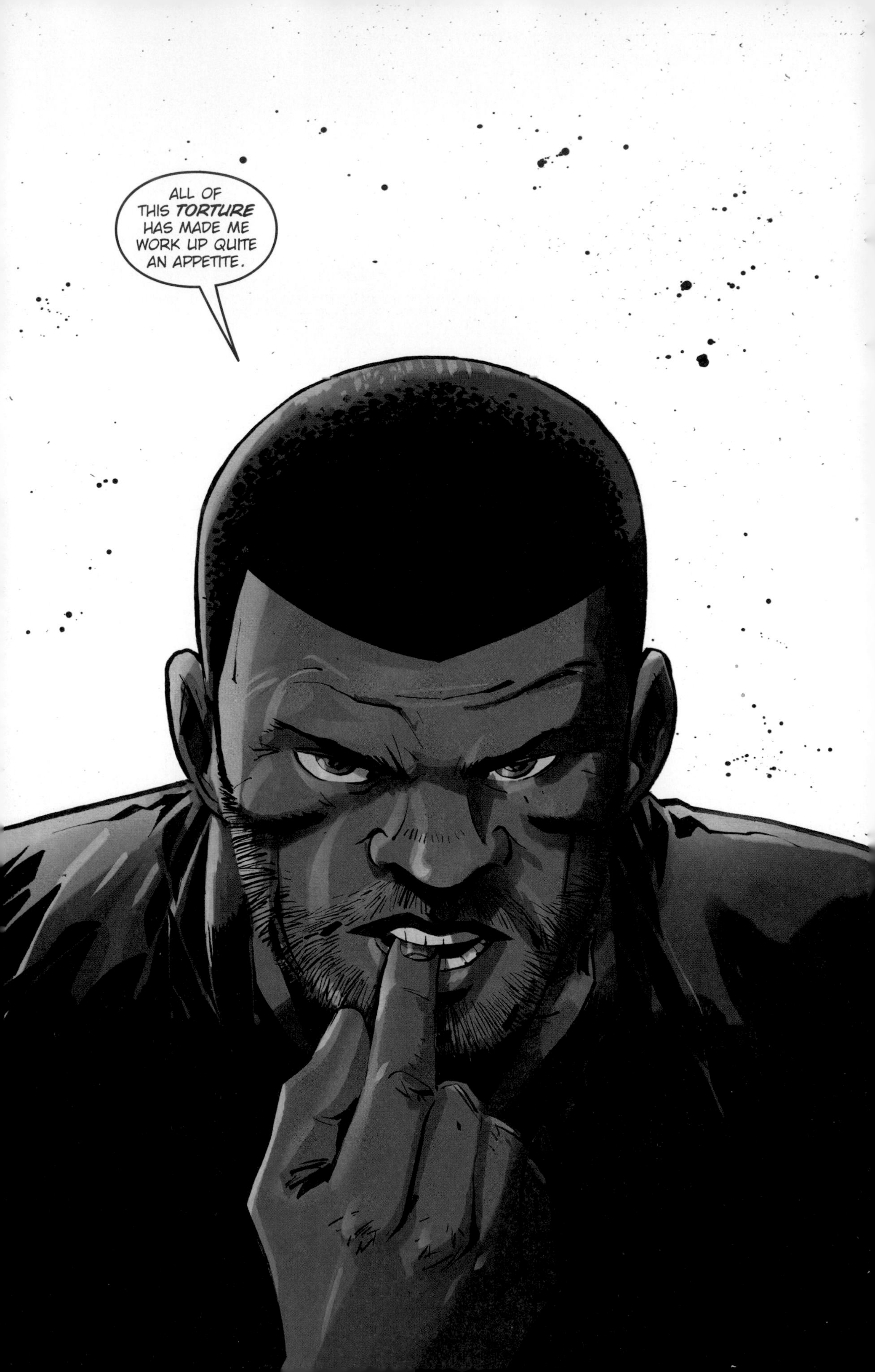
ALL OF THIS *TORTURE* HAS MADE ME WORK UP QUITE AN APPETITE.

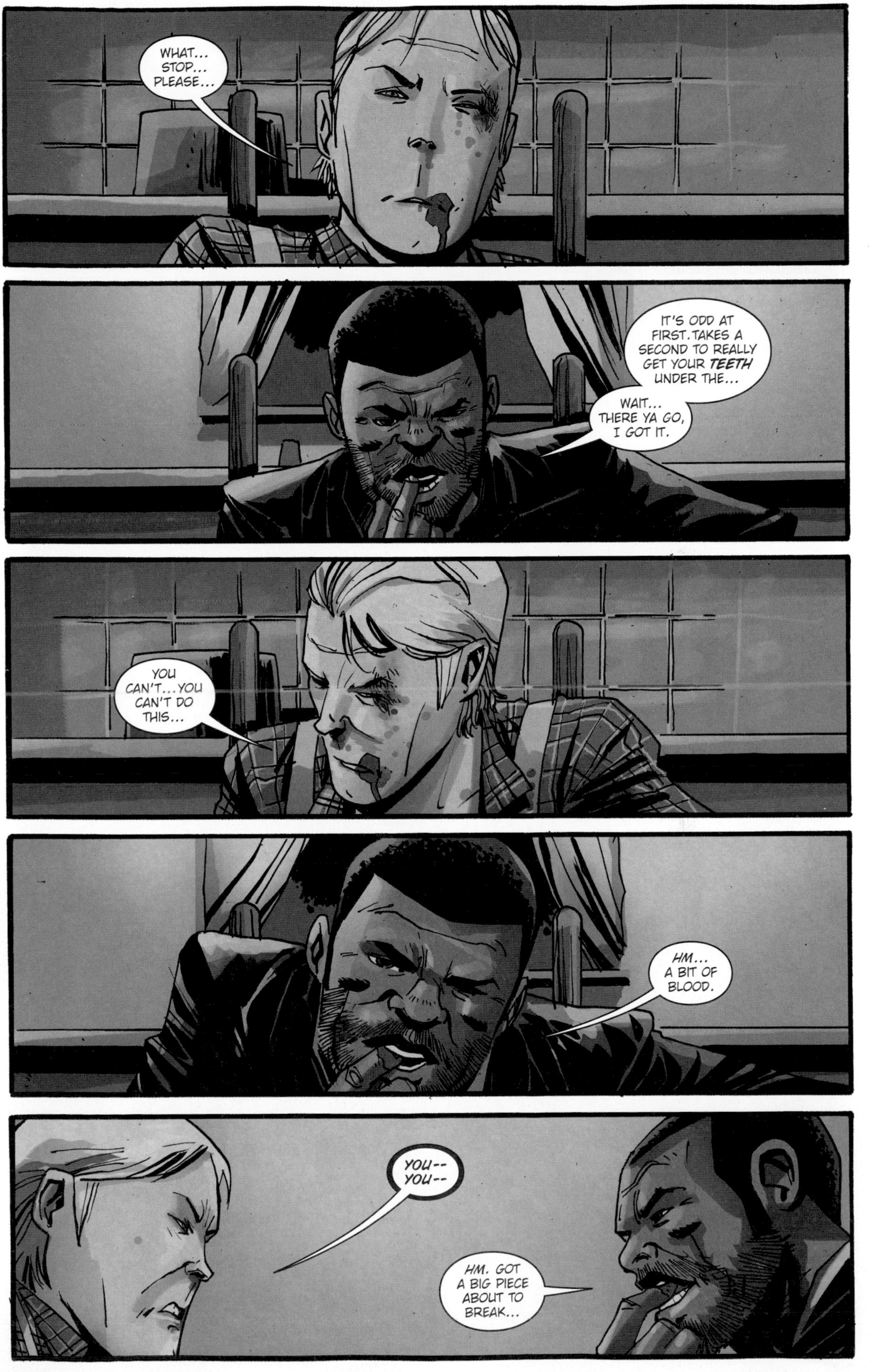
WHAT... STOP... PLEASE...
IT'S ODD AT FIRST. TAKES A SECOND TO REALLY GET YOUR *TEETH* UNDER THE...
WAIT... THERE YA GO, I GOT IT.
YOU CAN'T... YOU CAN'T DO THIS...
HM... A BIT OF BLOOD.
YOU-- YOU--
HM. GOT A BIG PIECE ABOUT TO BREAK...

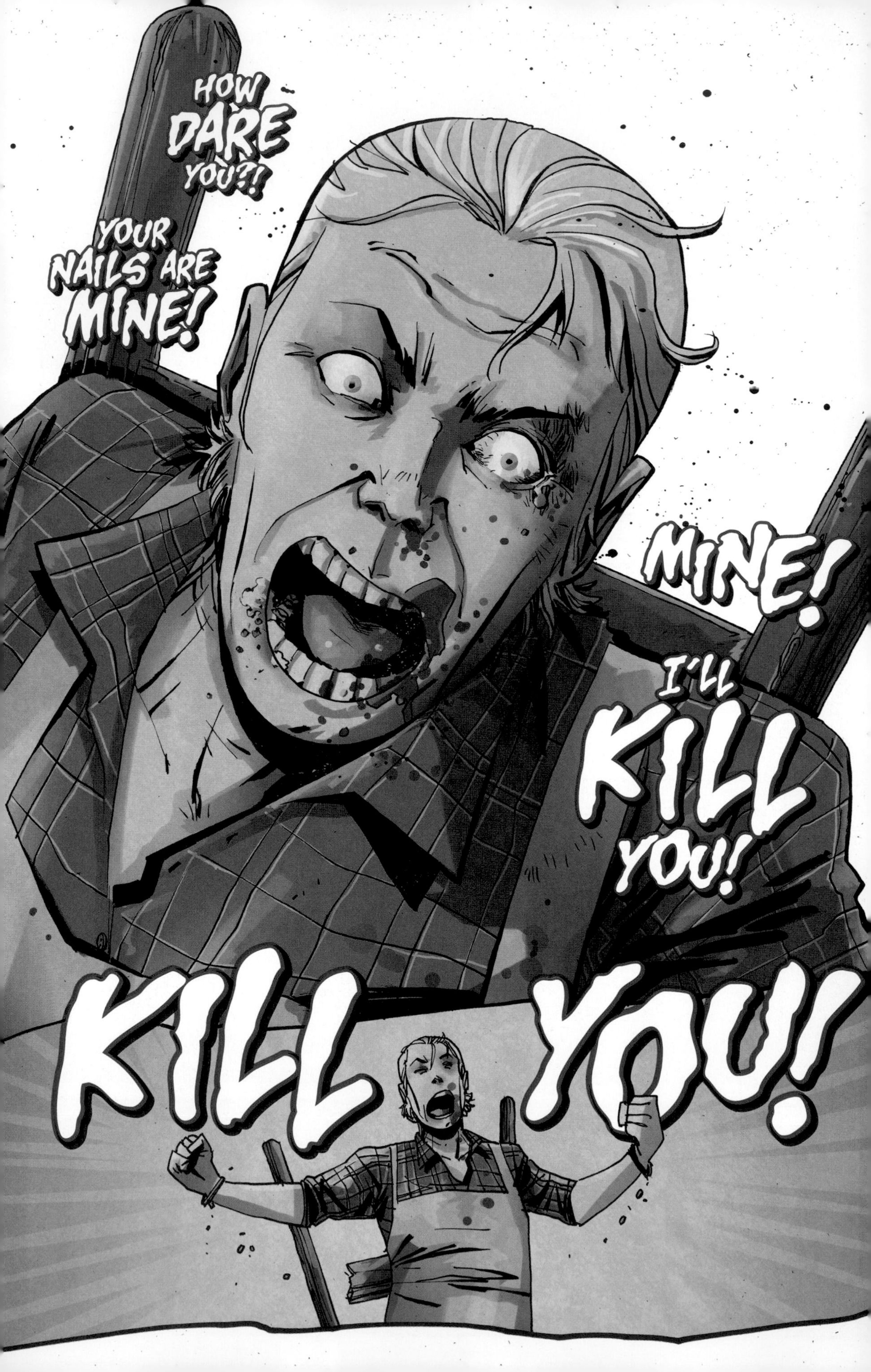
HOW DARE YOU?!
YOUR NAILS ARE MINE!
MINE!
I'LL KILL YOU!
KILL YOU!

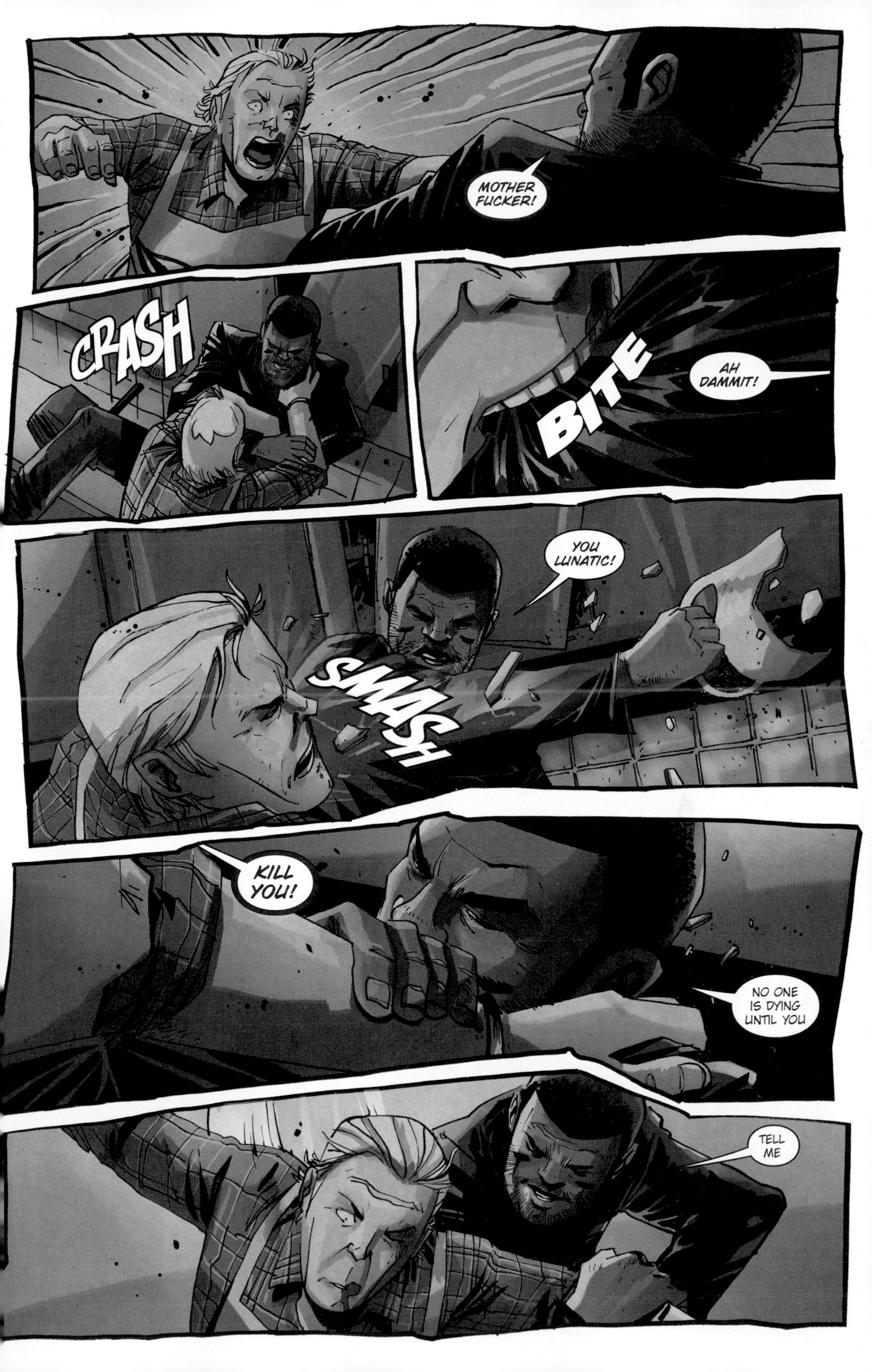
MOTHER FUCKER!
CRASH
BITE
AH DAMMIT!
YOU LUNATIC!
SMASH
KILL YOU!
NO ONE IS DYING UNTIL YOU
TELL ME

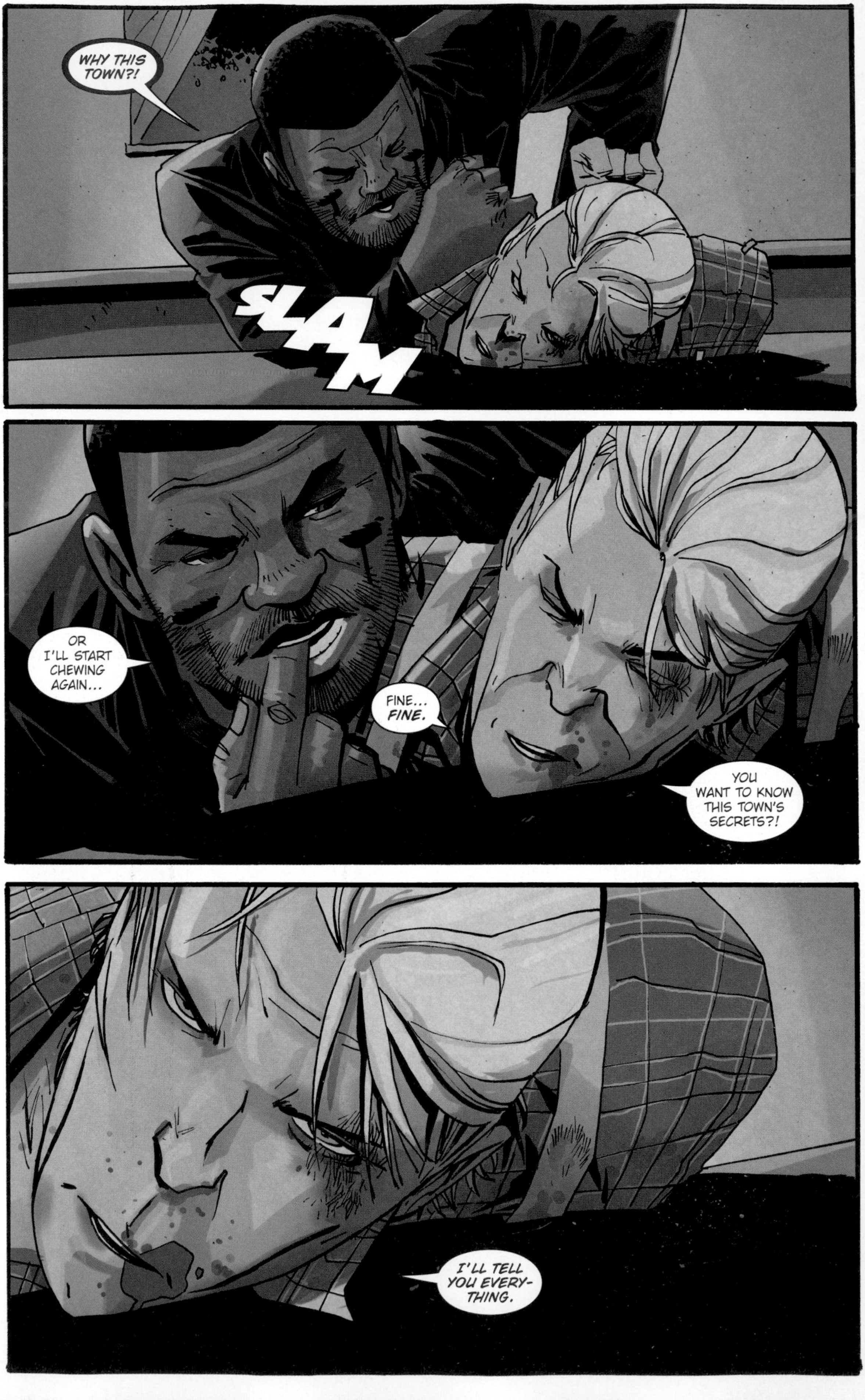
WHY THIS TOWN?!
SLAM
OR I'LL START CHEWING AGAIN...
FINE... FINE.
YOU WANT TO KNOW THIS TOWN'S SECRETS?!
I'LL TELL YOU EVERY-THING.

ISSUE TWELVE

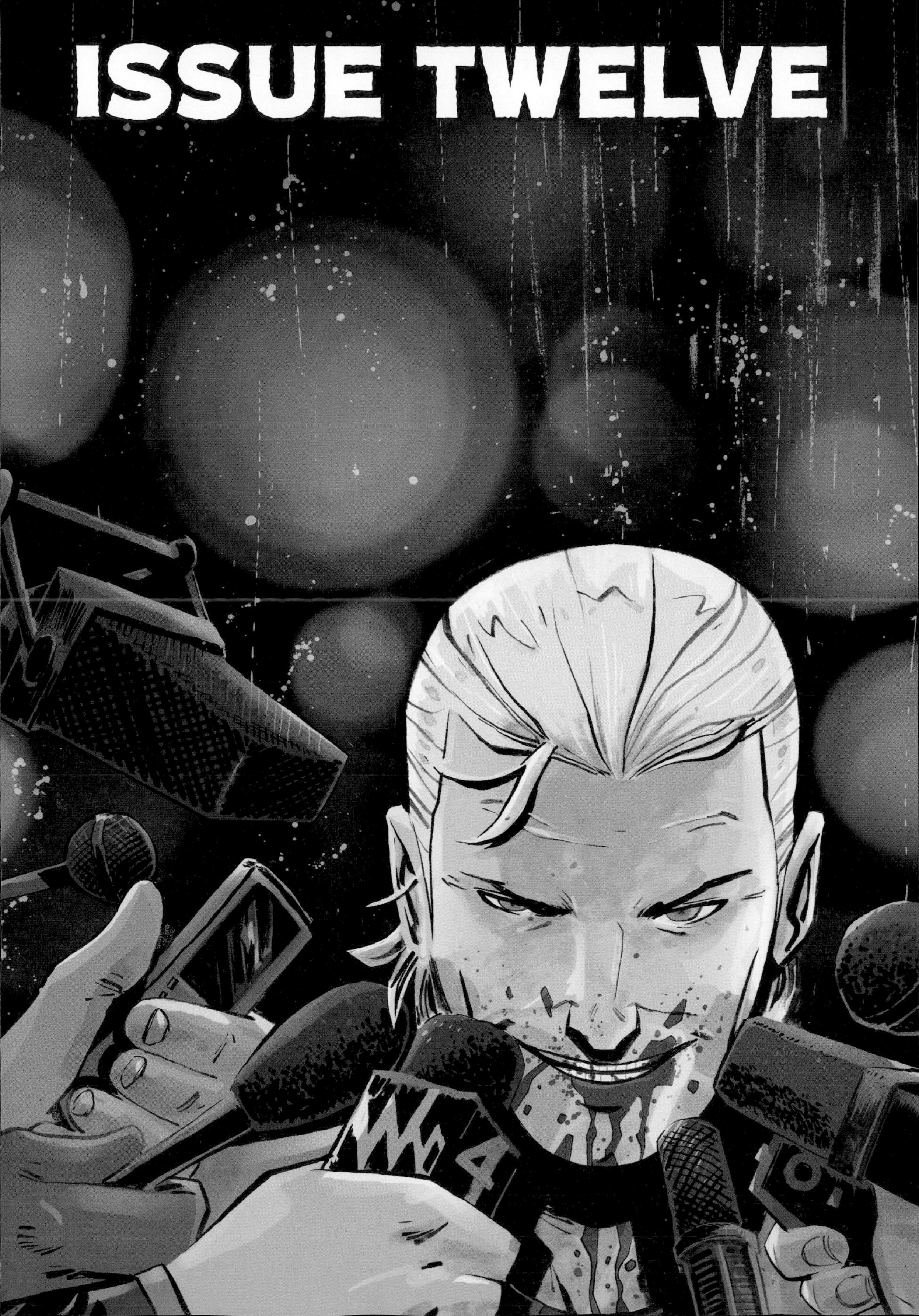

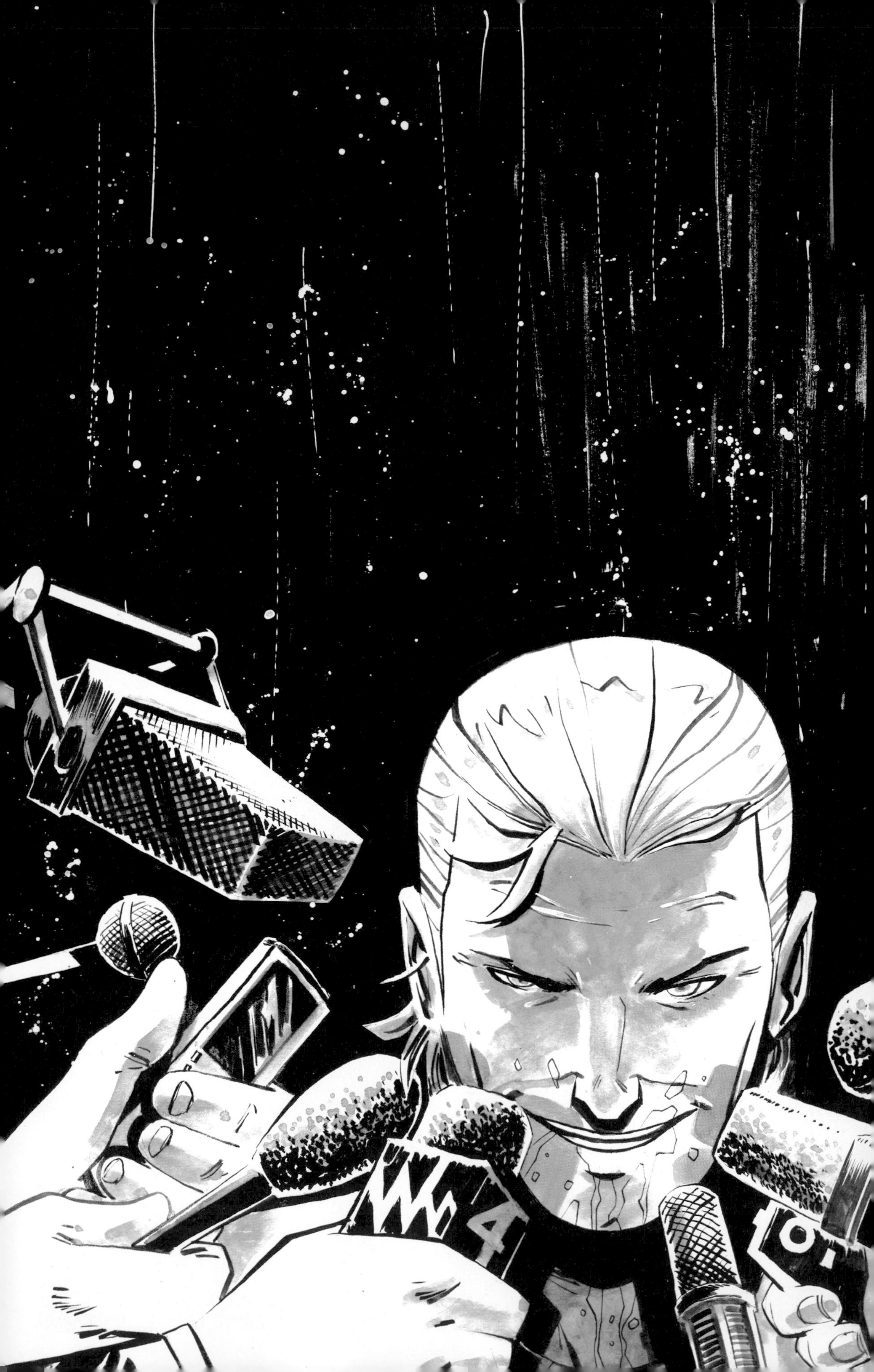

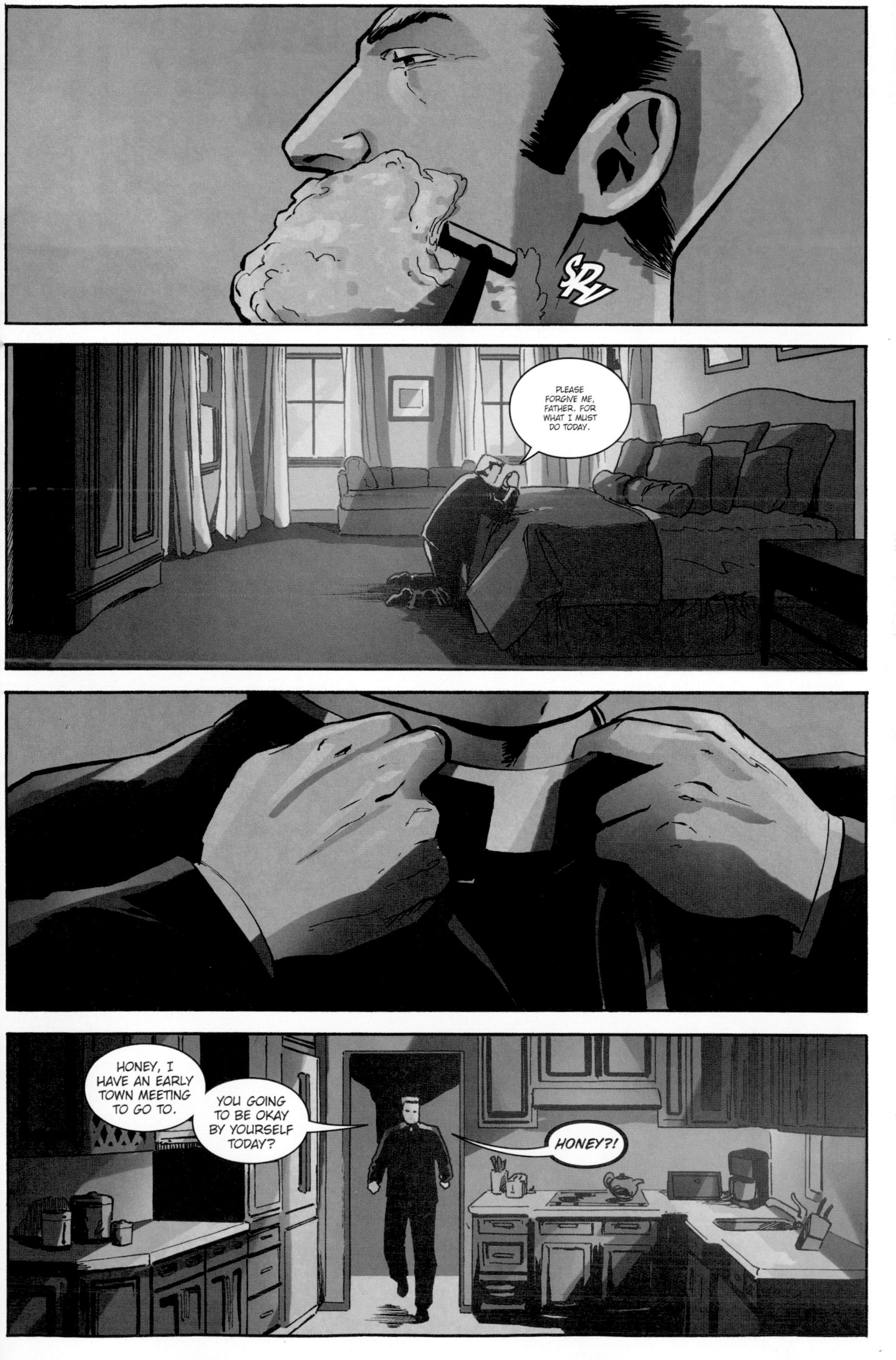
SRV
PLEASE FORGIVE ME, FATHER. FOR WHAT I MUST DO TODAY.
HONEY, I HAVE AN EARLY TOWN MEETING TO GO TO.
YOU GOING TO BE OKAY BY YOURSELF TODAY?
HONEY?!

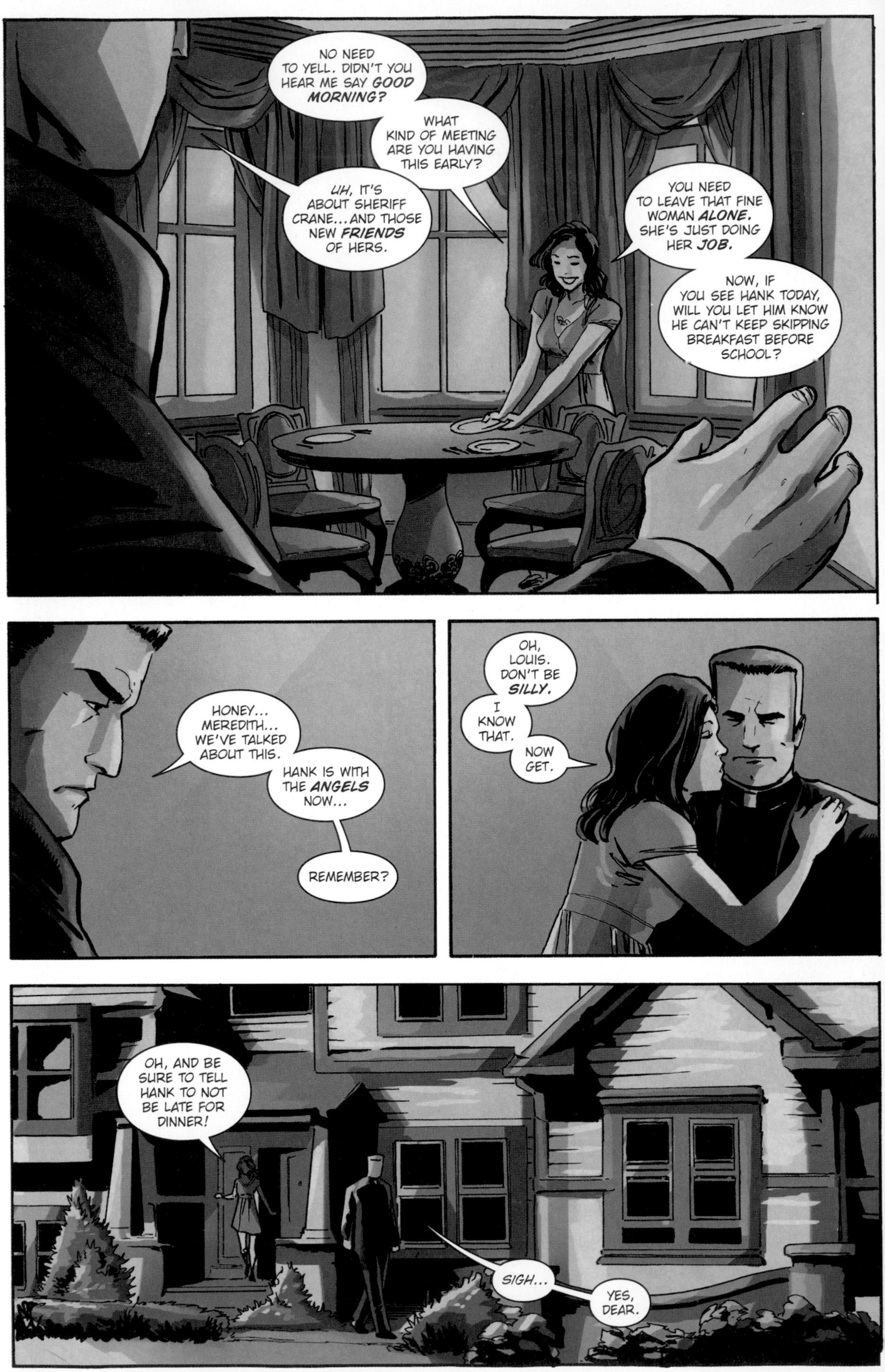
NO NEED TO YELL. DIDN'T YOU HEAR ME SAY GOOD MORNING?
WHAT KIND OF MEETING ARE YOU HAVING THIS EARLY?
UH, IT'S ABOUT SHERIFF CRANE... AND THOSE NEW FRIENDS OF HERS.
YOU NEED TO LEAVE THAT FINE WOMAN ALONE. SHE'S JUST DOING HER JOB.
NOW, IF YOU SEE HANK TODAY, WILL YOU LET HIM KNOW HE CAN'T KEEP SKIPPING BREAKFAST BEFORE SCHOOL?
HONEY... MEREDITH... WE'VE TALKED ABOUT THIS.
HANK IS WITH THE ANGELS NOW...
REMEMBER?
OH, LOUIS. DON'T BE SILLY.
I KNOW THAT.
NOW GET.
OH, AND BE SURE TO TELL HANK TO NOT BE LATE FOR DINNER!
SIGH...
YES, DEAR.

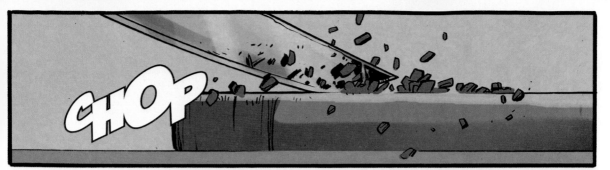

CHOP

CHOP CHOP
CHOP CHOP
CHOP

AH. SHIT.

GODDAMMIT.

THUK

SSSSSH-AH.

NOT SO BAD...NO E.R. TRIP ON MY DAY OFF AT LEAST...

KNOCK KNOCK

SORRY...IF YOU NEED HELP YOU NEED TO CALL...

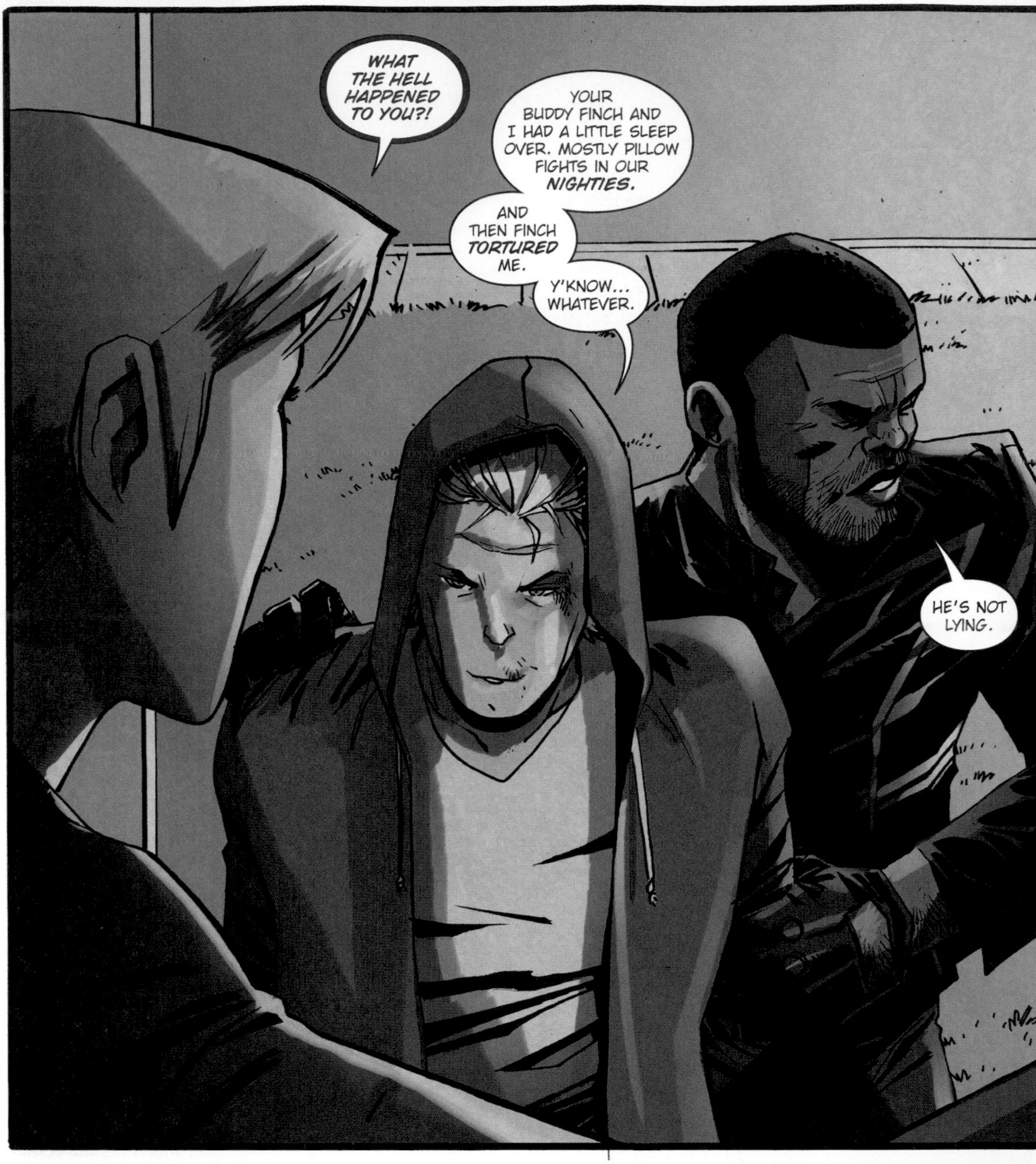
WHAT THE HELL HAPPENED TO YOU?!
YOUR BUDDY FINCH AND I HAD A LITTLE SLEEP OVER. MOSTLY PILLOW FIGHTS IN OUR NIGHTIES.
AND THEN FINCH TORTURED ME.
Y'KNOW... WHATEVER.
HE'S NOT LYING.

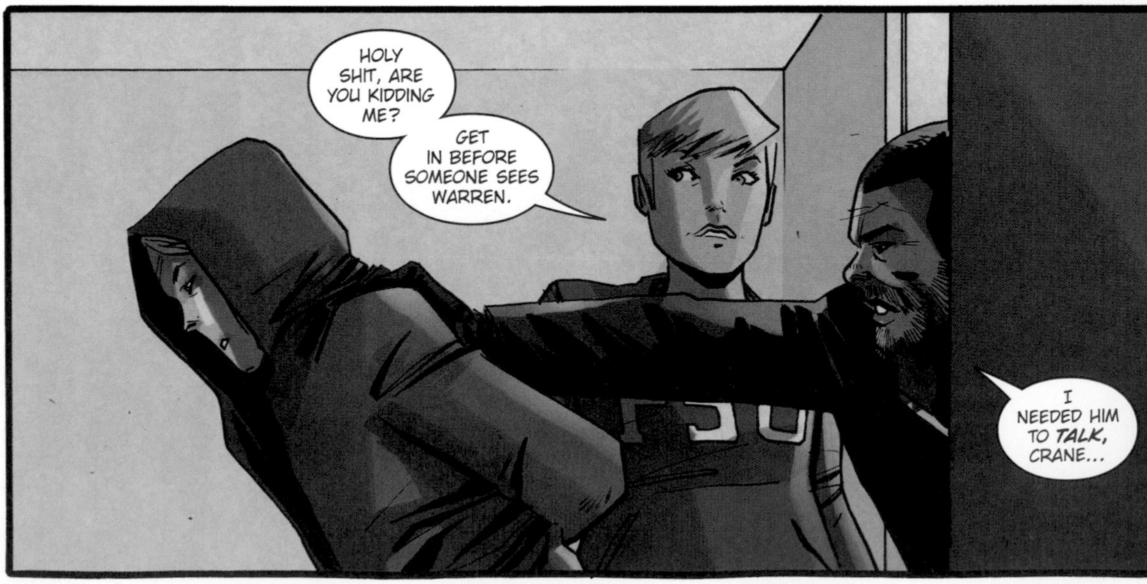
HOLY SHIT, ARE YOU KIDDING ME?
GET IN BEFORE SOMEONE SEES WARREN.
I NEEDED HIM TO TALK, CRANE...

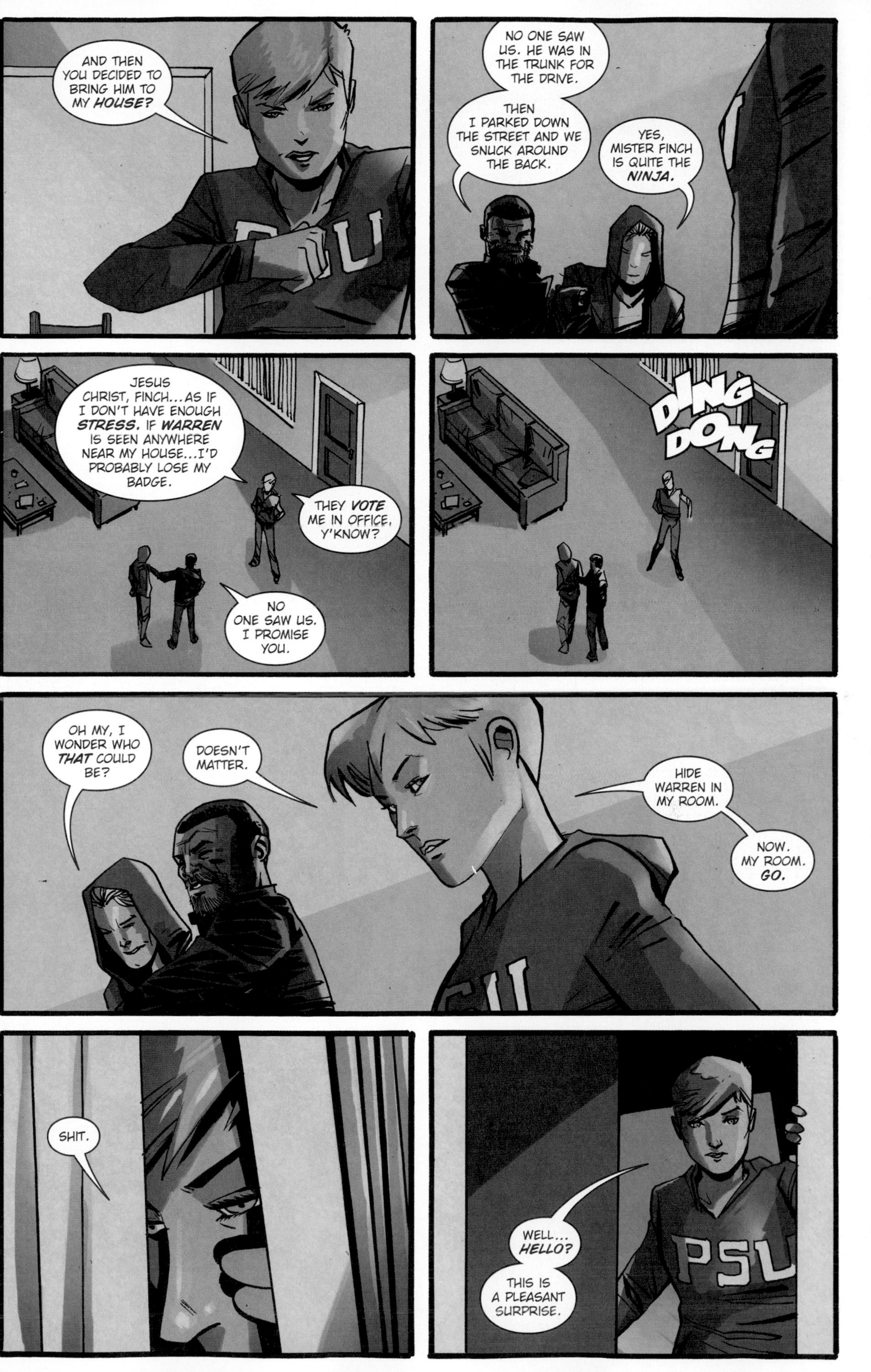

AND THEN YOU DECIDED TO BRING HIM TO MY HOUSE?
NO ONE SAW US. HE WAS IN THE TRUNK FOR THE DRIVE.
THEN I PARKED DOWN THE STREET AND WE SNUCK AROUND THE BACK.
YES, MISTER FINCH IS QUITE THE NINJA.
JESUS CHRIST, FINCH...AS IF I DON'T HAVE ENOUGH STRESS. IF WARREN IS SEEN ANYWHERE NEAR MY HOUSE...I'D PROBABLY LOSE MY BADGE.
THEY VOTE ME IN OFFICE, Y'KNOW?
NO ONE SAW US. I PROMISE YOU.
DING DONG
OH MY, I WONDER WHO THAT COULD BE?
DOESN'T MATTER.
HIDE WARREN IN MY ROOM.
NOW. MY ROOM. GO.
SHIT.
WELL... HELLO?
THIS IS A PLEASANT SURPRISE.
PSU

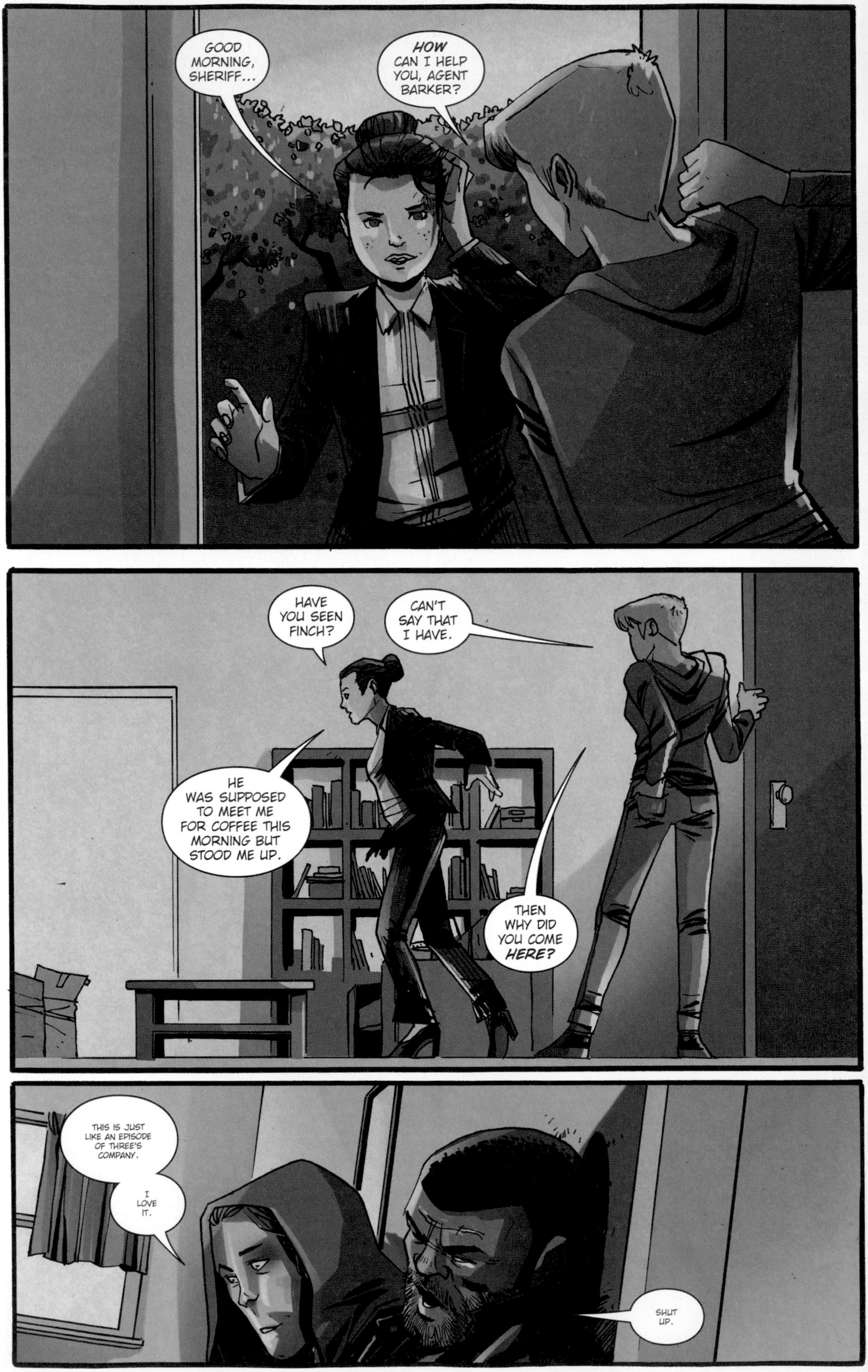
GOOD MORNING, SHERIFF...
HOW CAN I HELP YOU, AGENT BARKER?
HAVE YOU SEEN FINCH?
CAN'T SAY THAT I HAVE.
HE WAS SUPPOSED TO MEET ME FOR COFFEE THIS MORNING BUT STOOD ME UP.
THEN WHY DID YOU COME HERE?
THIS IS JUST LIKE AN EPISODE OF THREE'S COMPANY.
I LOVE IT.
SHUT UP.

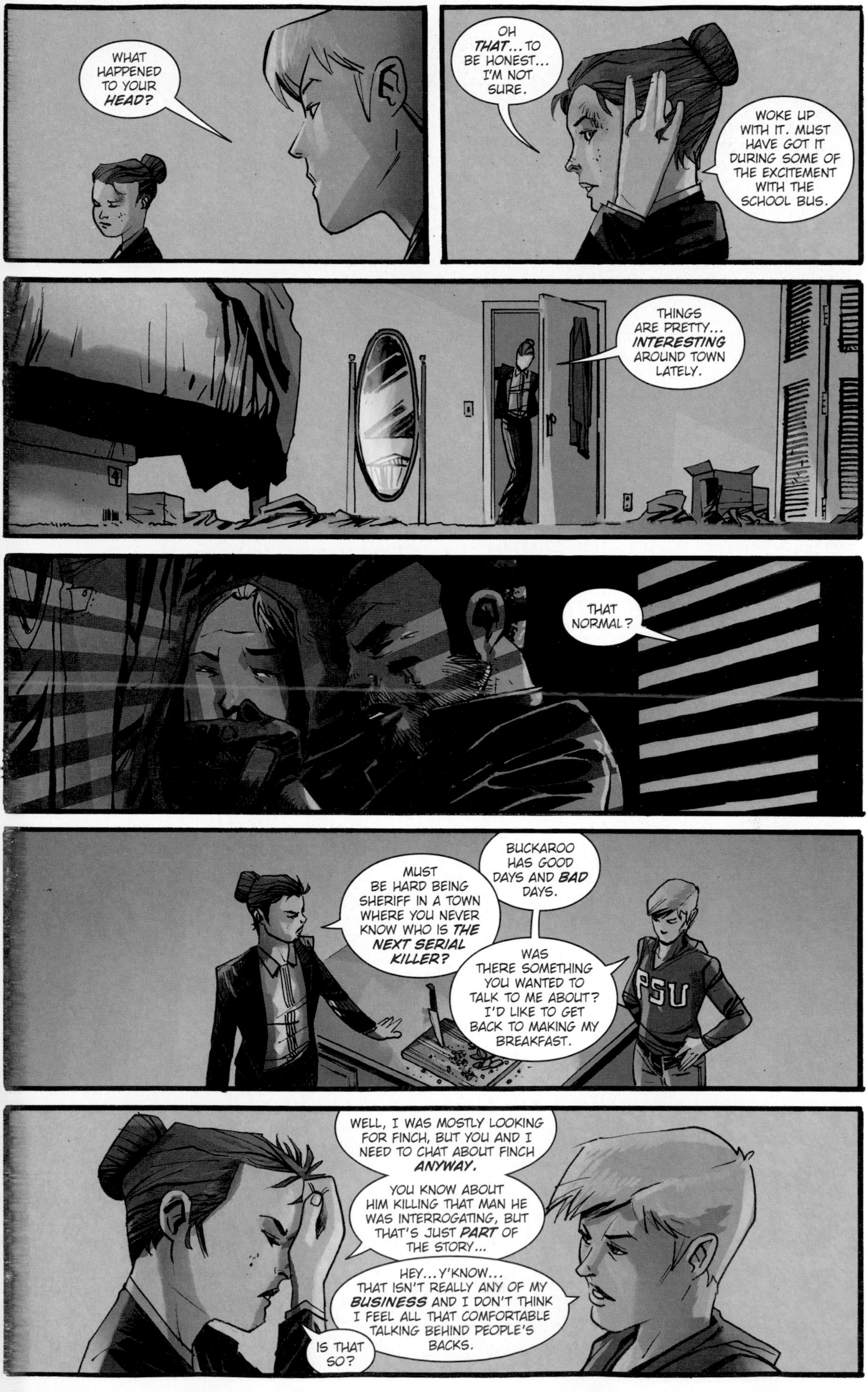
WHAT HAPPENED TO YOUR HEAD?
OH THAT... TO BE HONEST... I'M NOT SURE.
WOKE UP WITH IT. MUST HAVE GOT IT DURING SOME OF THE EXCITEMENT WITH THE SCHOOL BUS.
THINGS ARE PRETTY... INTERESTING AROUND TOWN LATELY.
THAT NORMAL?
MUST BE HARD BEING SHERIFF IN A TOWN WHERE YOU NEVER KNOW WHO IS THE NEXT SERIAL KILLER?
BUCKAROO HAS GOOD DAYS AND BAD DAYS.
WAS THERE SOMETHING YOU WANTED TO TALK TO ME ABOUT? I'D LIKE TO GET BACK TO MAKING MY BREAKFAST.
PSU
WELL, I WAS MOSTLY LOOKING FOR FINCH, BUT YOU AND I NEED TO CHAT ABOUT FINCH ANYWAY.
YOU KNOW ABOUT HIM KILLING THAT MAN HE WAS INTERROGATING, BUT THAT'S JUST PART OF THE STORY...
HEY... Y'KNOW... THAT ISN'T REALLY ANY OF MY BUSINESS AND I DON'T THINK I FEEL ALL THAT COMFORTABLE TALKING BEHIND PEOPLE'S BACKS.
IS THAT SO?

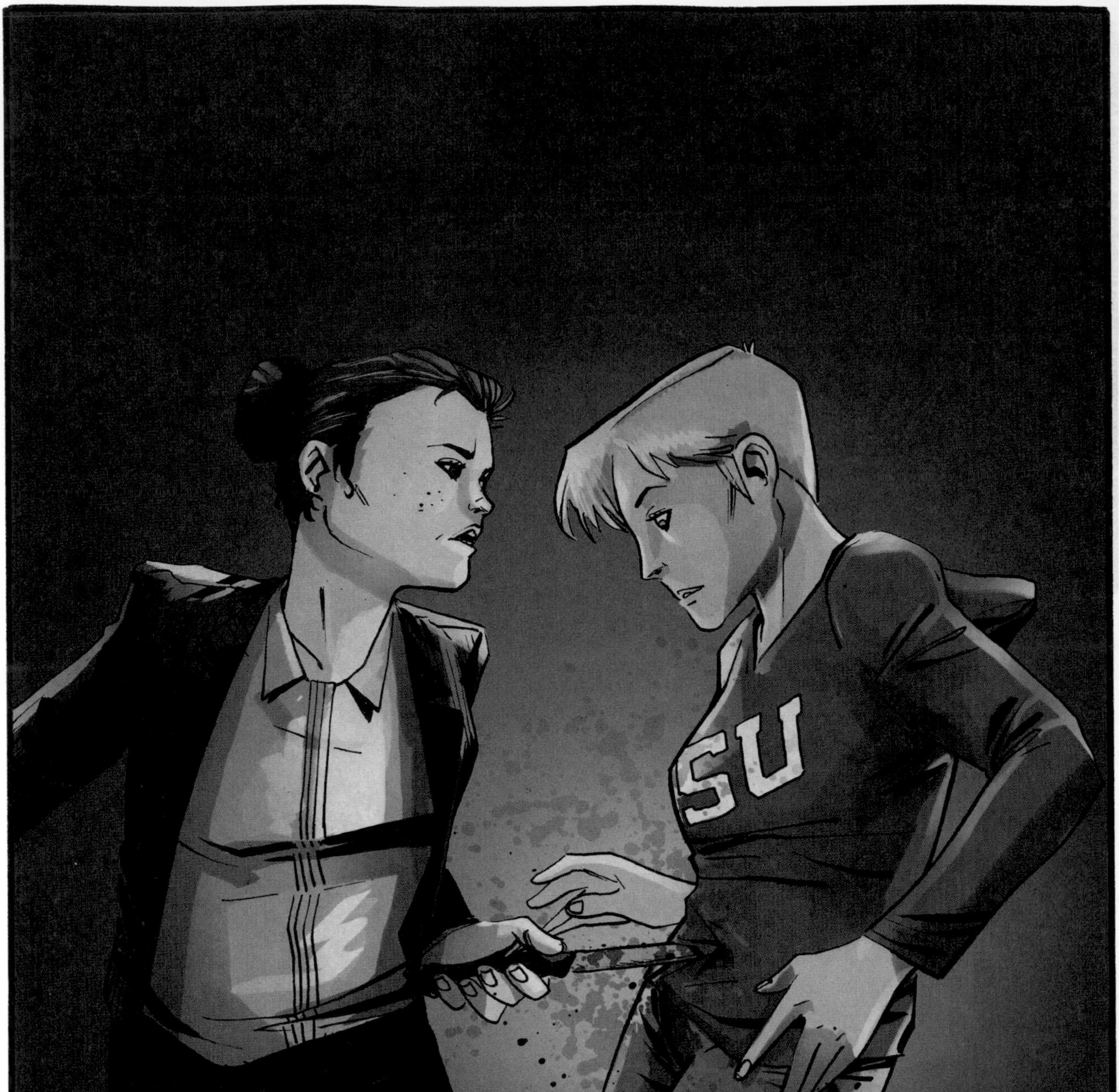

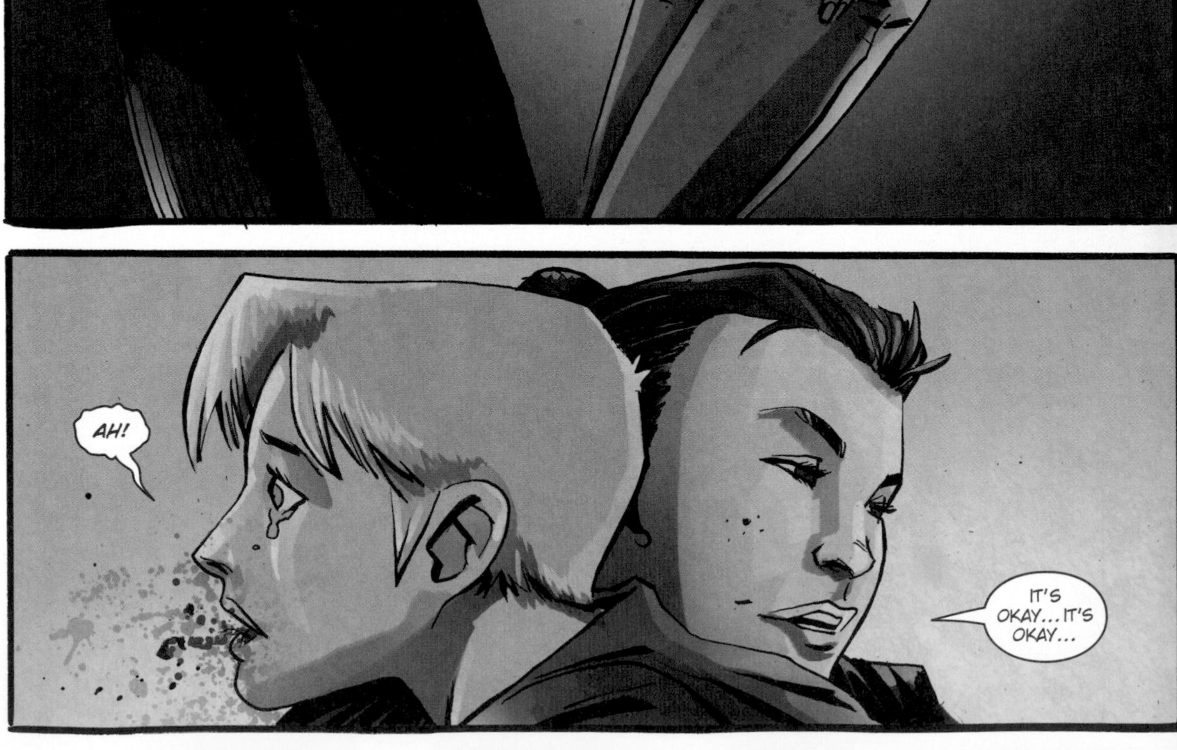
AH!
IT'S OKAY... IT'S OKAY...

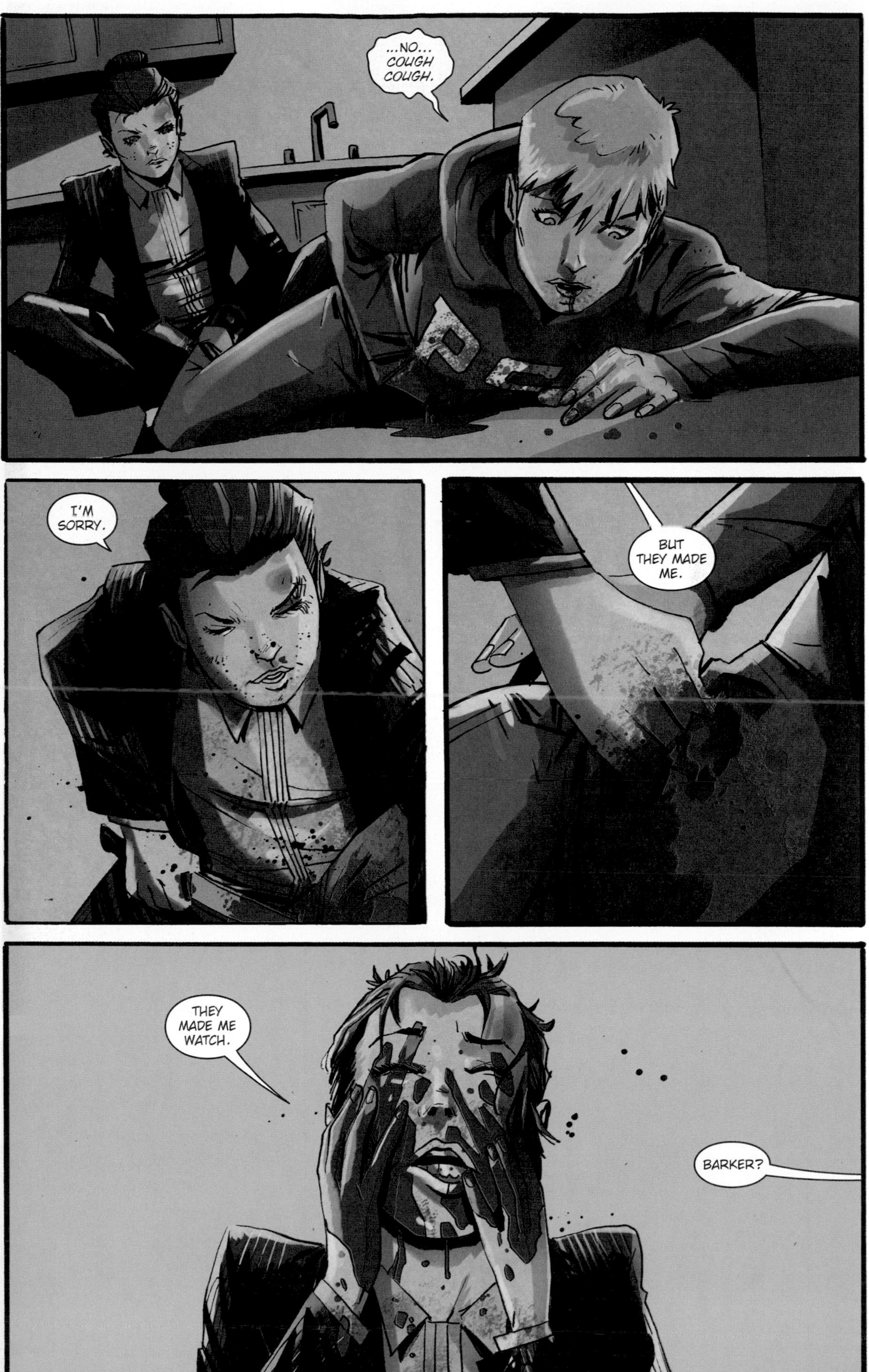
...NO... COUGH COUGH.
I'M SORRY.
BUT THEY MADE ME.
THEY MADE ME WATCH.
BARKER?

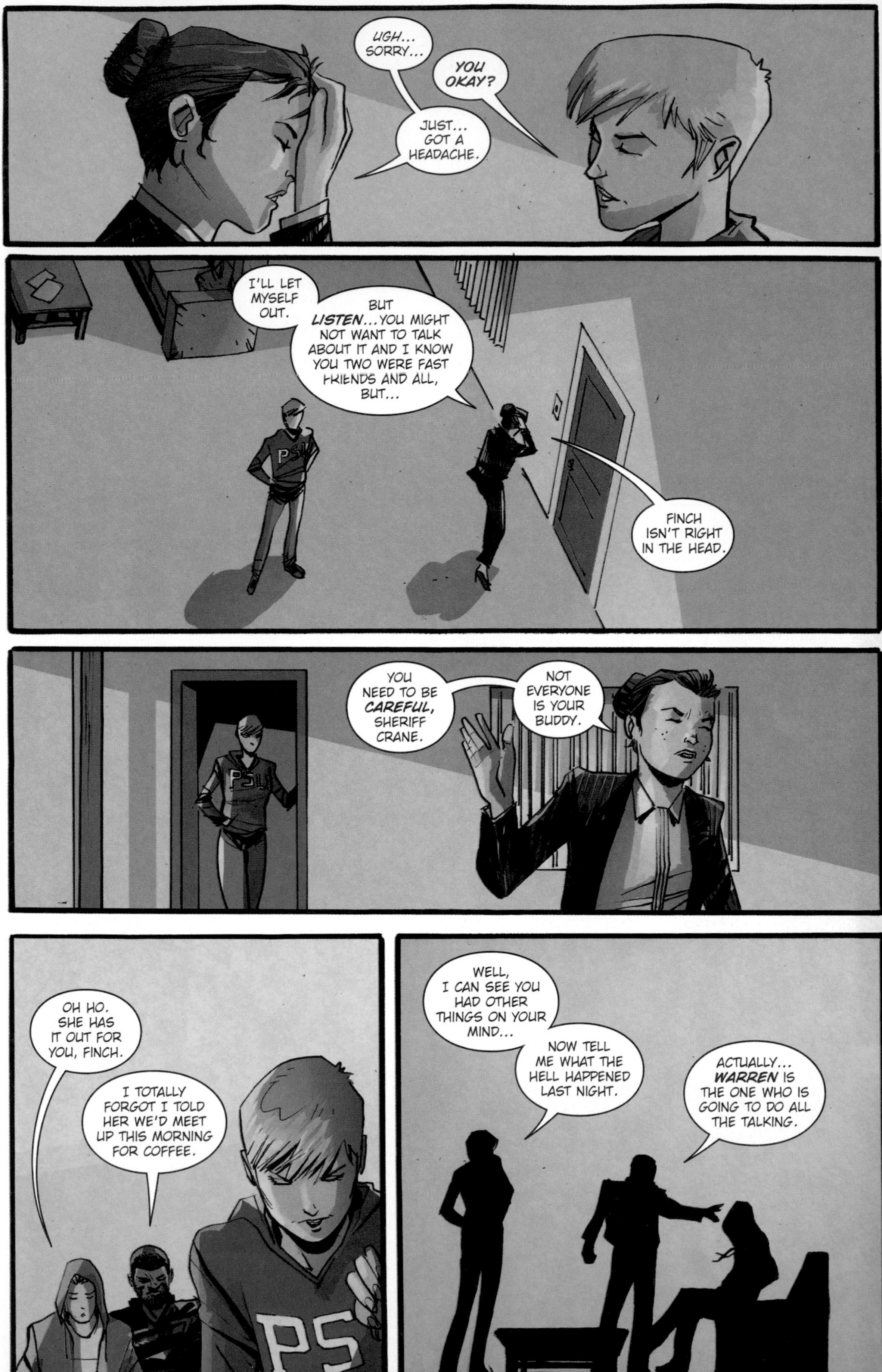
UGH... SORRY...
YOU OKAY?
JUST... GOT A HEADACHE.
I'LL LET MYSELF OUT.
BUT LISTEN...YOU MIGHT NOT WANT TO TALK ABOUT IT AND I KNOW YOU TWO WERE FAST FRIENDS AND ALL, BUT...
FINCH ISN'T RIGHT IN THE HEAD.
YOU NEED TO BE CAREFUL, SHERIFF CRANE.
NOT EVERYONE IS YOUR BUDDY.
OH HO. SHE HAS IT OUT FOR YOU, FINCH.
I TOTALLY FORGOT I TOLD HER WE'D MEET UP THIS MORNING FOR COFFEE.
WELL, I CAN SEE YOU HAD OTHER THINGS ON YOUR MIND...
NOW TELL ME WHAT THE HELL HAPPENED LAST NIGHT.
ACTUALLY... WARREN IS THE ONE WHO IS GOING TO DO ALL THE TALKING.

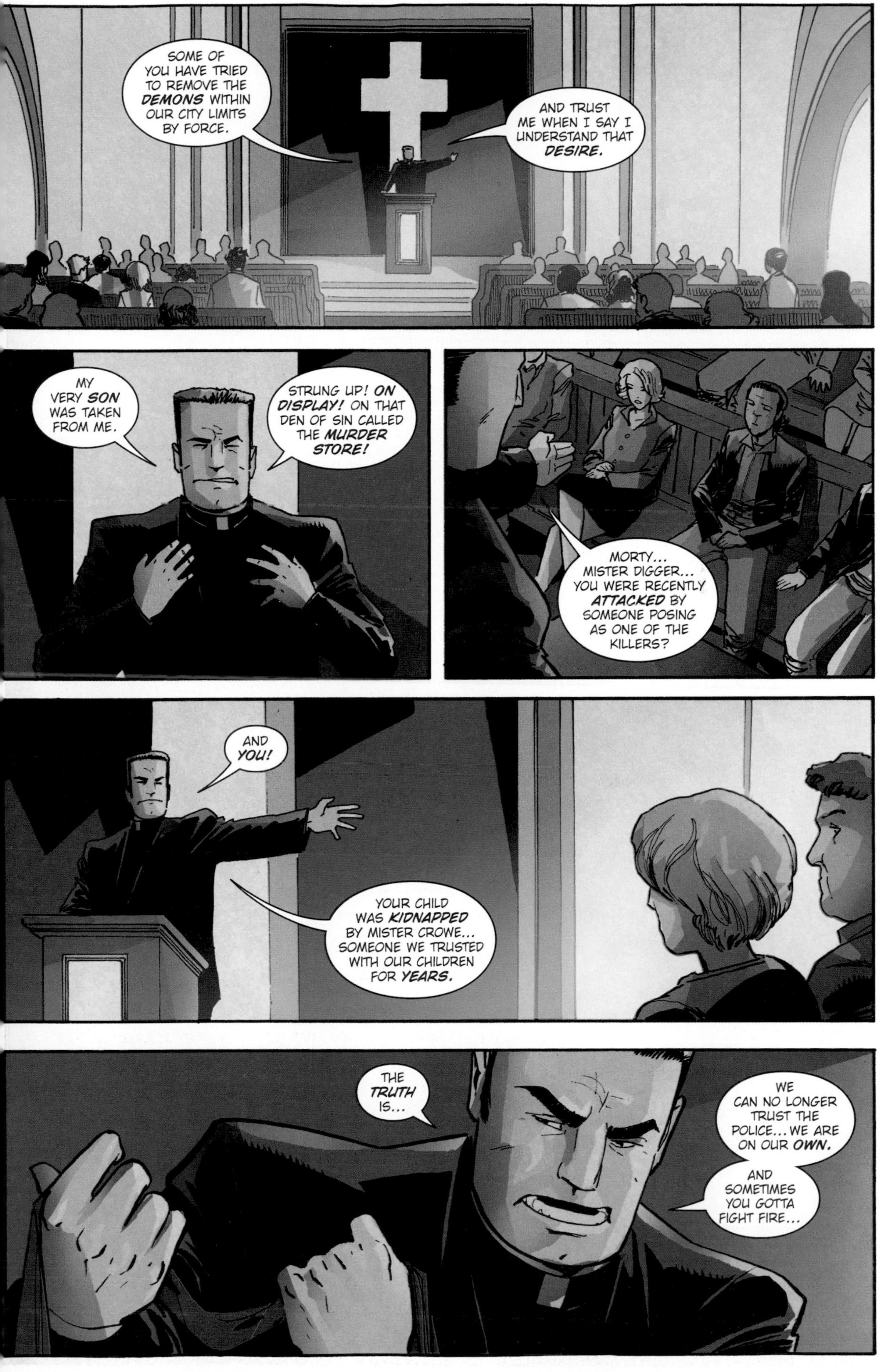
SOME OF YOU HAVE TRIED TO REMOVE THE DEMONS WITHIN OUR CITY LIMITS BY FORCE.
AND TRUST ME WHEN I SAY I UNDERSTAND THAT DESIRE.
MY VERY SON WAS TAKEN FROM ME.
STRUNG UP! ON DISPLAY! ON THAT DEN OF SIN CALLED THE MURDER STORE!
MORTY... MISTER DIGGER... YOU WERE RECENTLY ATTACKED BY SOMEONE POSING AS ONE OF THE KILLERS?
AND YOU!
YOUR CHILD WAS KIDNAPPED BY MISTER CROWE... SOMEONE WE TRUSTED WITH OUR CHILDREN FOR YEARS.
THE TRUTH IS...
WE CAN NO LONGER TRUST THE POLICE... WE ARE ON OUR OWN.
AND SOMETIMES YOU GOTTA FIGHT FIRE...

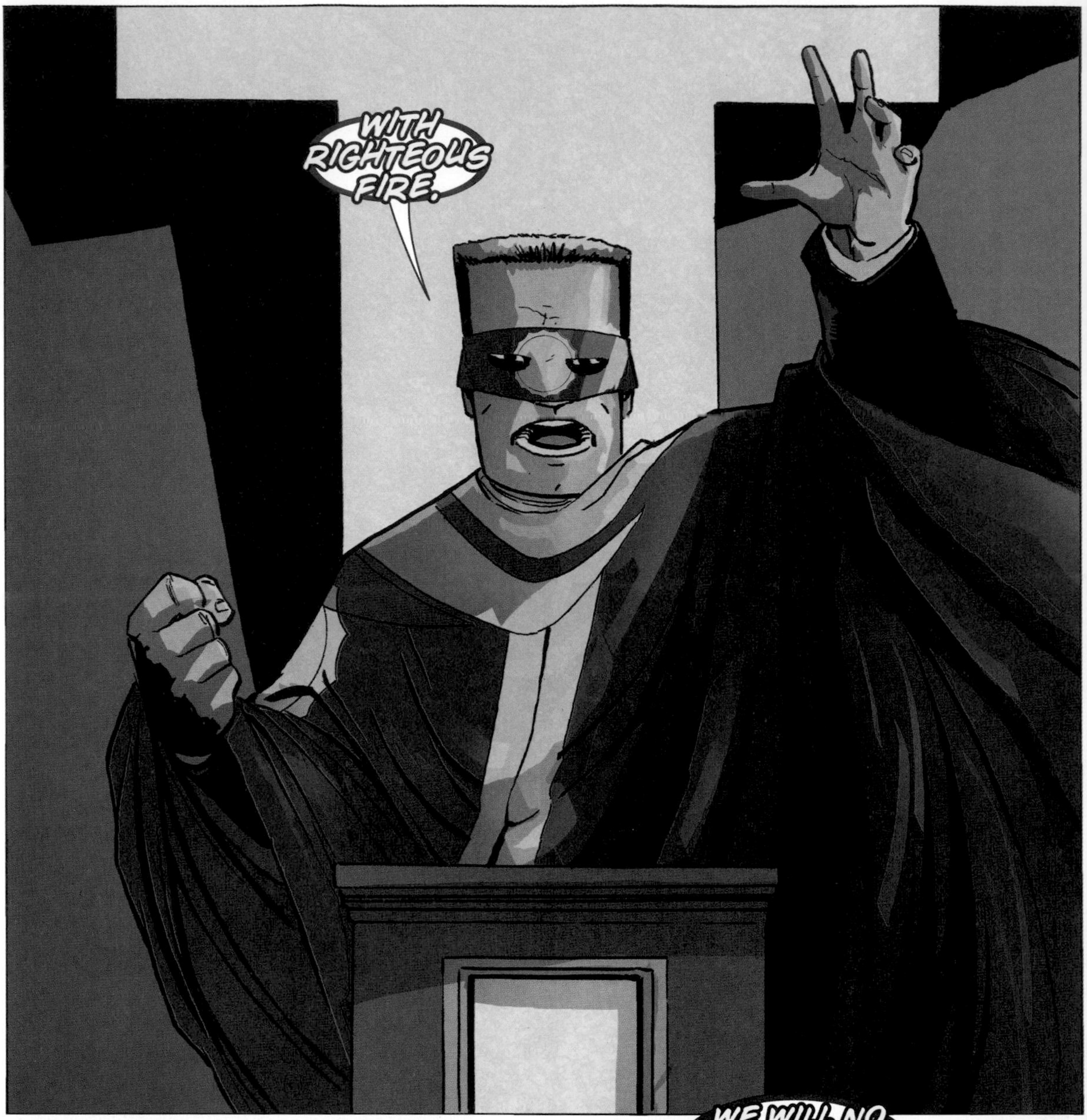
WITH RIGHTEOUS FIRE.

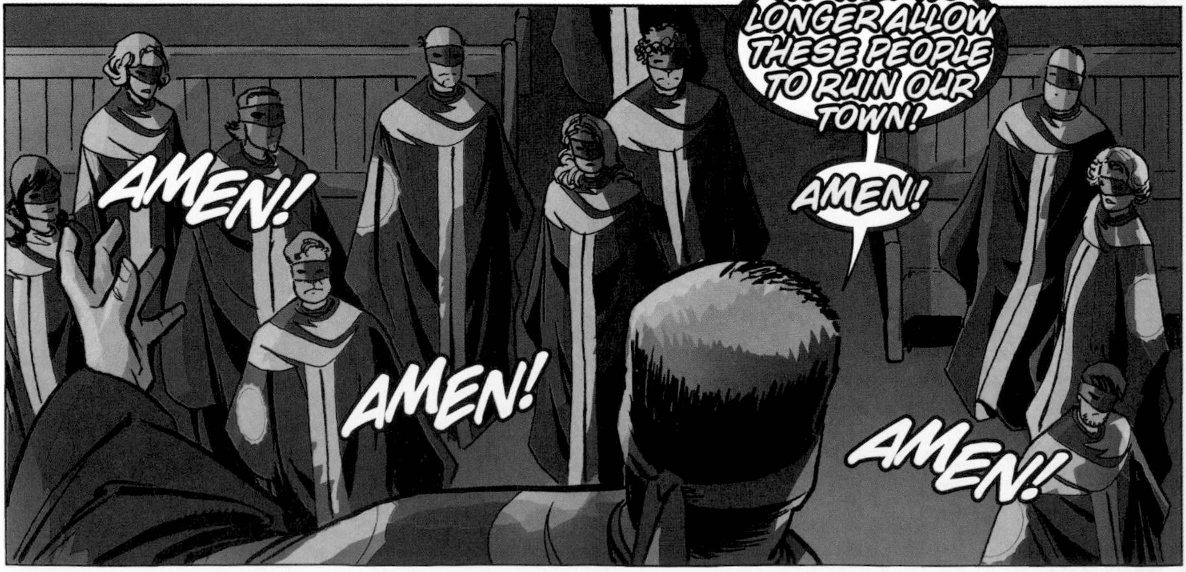
WE WILL NO LONGER ALLOW THESE PEOPLE TO RUIN OUR TOWN!
AMEN!
AMEN!
AMEN!
AMEN!

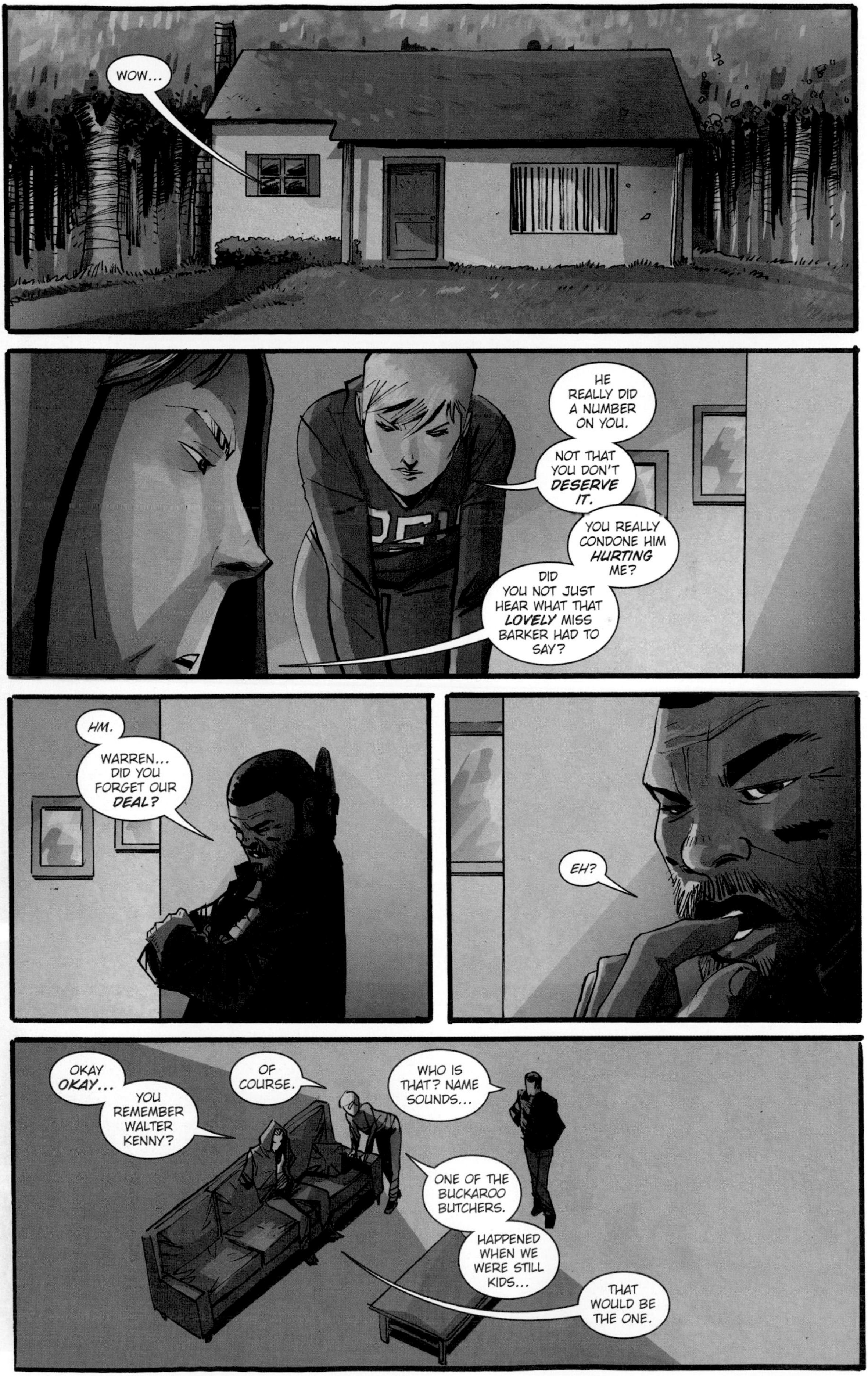
WOW...
HE REALLY DID A NUMBER ON YOU.
NOT THAT YOU DON'T DESERVE IT.
YOU REALLY CONDONE HIM HURTING ME?
DID YOU NOT JUST HEAR WHAT THAT LOVELY MISS BARKER HAD TO SAY?
HM.
WARREN... DID YOU FORGET OUR DEAL?
EH?
OKAY OKAY...
YOU REMEMBER WALTER KENNY?
OF COURSE.
WHO IS THAT? NAME SOUNDS...
ONE OF THE BUCKAROO BUTCHERS.
HAPPENED WHEN WE WERE STILL KIDS...
THAT WOULD BE THE ONE.

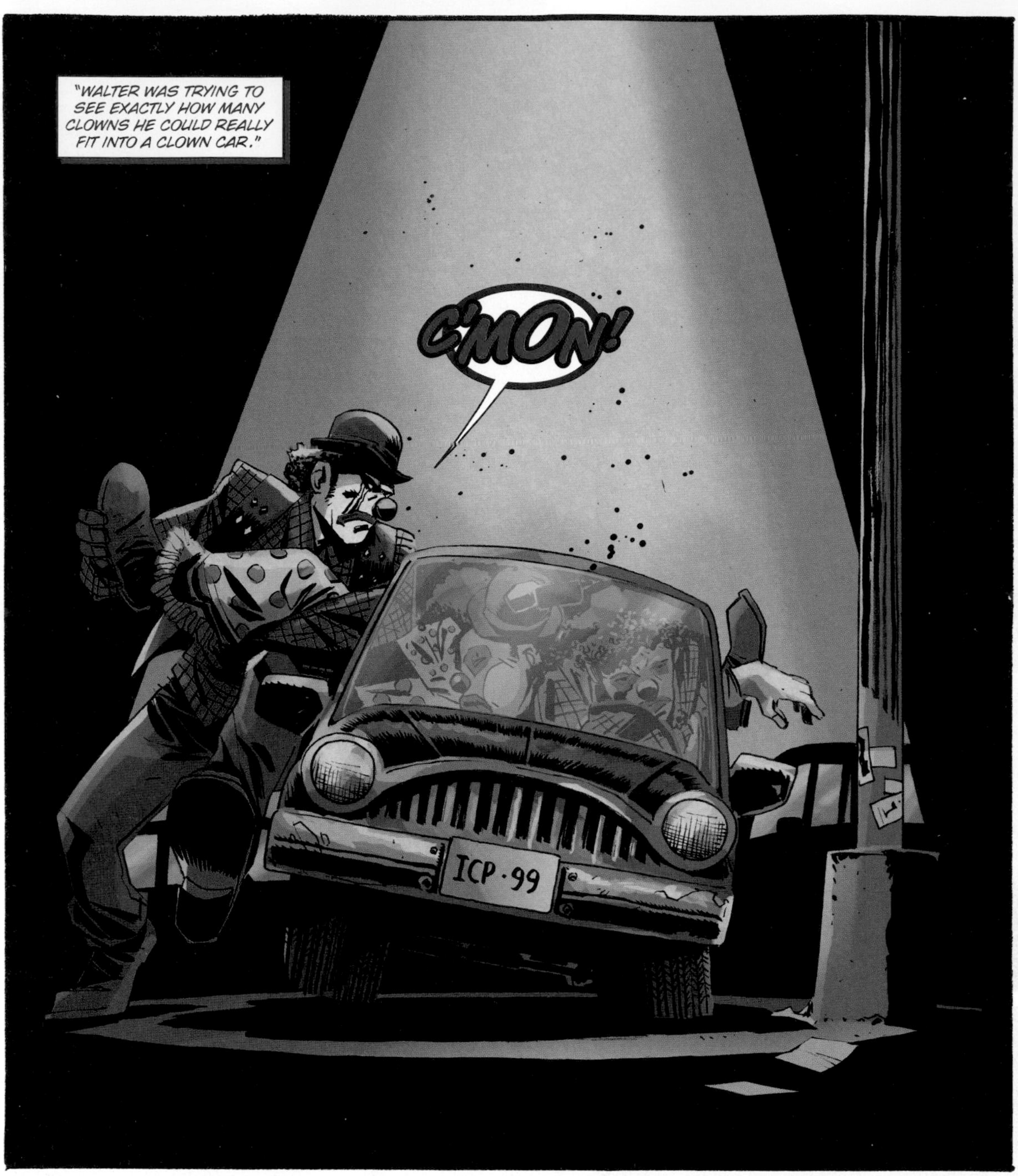
"WALTER WAS TRYING TO SEE EXACTLY HOW MANY CLOWNS HE COULD REALLY FIT INTO A CLOWN CAR."
C'MON!
ICP-99

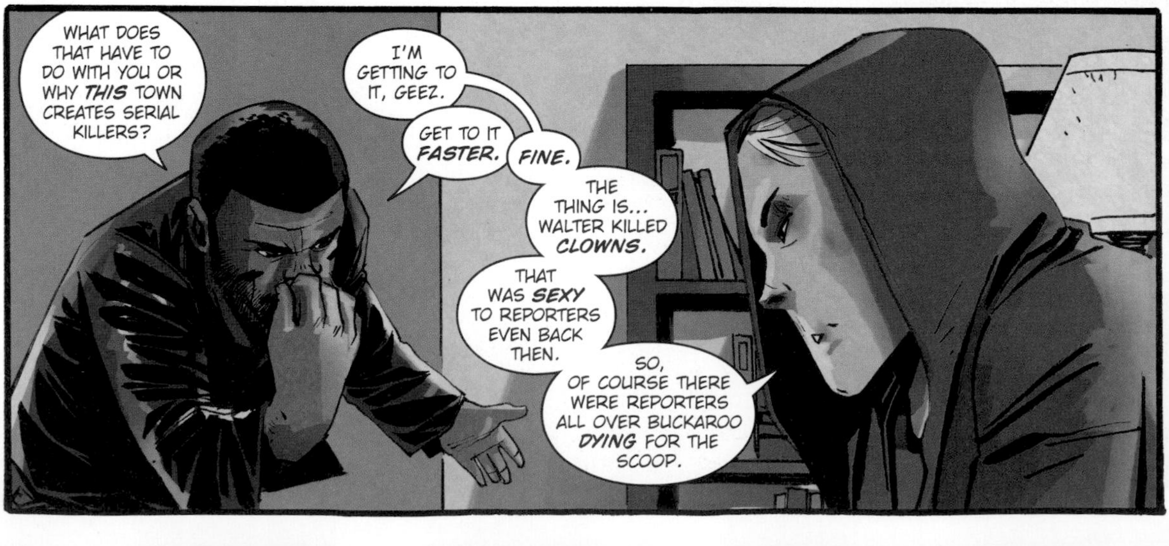
WHAT DOES THAT HAVE TO DO WITH YOU OR WHY THIS TOWN CREATES SERIAL KILLERS?
I'M GETTING TO IT, GEEZ.
GET TO IT FASTER.
FINE.
THE THING IS... WALTER KILLED CLOWNS.
THAT WAS SEXY TO REPORTERS EVEN BACK THEN.
SO, OF COURSE THERE WERE REPORTERS ALL OVER BUCKAROO DYING FOR THE SCOOP.

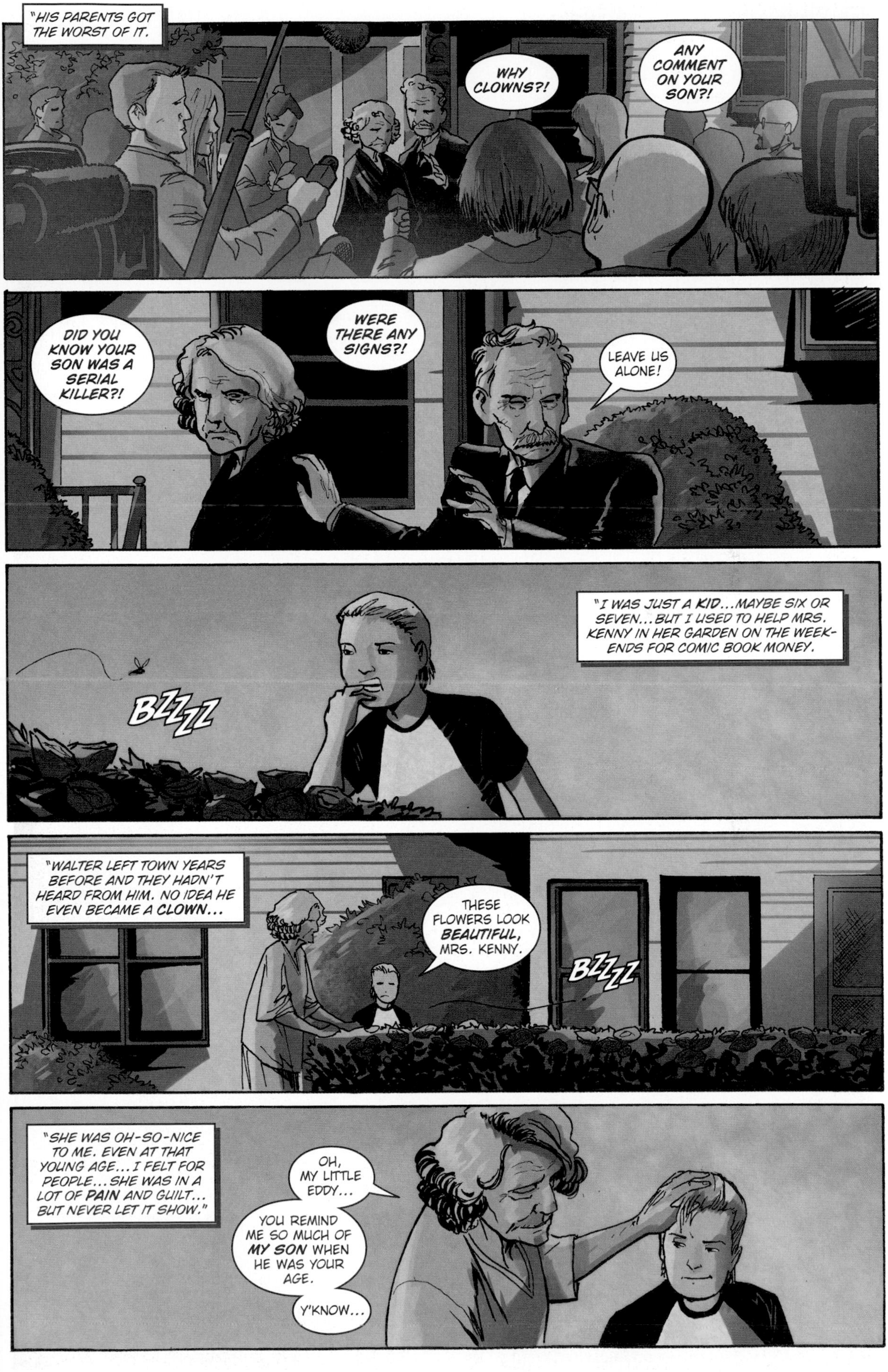
"HIS PARENTS GOT THE WORST OF IT.
WHY CLOWNS?!
ANY COMMENT ON YOUR SON?!
DID YOU KNOW YOUR SON WAS A SERIAL KILLER?!
WERE THERE ANY SIGNS?!
LEAVE US ALONE!
"I WAS JUST A KID...MAYBE SIX OR SEVEN...BUT I USED TO HELP MRS. KENNY IN HER GARDEN ON THE WEEK-ENDS FOR COMIC BOOK MONEY.
BZZZZ
"WALTER LEFT TOWN YEARS BEFORE AND THEY HADN'T HEARD FROM HIM. NO IDEA HE EVEN BECAME A CLOWN...
THESE FLOWERS LOOK BEAUTIFUL, MRS. KENNY.
BZZZZ
"SHE WAS OH-SO-NICE TO ME. EVEN AT THAT YOUNG AGE...I FELT FOR PEOPLE...SHE WAS IN A LOT OF PAIN AND GUILT... BUT NEVER LET IT SHOW."
OH, MY LITTLE EDDY...
YOU REMIND ME SO MUCH OF MY SON WHEN HE WAS YOUR AGE.
Y'KNOW...

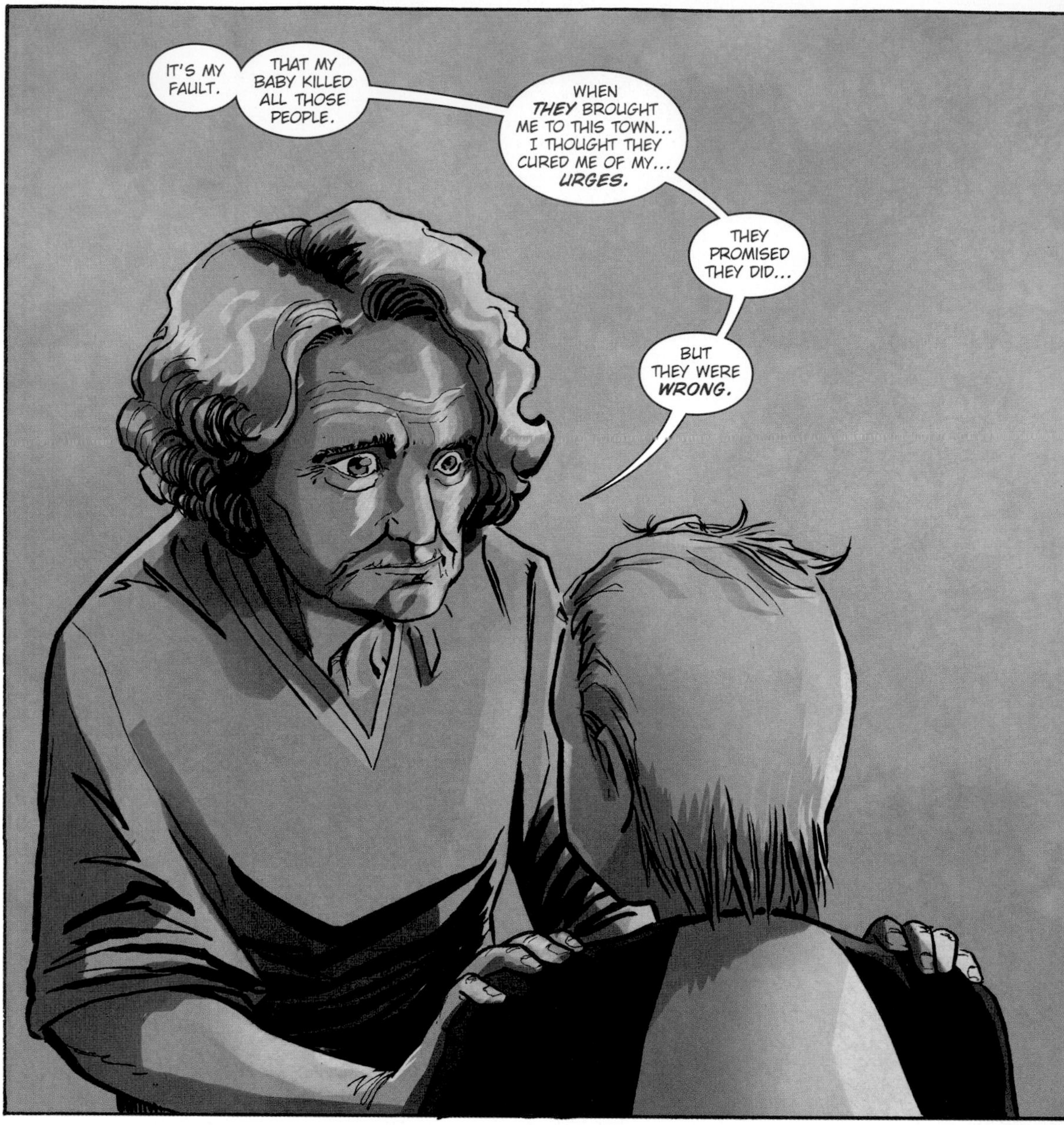
IT'S MY FAULT.
THAT MY BABY KILLED ALL THOSE PEOPLE.
WHEN *THEY* BROUGHT ME TO THIS TOWN... I THOUGHT THEY CURED ME OF MY... *URGES.*
THEY PROMISED THEY DID...
BUT THEY WERE *WRONG.*

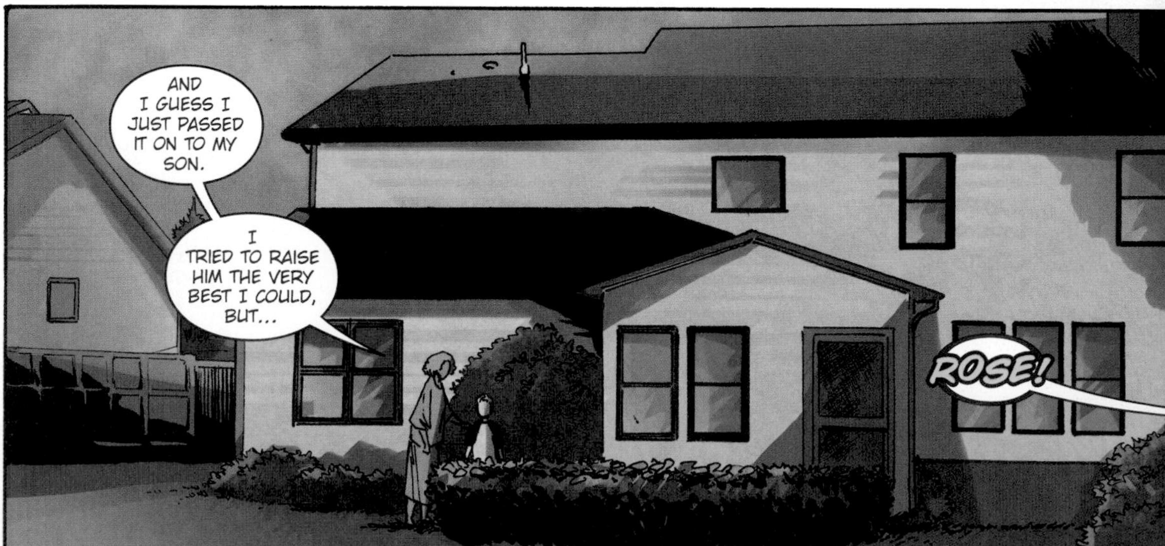
AND I GUESS I JUST PASSED IT ON TO MY SON.
I TRIED TO RAISE HIM THE VERY BEST I COULD, BUT...
ROSE!

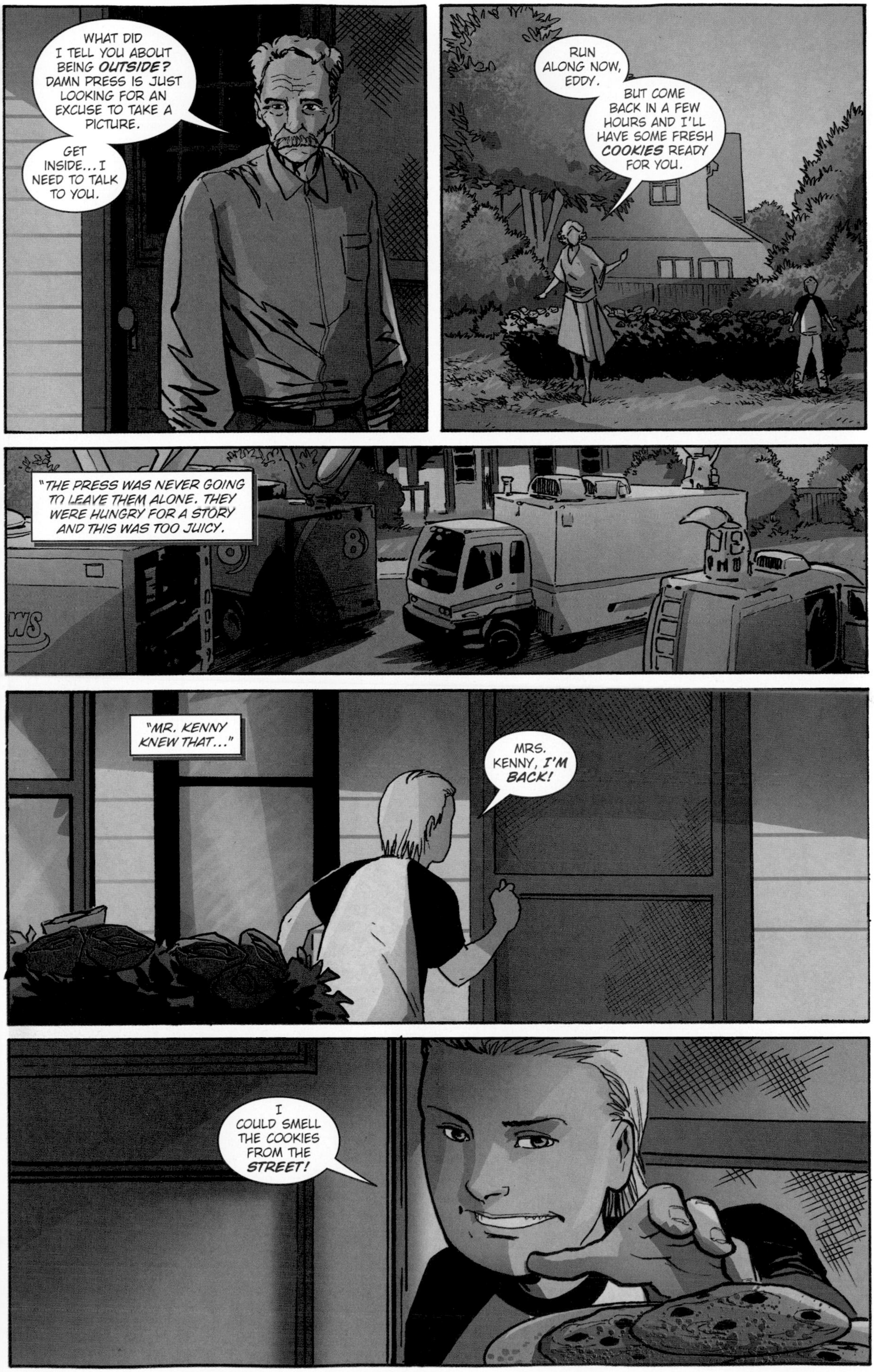
WHAT DID I TELL YOU ABOUT BEING OUTSIDE? DAMN PRESS IS JUST LOOKING FOR AN EXCUSE TO TAKE A PICTURE.
GET INSIDE... I NEED TO TALK TO YOU.
RUN ALONG NOW, EDDY.
BUT COME BACK IN A FEW HOURS AND I'LL HAVE SOME FRESH COOKIES READY FOR YOU.
"THE PRESS WAS NEVER GOING TO LEAVE THEM ALONE. THEY WERE HUNGRY FOR A STORY AND THIS WAS TOO JUICY.
"MR. KENNY KNEW THAT..."
MRS. KENNY, I'M BACK!
I COULD SMELL THE COOKIES FROM THE STREET!

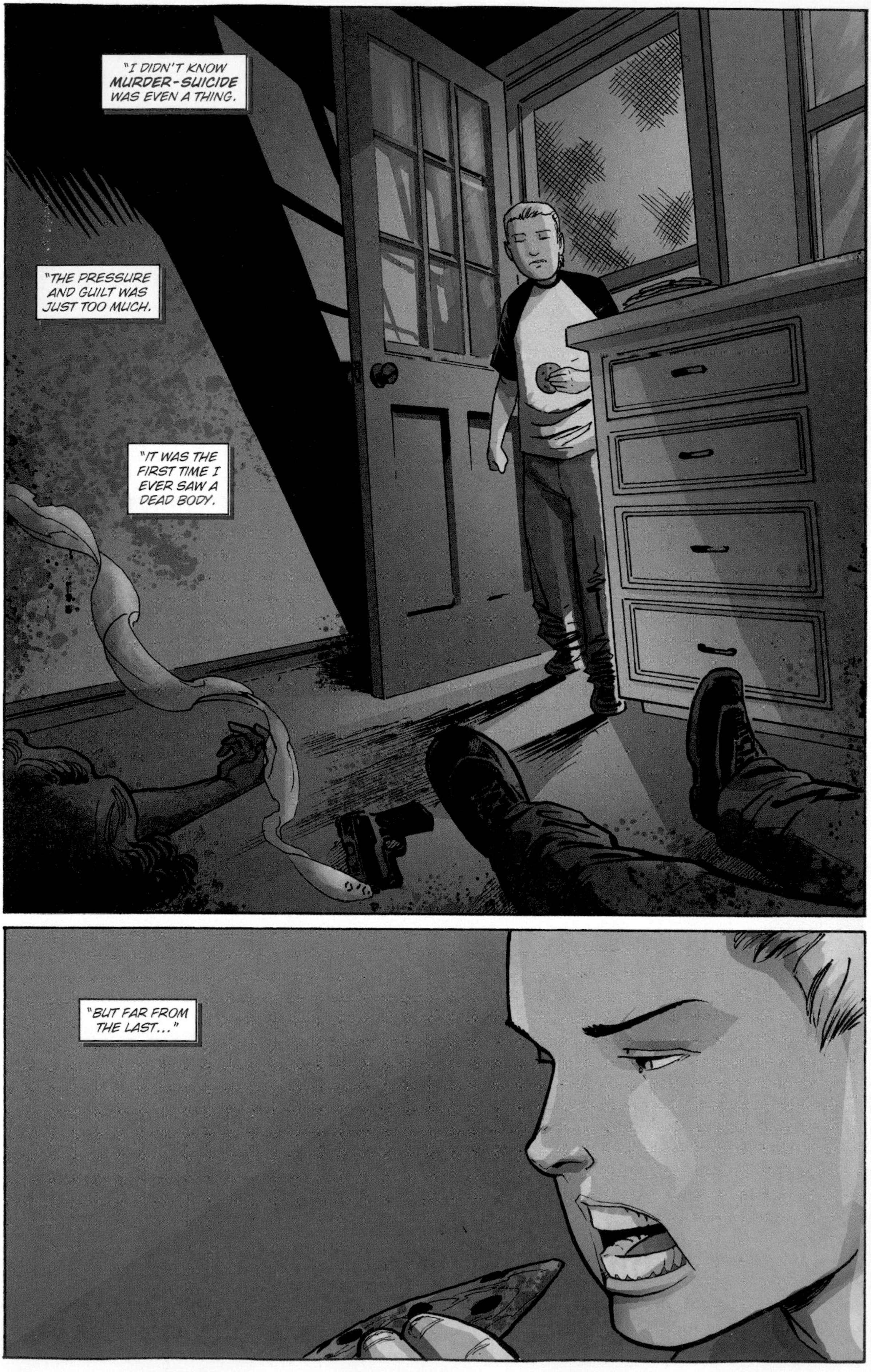
"I DIDN'T KNOW MURDER-SUICIDE WAS EVEN A THING.
"THE PRESSURE AND GUILT WAS JUST TOO MUCH.
"IT WAS THE FIRST TIME I EVER SAW A DEAD BODY.
"BUT FAR FROM THE LAST..."

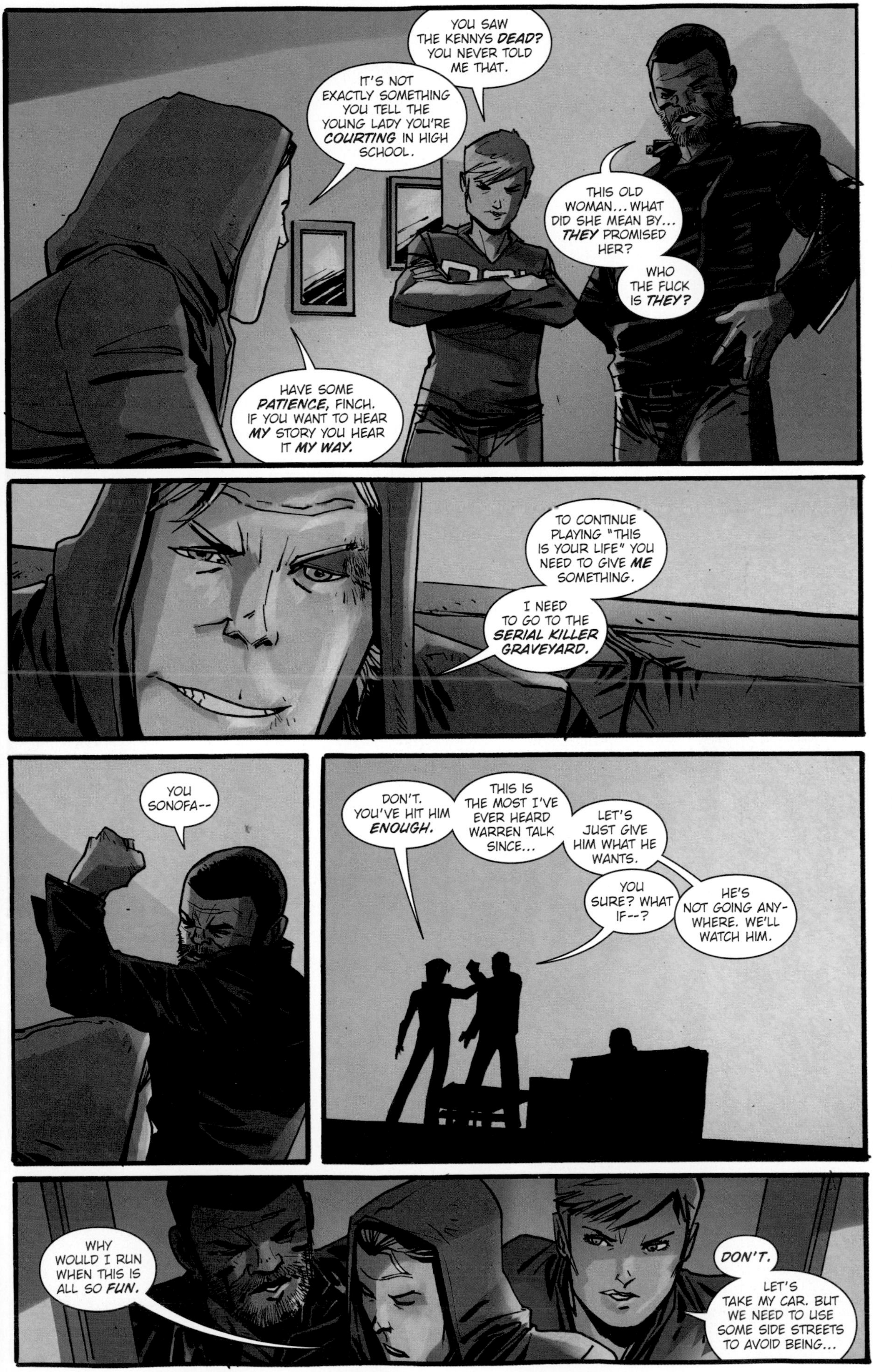

YOU SAW THE KENNYS *DEAD?* YOU NEVER TOLD ME THAT.
IT'S NOT EXACTLY SOMETHING YOU TELL THE YOUNG LADY YOU'RE *COURTING* IN HIGH SCHOOL.
THIS OLD WOMAN... WHAT DID SHE MEAN BY... *THEY* PROMISED HER?
WHO THE FUCK IS *THEY?*
HAVE SOME *PATIENCE,* FINCH. IF YOU WANT TO HEAR *MY* STORY YOU HEAR IT *MY WAY.*
TO CONTINUE PLAYING "THIS IS YOUR LIFE" YOU NEED TO GIVE *ME* SOMETHING.
I NEED TO GO TO THE *SERIAL KILLER GRAVEYARD.*
YOU SONOFA--
DON'T. YOU'VE HIT HIM *ENOUGH.*
THIS IS THE MOST I'VE EVER HEARD WARREN TALK SINCE...
LET'S JUST GIVE HIM WHAT HE WANTS.
YOU SURE? WHAT IF--?
HE'S NOT GOING ANY-WHERE. WE'LL WATCH HIM.
WHY WOULD I RUN WHEN THIS IS ALL SO *FUN.*
DON'T.
LET'S TAKE MY CAR. BUT WE NEED TO USE SOME SIDE STREETS TO AVOID BEING...

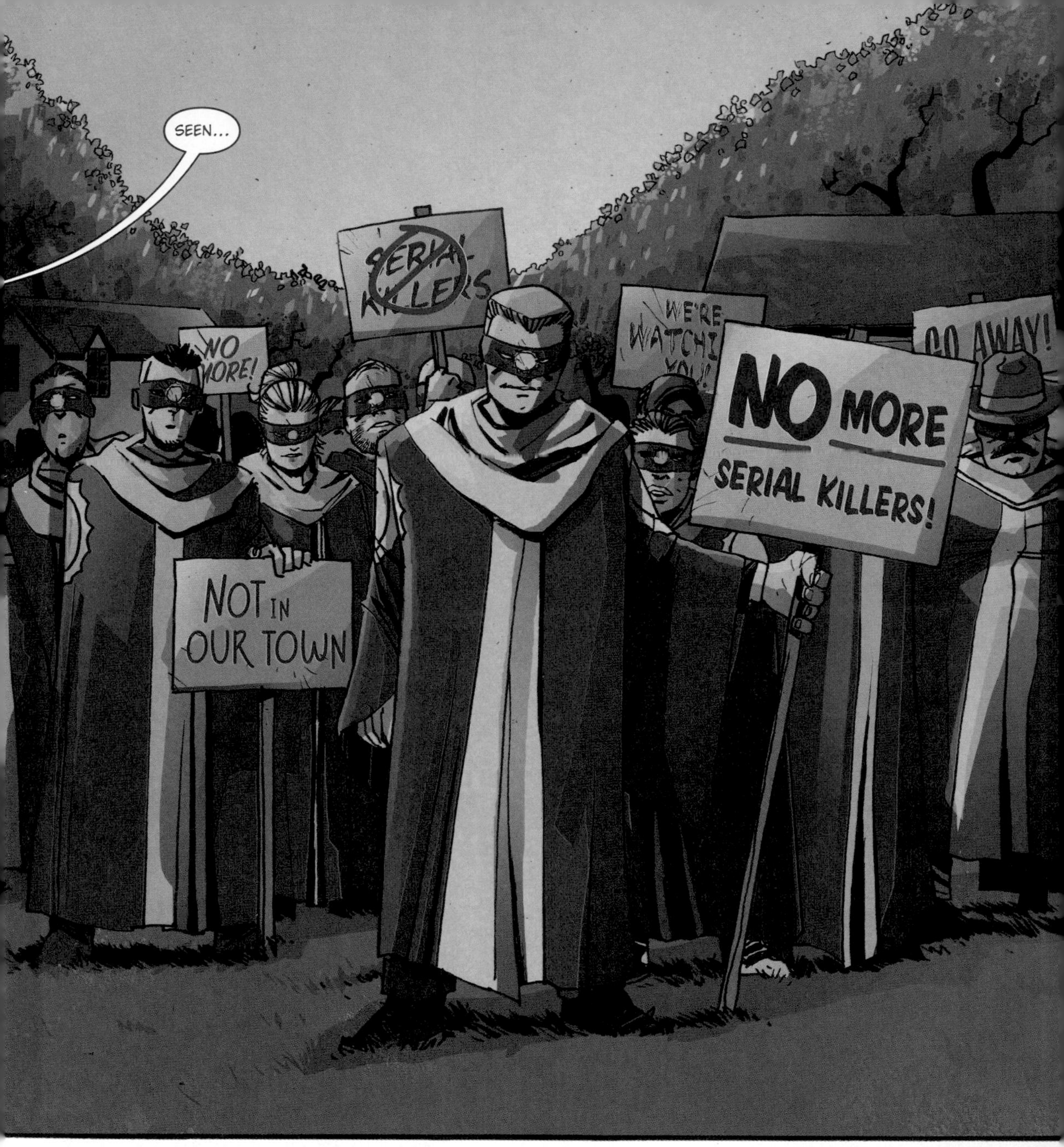
SEEN...
SERIAL KILLERS
NO MORE!
WE'RE WATCHI
NOT IN OUR TOWN
NO MORE SERIAL KILLERS!
GO AWAY!

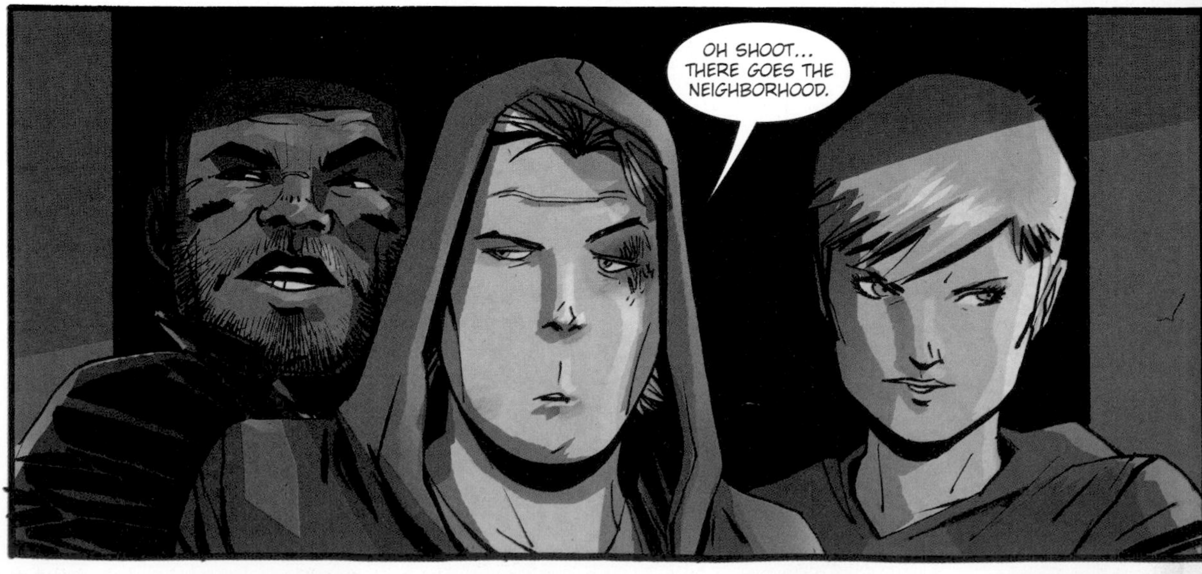
OH SHOOT... THERE GOES THE NEIGHBORHOOD.

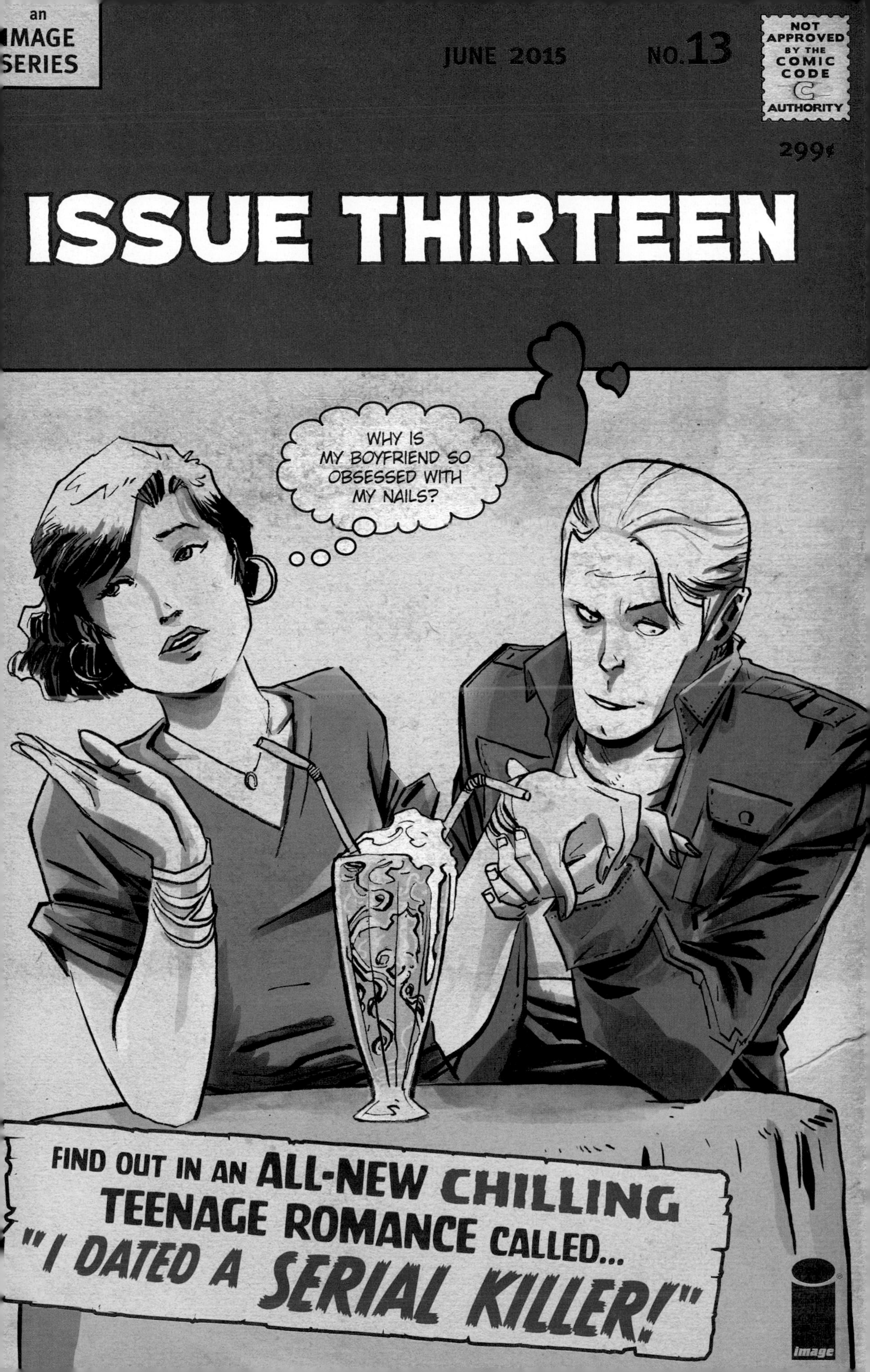

an IMAGE SERIES
JUNE 2015
NO.13
NOT APPROVED BY THE COMIC CODE AUTHORITY
299¢
ISSUE THIRTEEN
WHY IS MY BOYFRIEND SO OBSESSED WITH MY NAILS?
FIND OUT IN AN ALL-NEW CHILLING TEENAGE ROMANCE CALLED... "I DATED A SERIAL KILLER!"
image

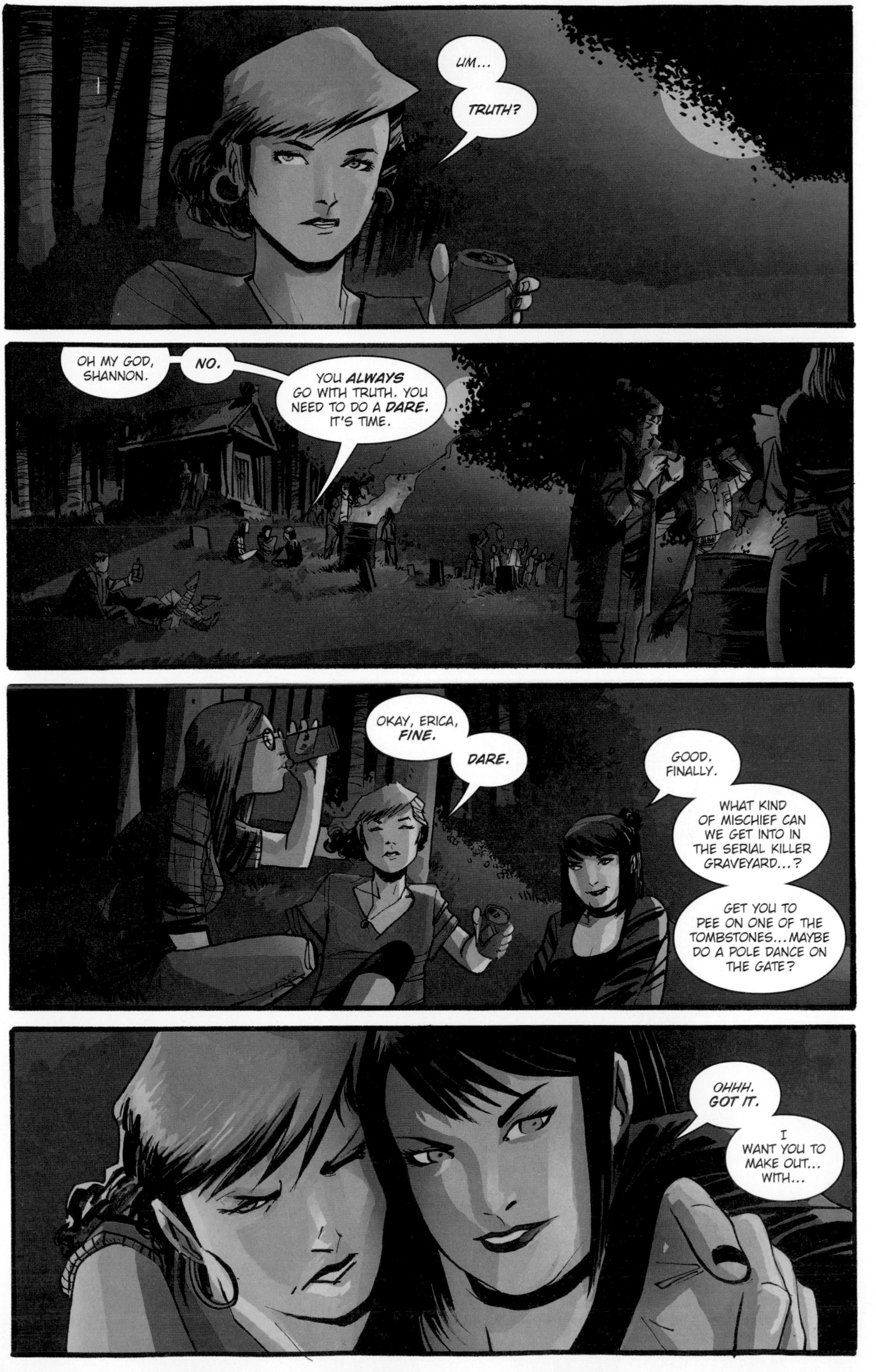
UM...
TRUTH?
OH MY GOD, SHANNON.
NO.
YOU ALWAYS GO WITH TRUTH. YOU NEED TO DO A DARE. IT'S TIME.
OKAY, ERICA, FINE.
DARE.
GOOD. FINALLY.
WHAT KIND OF MISCHIEF CAN WE GET INTO IN THE SERIAL KILLER GRAVEYARD...?
GET YOU TO PEE ON ONE OF THE TOMBSTONES... MAYBE DO A POLE DANCE ON THE GATE?
OHHH. GOT IT.
I WANT YOU TO MAKE OUT... WITH...

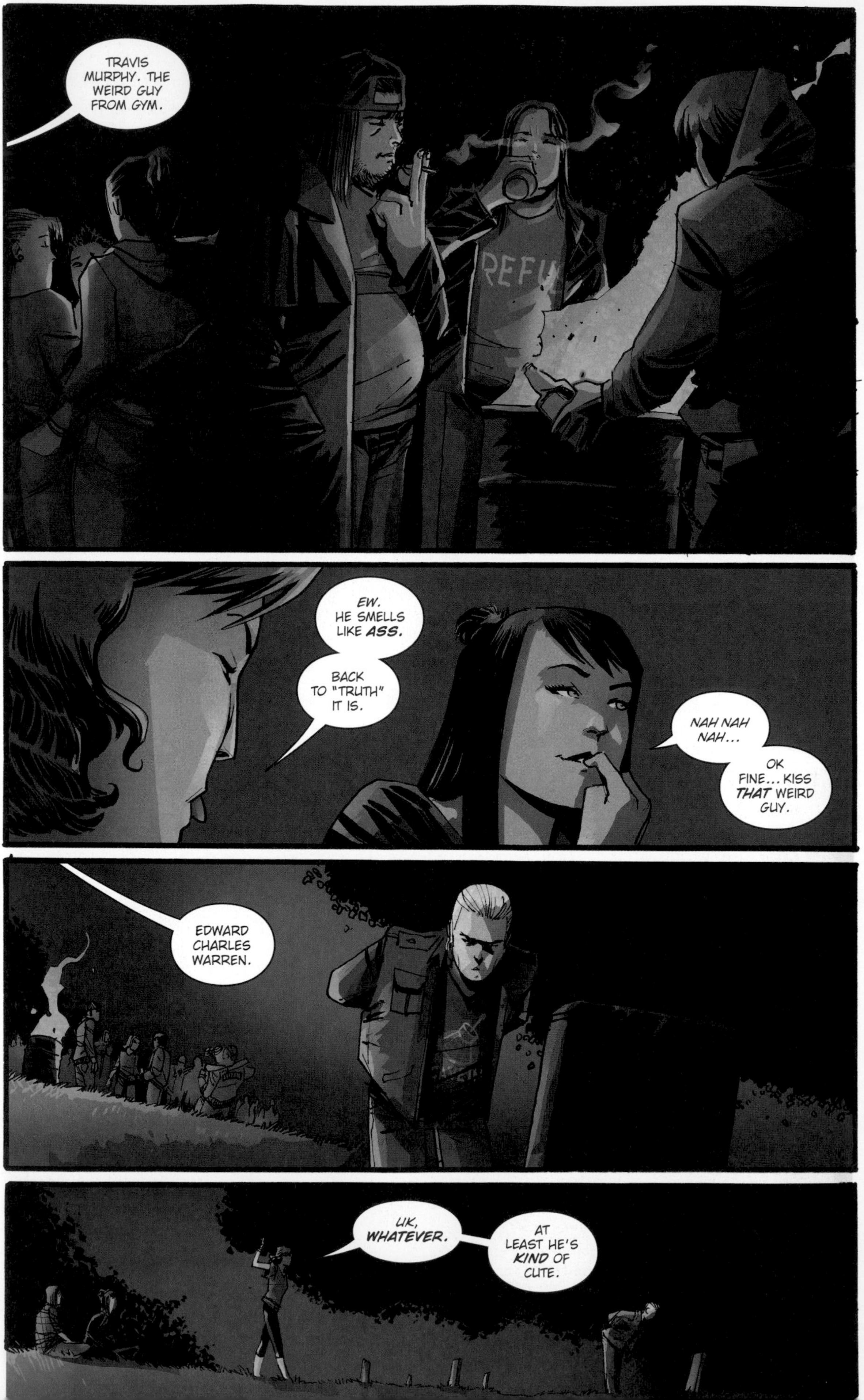
TRAVIS MURPHY. THE WEIRD GUY FROM GYM.
REFU
EW. HE SMELLS LIKE **ASS.**
BACK TO "TRUTH" IT IS.
NAH NAH NAH...
OK FINE... KISS ***THAT*** WEIRD GUY.
EDWARD CHARLES WARREN.
UK, ***WHATEVER.***
AT LEAST HE'S ***KIND*** OF CUTE.

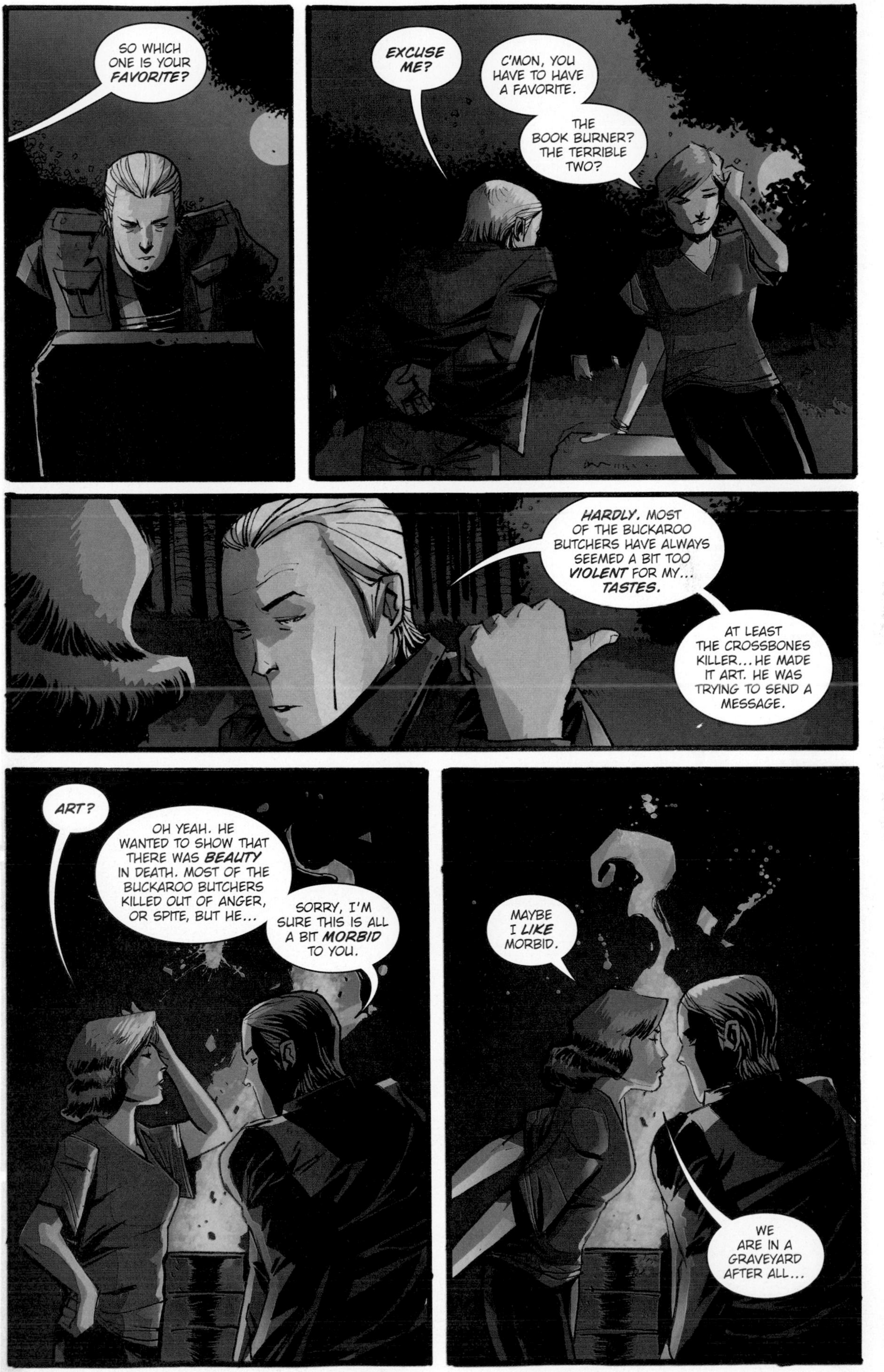
SO WHICH ONE IS YOUR *FAVORITE?*
EXCUSE ME?
C'MON, YOU HAVE TO HAVE A FAVORITE.
THE BOOK BURNER? THE TERRIBLE TWO?
HARDLY. MOST OF THE BUCKAROO BUTCHERS HAVE ALWAYS SEEMED A BIT TOO *VIOLENT* FOR MY... *TASTES.*
AT LEAST THE CROSSBONES KILLER... HE MADE IT ART. HE WAS TRYING TO SEND A MESSAGE.
ART?
OH YEAH. HE WANTED TO SHOW THAT THERE WAS *BEAUTY* IN DEATH. MOST OF THE BUCKAROO BUTCHERS KILLED OUT OF ANGER, OR SPITE, BUT HE...
SORRY, I'M SURE THIS IS ALL A BIT *MORBID* TO YOU.
MAYBE I *LIKE* MORBID.
WE ARE IN A GRAVEYARD AFTER ALL...

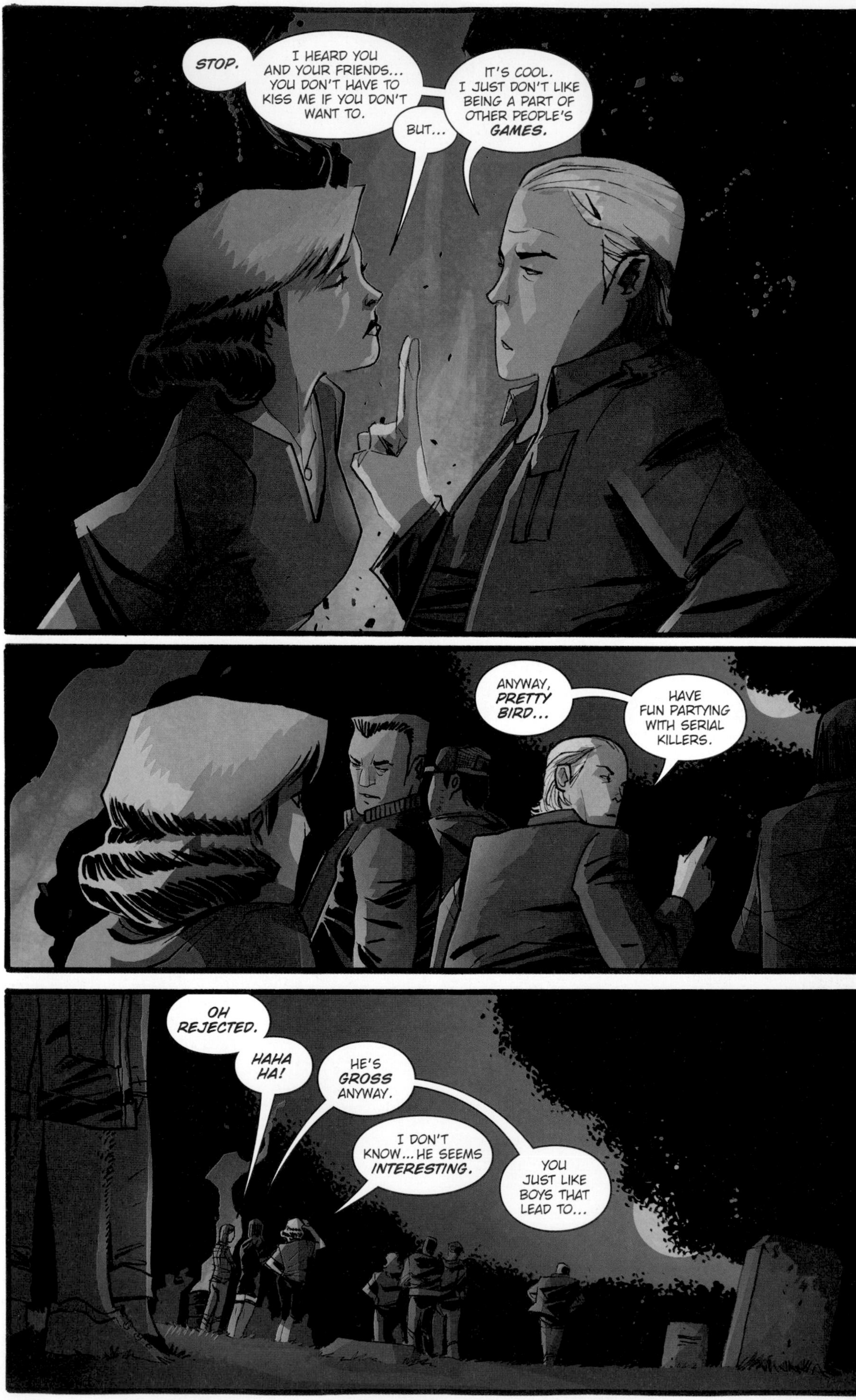
STOP.
I HEARD YOU AND YOUR FRIENDS... YOU DON'T HAVE TO KISS ME IF YOU DON'T WANT TO.
BUT...
IT'S COOL. I JUST DON'T LIKE BEING A PART OF OTHER PEOPLE'S GAMES.
ANYWAY, PRETTY BIRD...
HAVE FUN PARTYING WITH SERIAL KILLERS.
OH REJECTED.
HAHA HA!
HE'S GROSS ANYWAY.
I DON'T KNOW...HE SEEMS INTERESTING.
YOU JUST LIKE BOYS THAT LEAD TO...

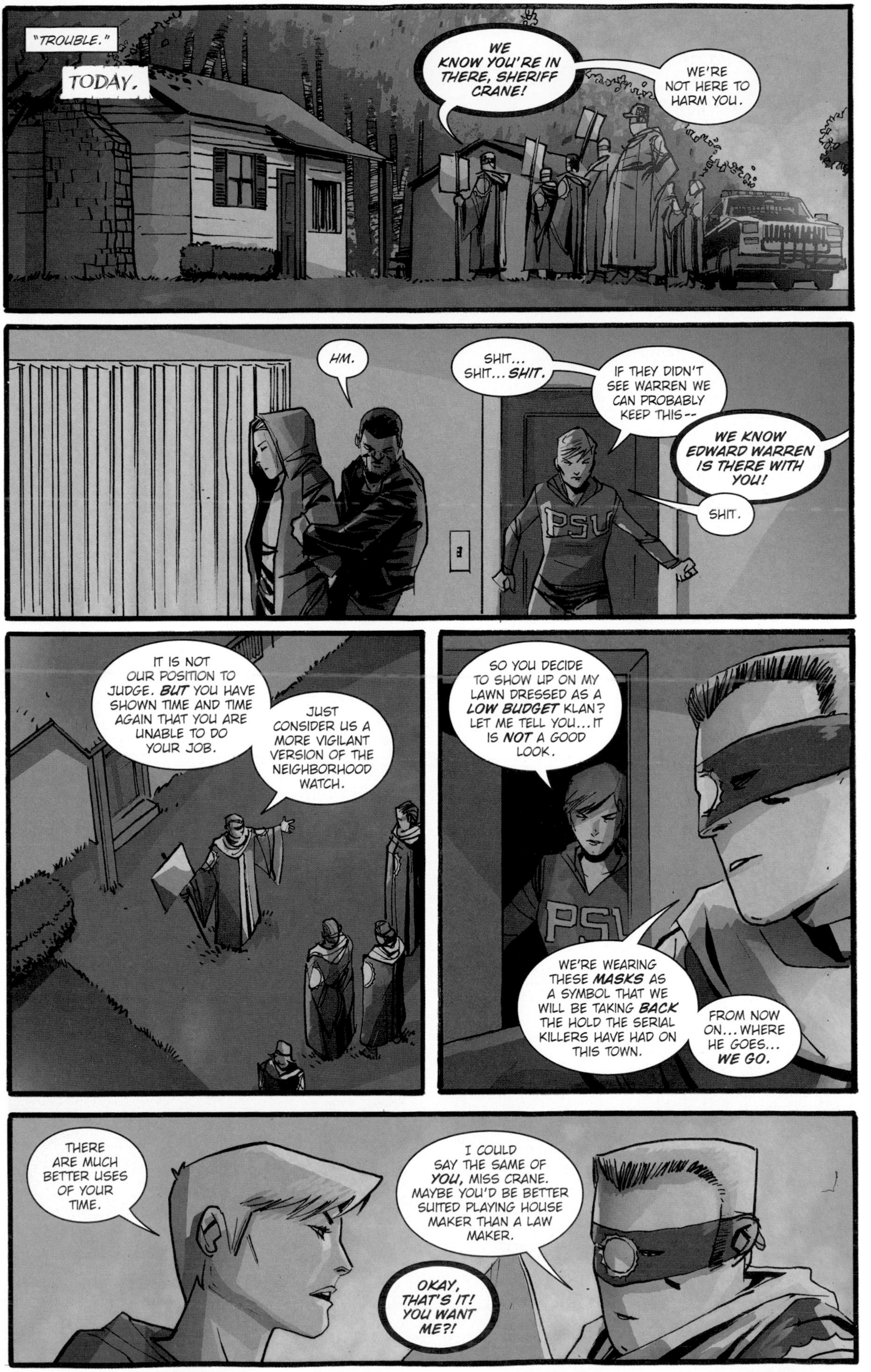
"TROUBLE."
TODAY.
WE KNOW YOU'RE IN THERE, SHERIFF CRANE!
WE'RE NOT HERE TO HARM YOU.
HM.
SHIT... SHIT... SHIT.
IF THEY DIDN'T SEE WARREN WE CAN PROBABLY KEEP THIS--
WE KNOW EDWARD WARREN IS THERE WITH YOU!
SHIT.
IT IS NOT OUR POSITION TO JUDGE. BUT YOU HAVE SHOWN TIME AND TIME AGAIN THAT YOU ARE UNABLE TO DO YOUR JOB.
JUST CONSIDER US A MORE VIGILANT VERSION OF THE NEIGHBORHOOD WATCH.
SO YOU DECIDE TO SHOW UP ON MY LAWN DRESSED AS A LOW BUDGET KLAN? LET ME TELL YOU... IT IS NOT A GOOD LOOK.
WE'RE WEARING THESE MASKS AS A SYMBOL THAT WE WILL BE TAKING BACK THE HOLD THE SERIAL KILLERS HAVE HAD ON THIS TOWN.
FROM NOW ON... WHERE HE GOES... WE GO.
THERE ARE MUCH BETTER USES OF YOUR TIME.
I COULD SAY THE SAME OF YOU, MISS CRANE. MAYBE YOU'D BE BETTER SUITED PLAYING HOUSE MAKER THAN A LAW MAKER.
OKAY, THAT'S IT! YOU WANT ME?!

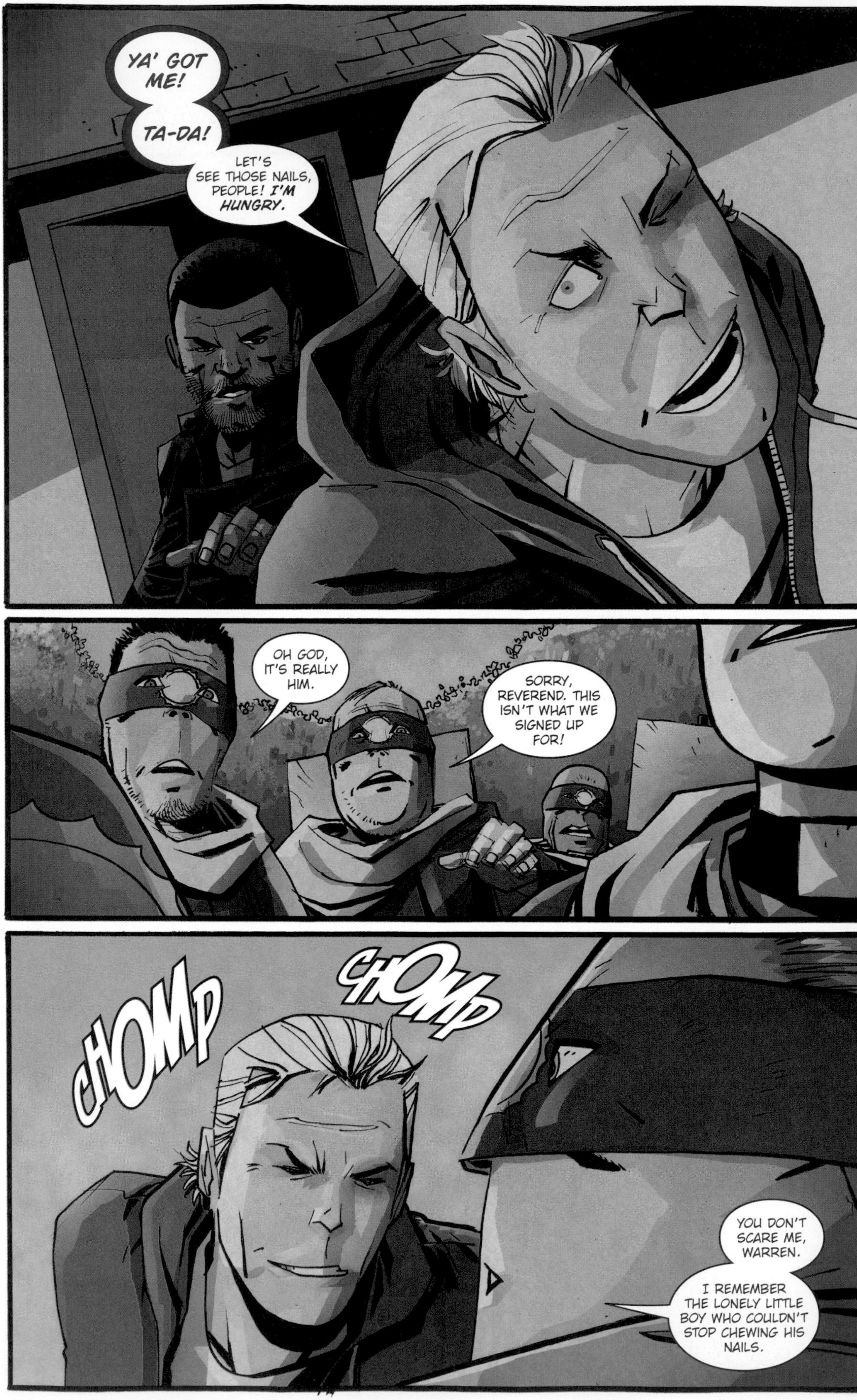
YA' GOT ME!
TA-DA!
LET'S SEE THOSE NAILS, PEOPLE! *I'M HUNGRY.*
OH GOD, IT'S REALLY HIM.
SORRY, REVEREND. THIS ISN'T WHAT WE SIGNED UP FOR!
CHOMP
CHOMP
YOU DON'T SCARE ME, WARREN.
I REMEMBER THE LONELY LITTLE BOY WHO COULDN'T STOP CHEWING HIS NAILS.

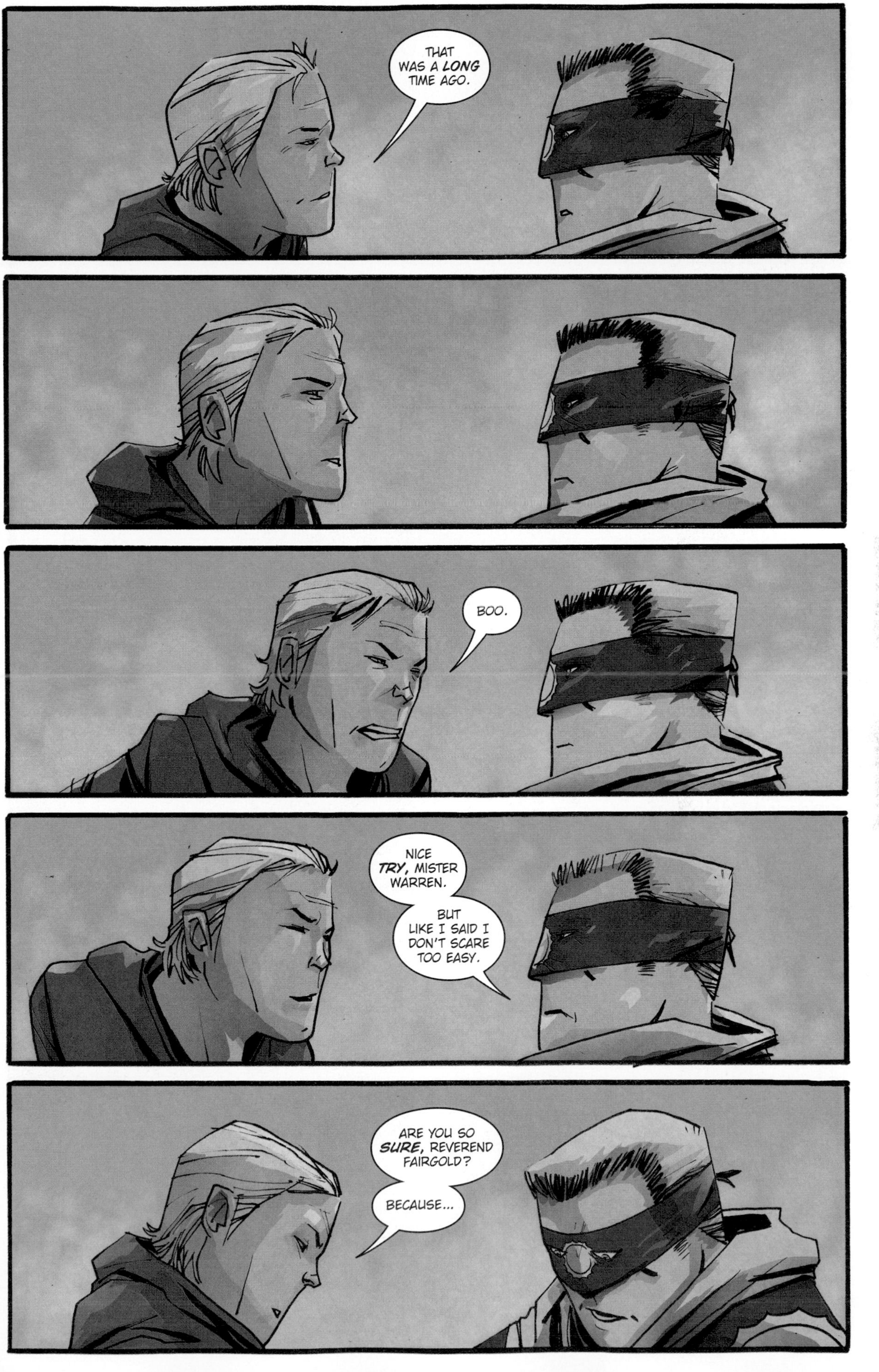
THAT WAS A LONG TIME AGO.
BOO.
NICE TRY, MISTER WARREN.
BUT LIKE I SAID I DON'T SCARE TOO EASY.
ARE YOU SO SURE, REVEREND FAIRGOLD?
BECAUSE...

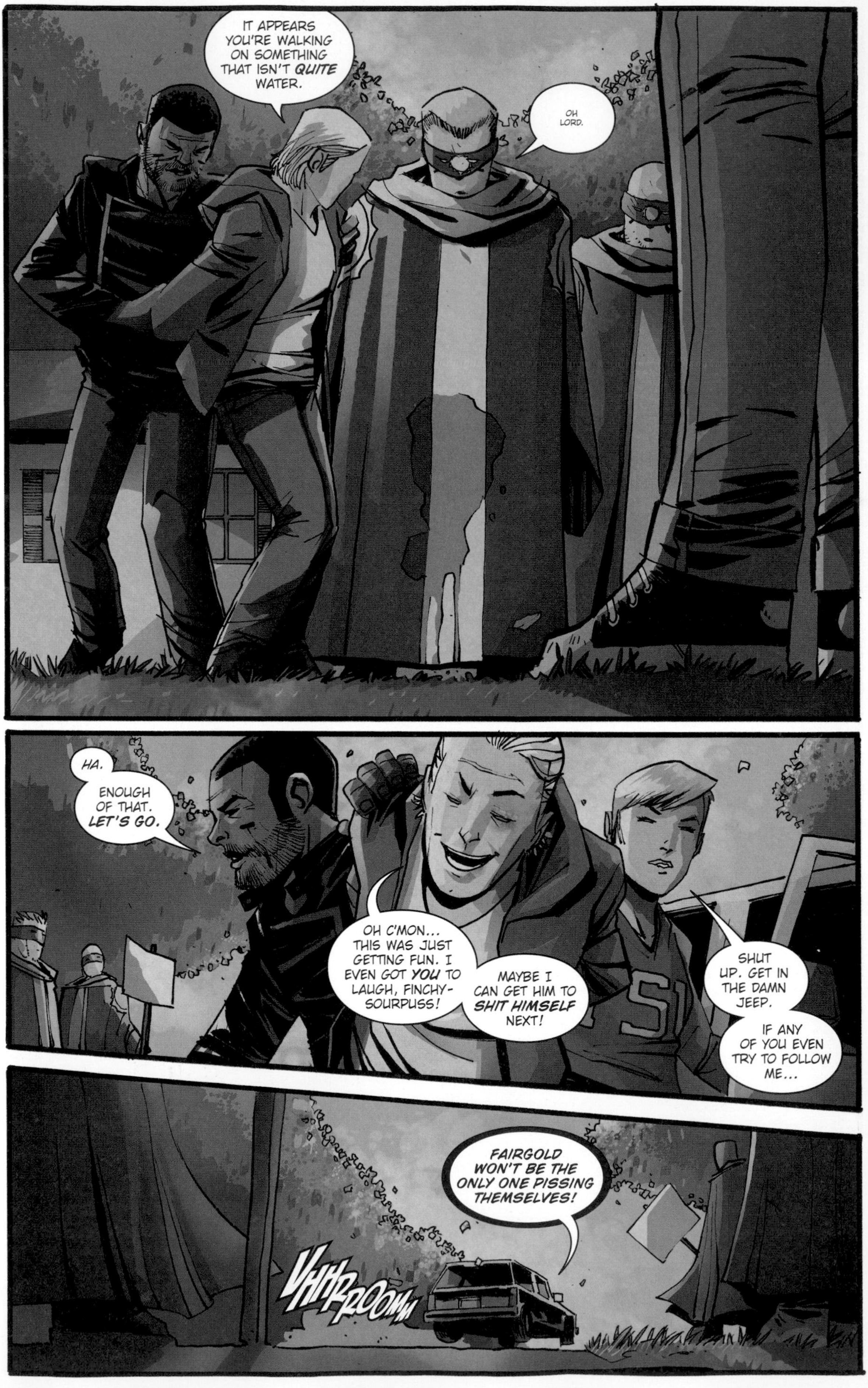

IT APPEARS YOU'RE WALKING ON SOMETHING THAT ISN'T QUITE WATER.
OH LORD.
HA.
ENOUGH OF THAT. LET'S GO.
OH C'MON... THIS WAS JUST GETTING FUN. I EVEN GOT YOU TO LAUGH, FINCHY-SOURPUSS!
MAYBE I CAN GET HIM TO SHIT HIMSELF NEXT!
SHUT UP. GET IN THE DAMN JEEP.
IF ANY OF YOU EVEN TRY TO FOLLOW ME...
FAIRGOLD WON'T BE THE ONLY ONE PISSING THEMSELVES!
VHHRROOMM

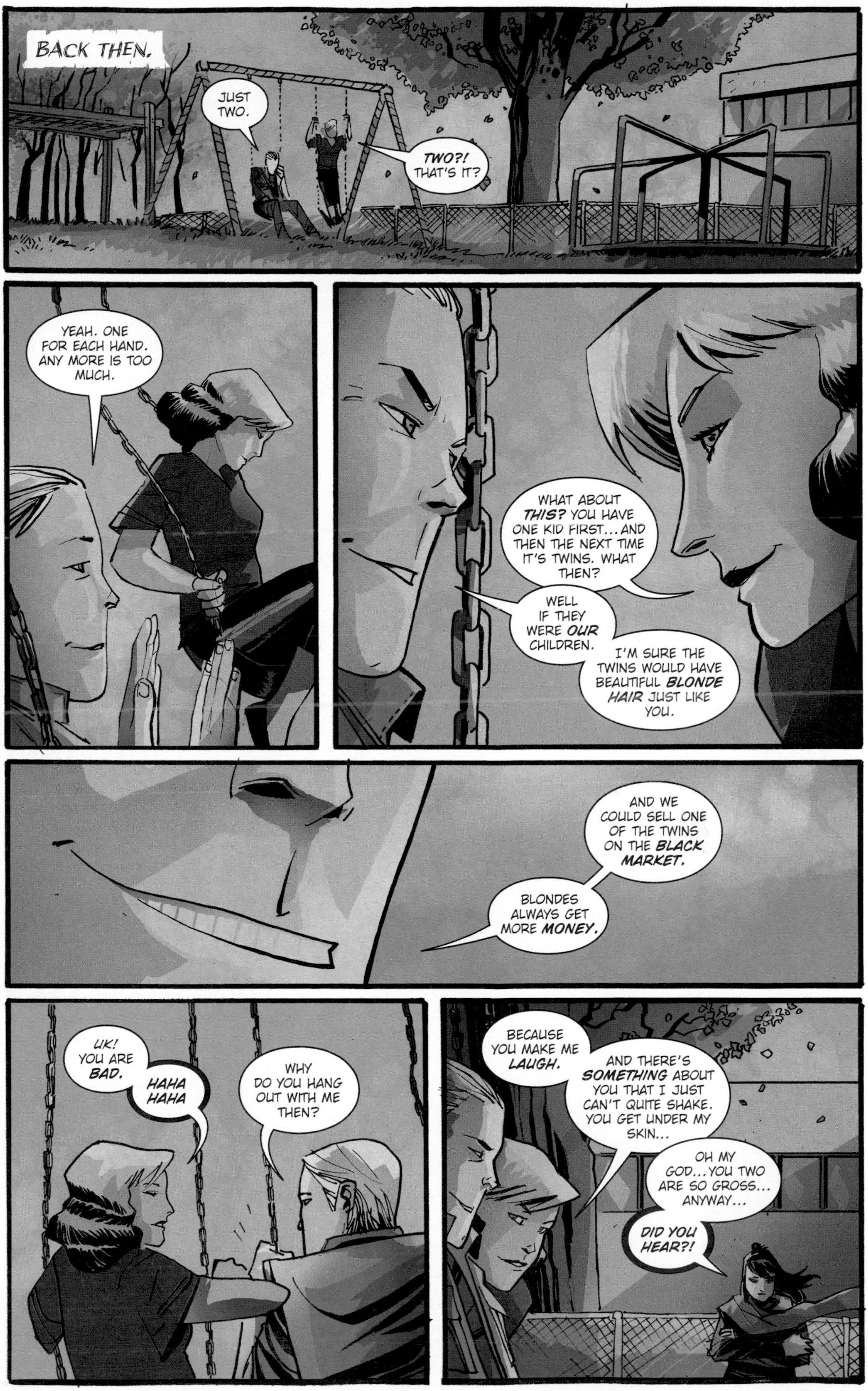
BACK THEN.
JUST TWO.
TWO?! THAT'S IT?
YEAH. ONE FOR EACH HAND. ANY MORE IS TOO MUCH.
WHAT ABOUT THIS? YOU HAVE ONE KID FIRST... AND THEN THE NEXT TIME IT'S TWINS. WHAT THEN?
WELL IF THEY WERE OUR CHILDREN.
I'M SURE THE TWINS WOULD HAVE BEAUTIFUL BLONDE HAIR JUST LIKE YOU.
AND WE COULD SELL ONE OF THE TWINS ON THE BLACK MARKET.
BLONDES ALWAYS GET MORE MONEY.
UK! YOU ARE BAD.
HAHA HAHA
WHY DO YOU HANG OUT WITH ME THEN?
BECAUSE YOU MAKE ME LAUGH.
AND THERE'S SOMETHING ABOUT YOU THAT I JUST CAN'T QUITE SHAKE. YOU GET UNDER MY SKIN...
OH MY GOD... YOU TWO ARE SO GROSS... ANYWAY...
DID YOU HEAR?!

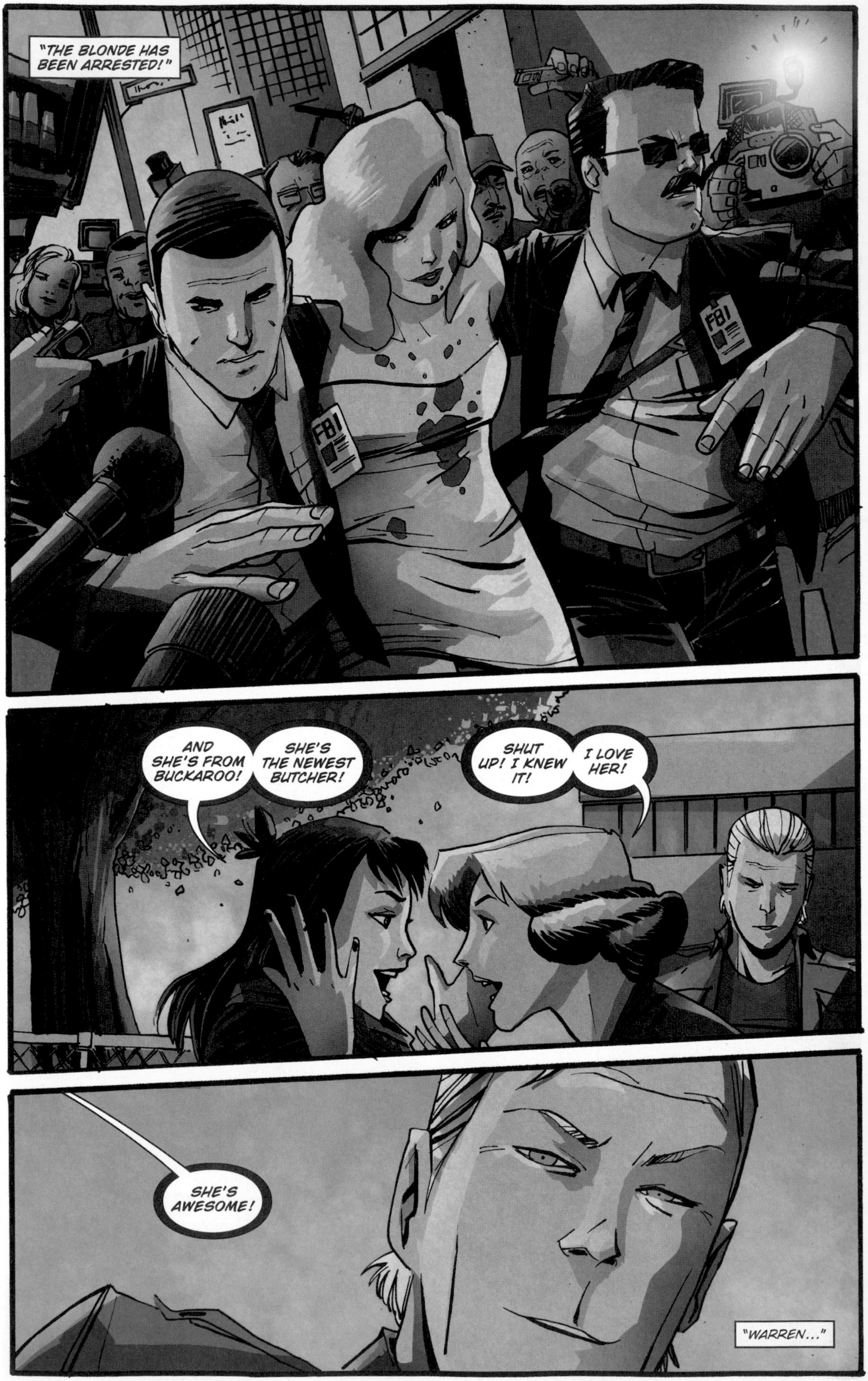
"THE BLONDE HAS BEEN ARRESTED!"
AND SHE'S FROM BUCKAROO!
SHE'S THE NEWEST BUTCHER!
SHUT UP! I KNEW IT!
I LOVE HER!
SHE'S AWESOME!
"WARREN..."

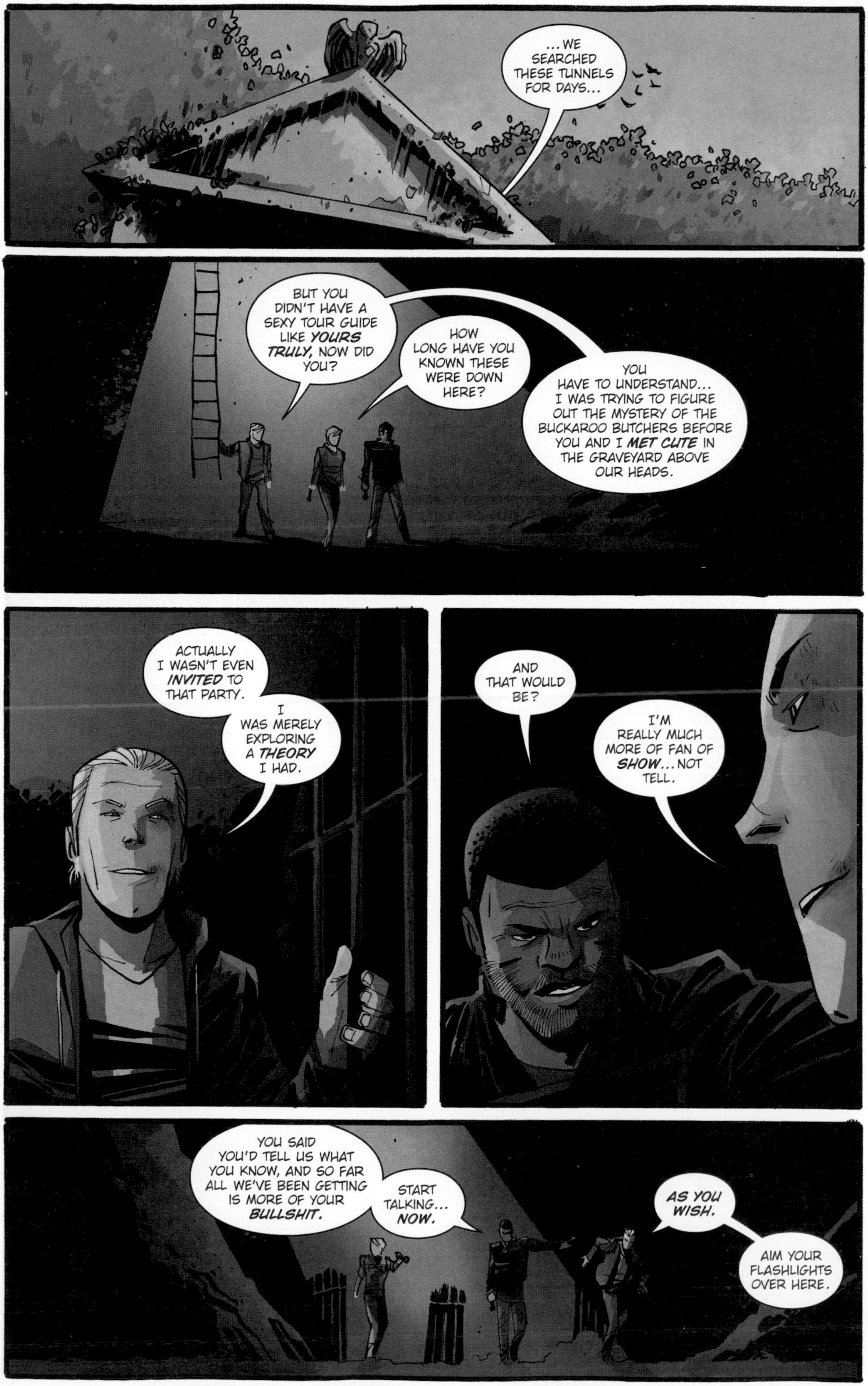
...WE SEARCHED THESE TUNNELS FOR DAYS...
BUT YOU DIDN'T HAVE A SEXY TOUR GUIDE LIKE YOURS TRULY, NOW DID YOU?
HOW LONG HAVE YOU KNOWN THESE WERE DOWN HERE?
YOU HAVE TO UNDERSTAND... I WAS TRYING TO FIGURE OUT THE MYSTERY OF THE BUCKAROO BUTCHERS BEFORE YOU AND I MET CUTE IN THE GRAVEYARD ABOVE OUR HEADS.
ACTUALLY I WASN'T EVEN INVITED TO THAT PARTY.
I WAS MERELY EXPLORING A THEORY I HAD.
AND THAT WOULD BE?
I'M REALLY MUCH MORE OF FAN OF SHOW... NOT TELL.
YOU SAID YOU'D TELL US WHAT YOU KNOW, AND SO FAR ALL WE'VE BEEN GETTING IS MORE OF YOUR BULLSHIT.
START TALKING... NOW.
AS YOU WISH.
AIM YOUR FLASHLIGHTS OVER HERE.

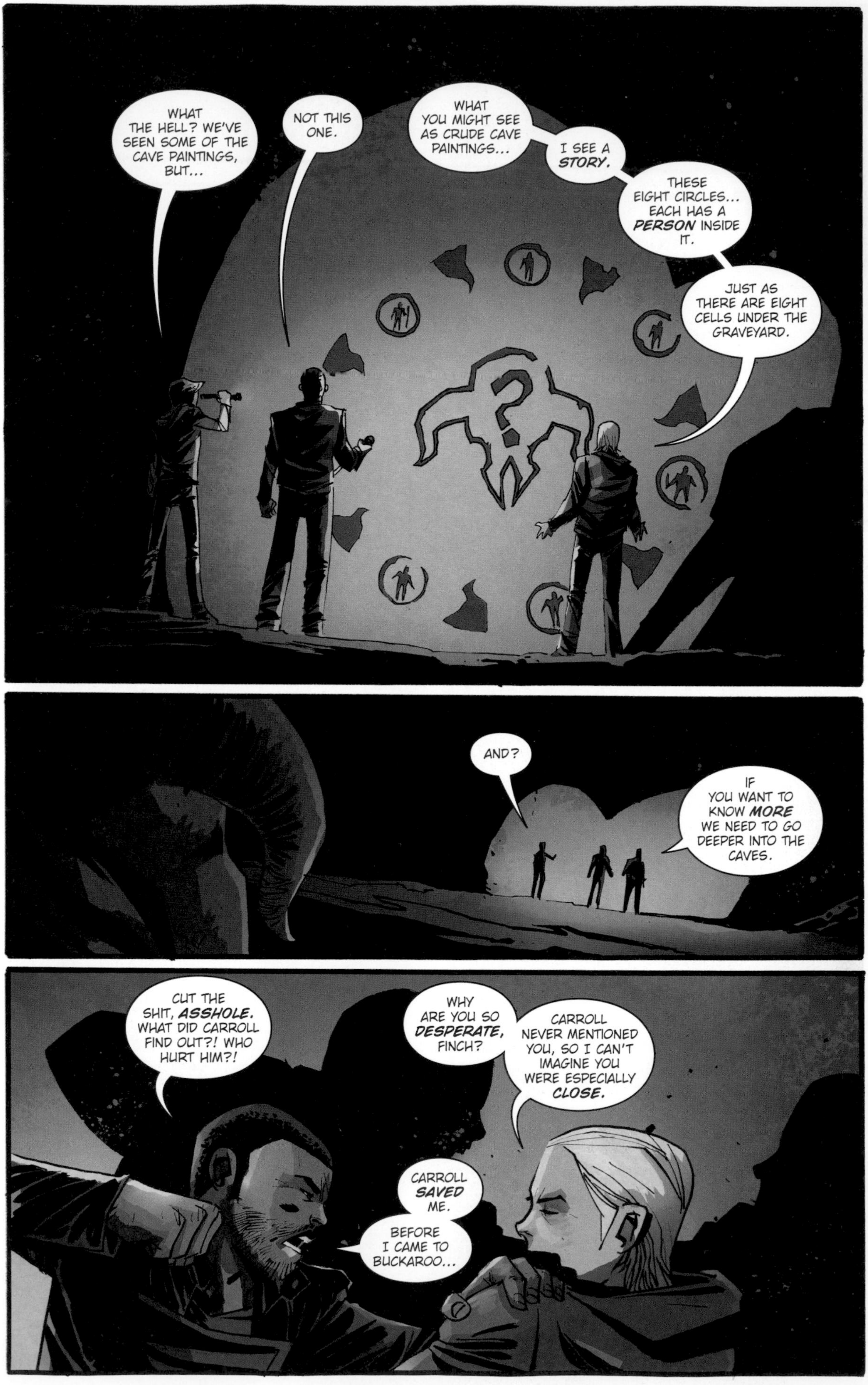
WHAT THE HELL? WE'VE SEEN SOME OF THE CAVE PAINTINGS, BUT...
NOT THIS ONE.
WHAT YOU MIGHT SEE AS CRUDE CAVE PAINTINGS...
I SEE A STORY.
THESE EIGHT CIRCLES... EACH HAS A PERSON INSIDE IT.
JUST AS THERE ARE EIGHT CELLS UNDER THE GRAVEYARD.
AND?
IF YOU WANT TO KNOW MORE WE NEED TO GO DEEPER INTO THE CAVES.
CUT THE SHIT, ASSHOLE. WHAT DID CARROLL FIND OUT?! WHO HURT HIM?!
WHY ARE YOU SO DESPERATE, FINCH?
CARROLL NEVER MENTIONED YOU, SO I CAN'T IMAGINE YOU WERE ESPECIALLY CLOSE.
CARROLL SAVED ME.
BEFORE I CAME TO BUCKAROO...

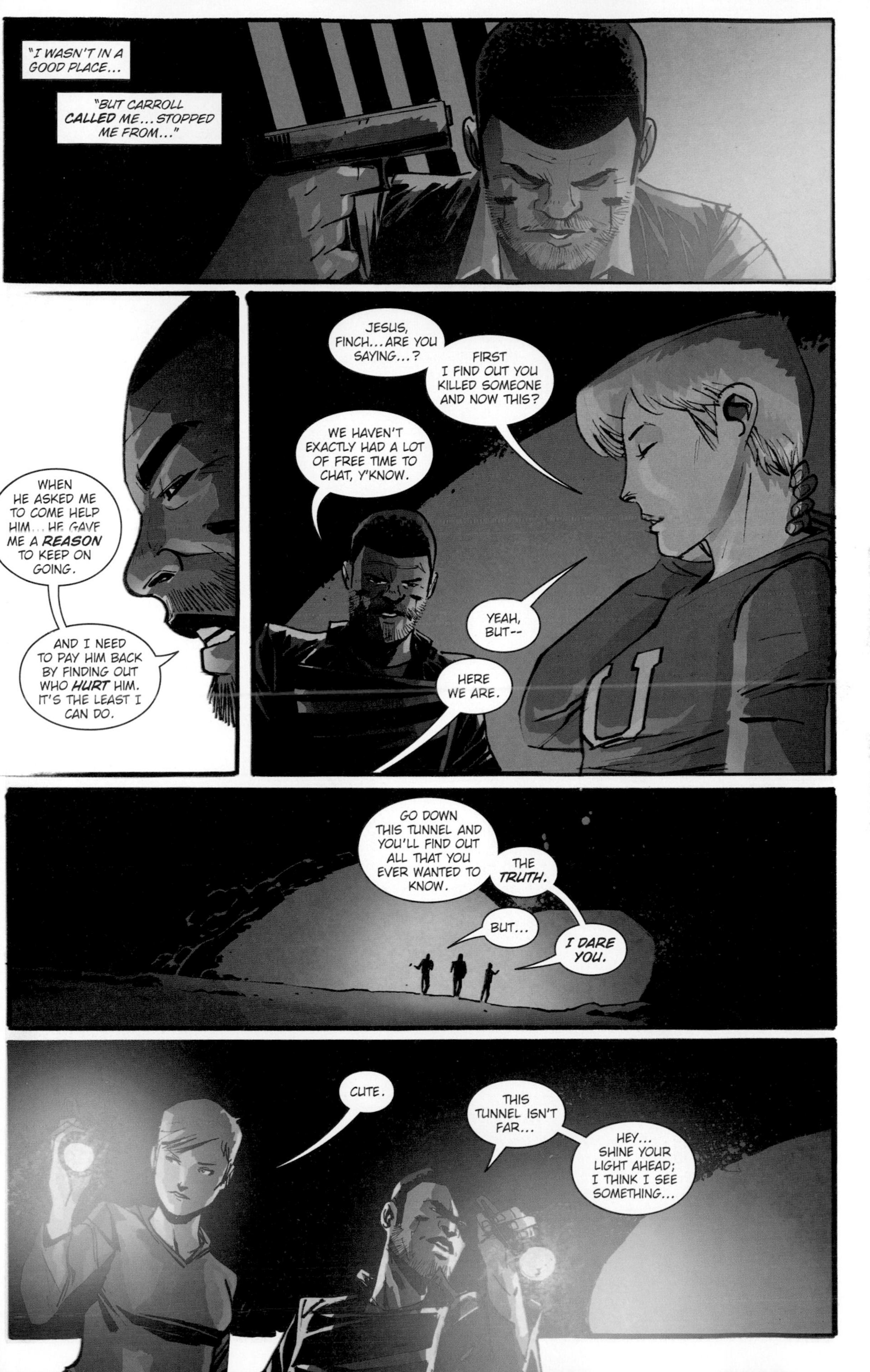
"I WASN'T IN A GOOD PLACE...
"BUT CARROLL CALLED ME... STOPPED ME FROM..."
WHEN HE ASKED ME TO COME HELP HIM... HE GAVE ME A REASON TO KEEP ON GOING.
AND I NEED TO PAY HIM BACK BY FINDING OUT WHO HURT HIM. IT'S THE LEAST I CAN DO.
JESUS, FINCH... ARE YOU SAYING...?
FIRST I FIND OUT YOU KILLED SOMEONE AND NOW THIS?
WE HAVEN'T EXACTLY HAD A LOT OF FREE TIME TO CHAT, Y'KNOW.
YEAH, BUT--
HERE WE ARE.
GO DOWN THIS TUNNEL AND YOU'LL FIND OUT ALL THAT YOU EVER WANTED TO KNOW.
THE TRUTH.
BUT...
I DARE YOU.
CUTE.
THIS TUNNEL ISN'T FAR...
HEY... SHINE YOUR LIGHT AHEAD; I THINK I SEE SOMETHING...

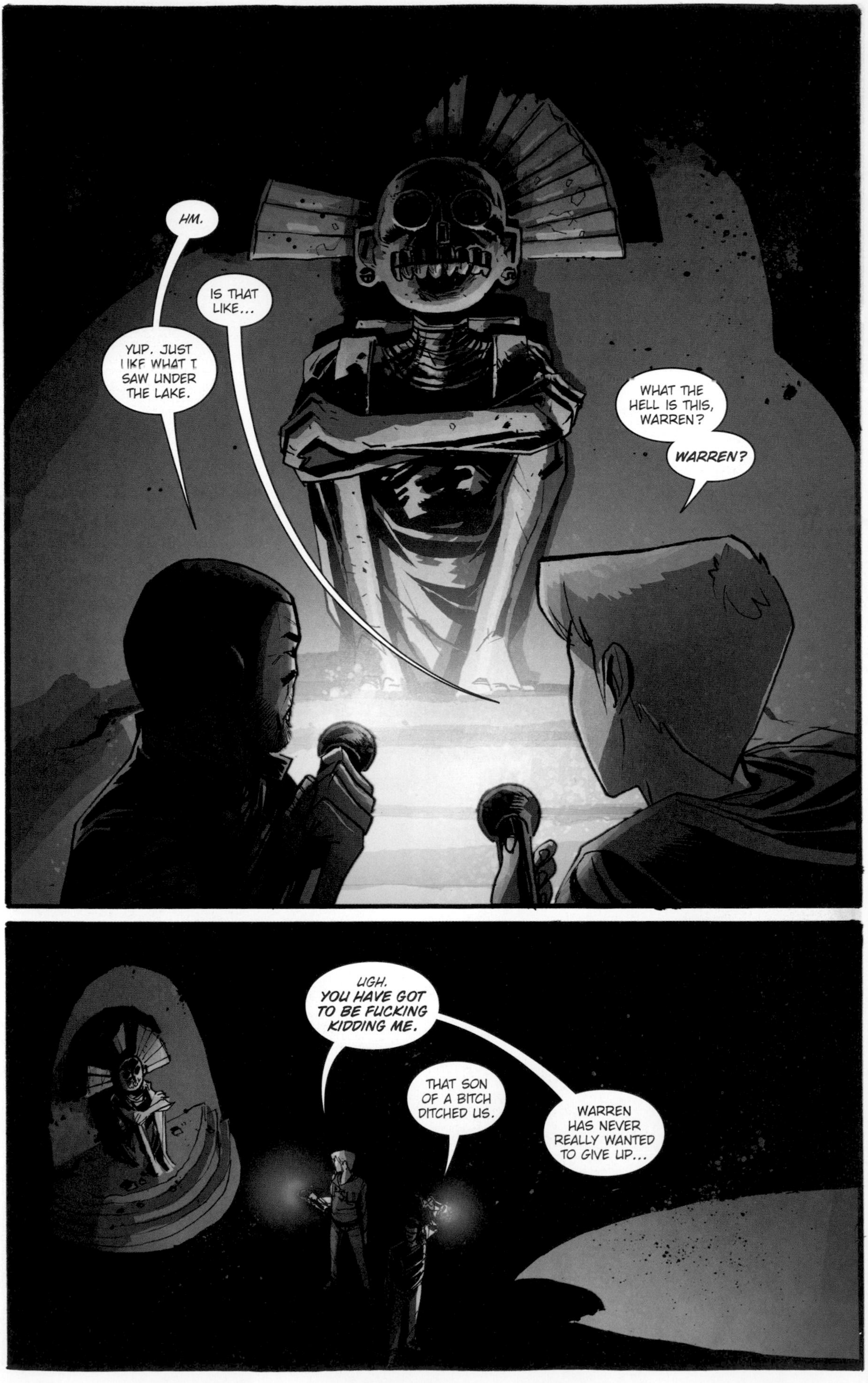
HM.
IS THAT LIKE...
YUP. JUST LIKE WHAT I SAW UNDER THE LAKE.
WHAT THE HELL IS THIS, WARREN?
WARREN?
UGH. ***YOU HAVE GOT TO BE FUCKING KIDDING ME.***
THAT SON OF A BITCH DITCHED US.
WARREN HAS NEVER REALLY WANTED TO GIVE UP...

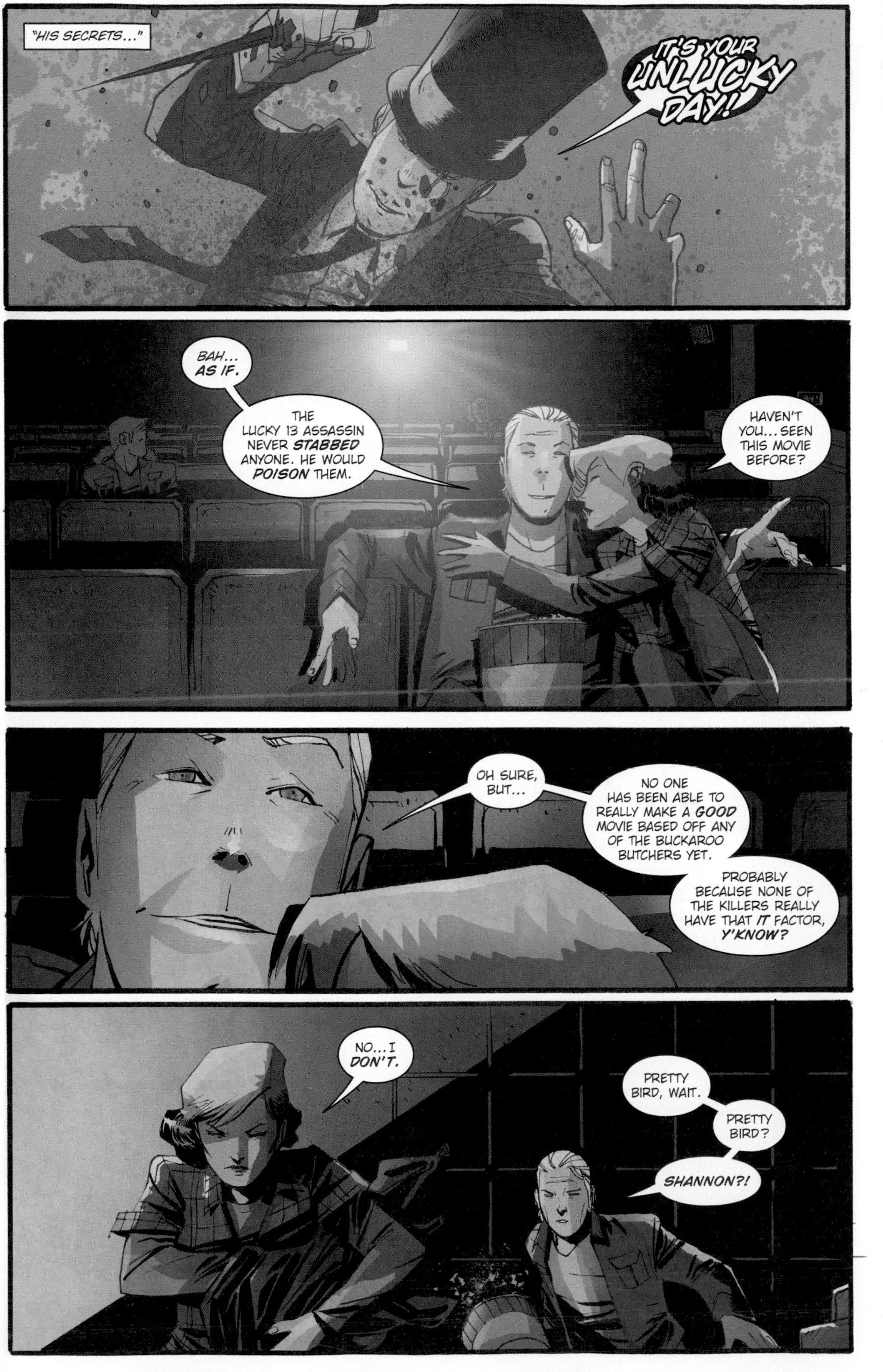
"HIS SECRETS..."
IT'S YOUR UNLUCKY DAY!
BAH... AS IF.
THE LUCKY 13 ASSASSIN NEVER STABBED ANYONE. HE WOULD POISON THEM.
HAVEN'T YOU... SEEN THIS MOVIE BEFORE?
OH SURE, BUT...
NO ONE HAS BEEN ABLE TO REALLY MAKE A GOOD MOVIE BASED OFF ANY OF THE BUCKAROO BUTCHERS YET.
PROBABLY BECAUSE NONE OF THE KILLERS REALLY HAVE THAT IT FACTOR, Y'KNOW?
NO... I DON'T.
PRETTY BIRD, WAIT.
PRETTY BIRD?
SHANNON?!

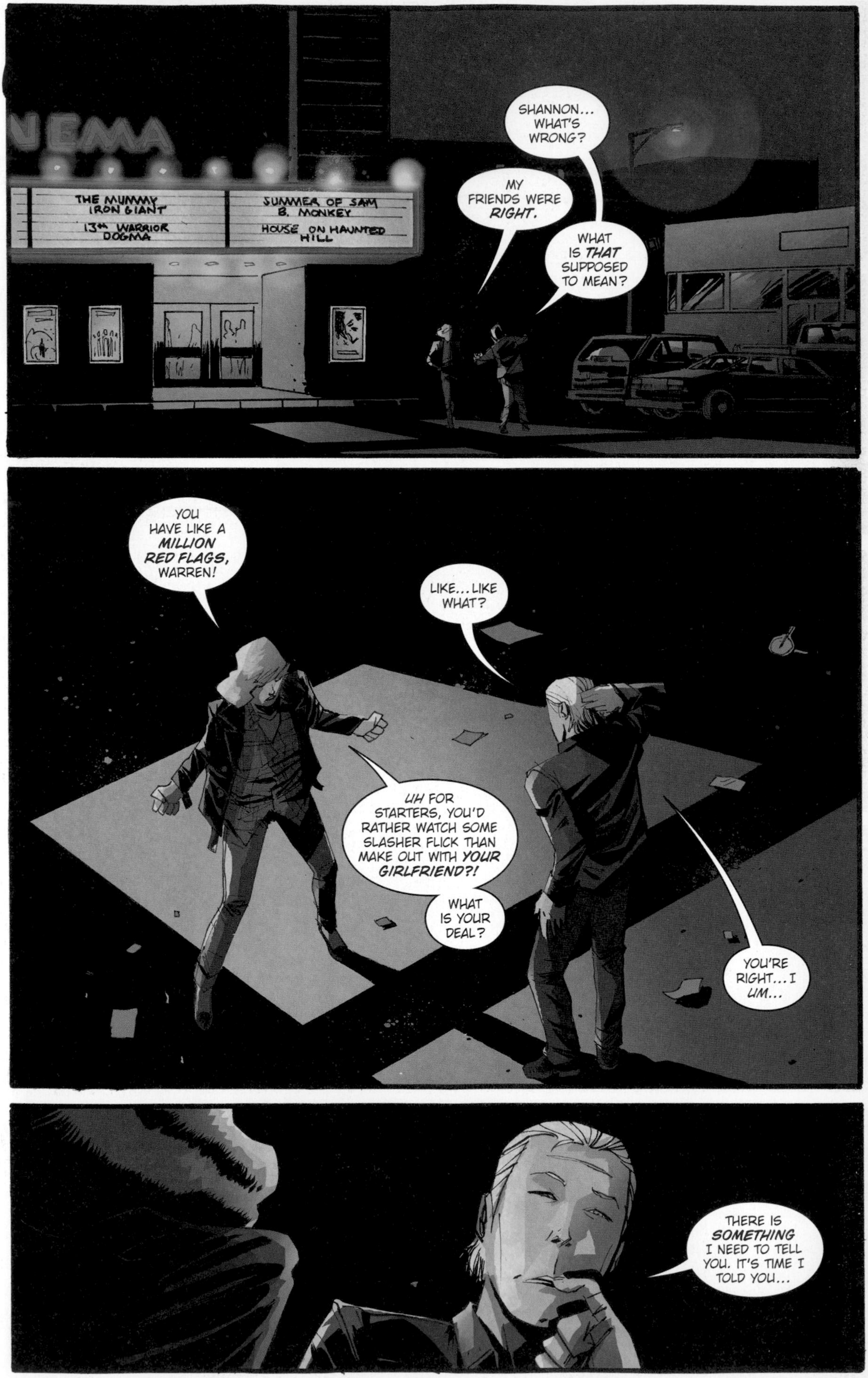
NEMA
THE MUMMY
IRON GIANT
13TH WARRIOR
DOGMA
SUMMER OF SAM
B. MONKEY
HOUSE ON HAUNTED HILL
SHANNON... WHAT'S WRONG?
MY FRIENDS WERE *RIGHT.*
WHAT IS *THAT* SUPPOSED TO MEAN?
YOU HAVE LIKE A *MILLION RED FLAGS,* WARREN!
LIKE... LIKE WHAT?
UH FOR STARTERS, YOU'D RATHER WATCH SOME SLASHER FLICK THAN MAKE OUT WITH *YOUR GIRLFRIEND?!*
WHAT IS YOUR DEAL?
YOU'RE RIGHT... I *UM...*
THERE IS *SOMETHING* I NEED TO TELL YOU. IT'S TIME I TOLD YOU...

"THE TRUTH."

BUCKAROO
HOSPITAL

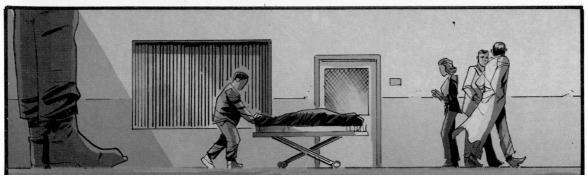

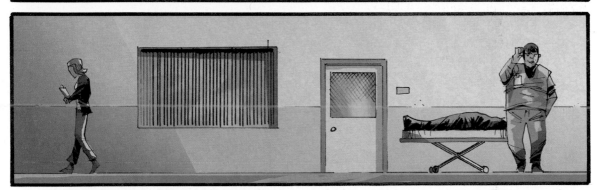

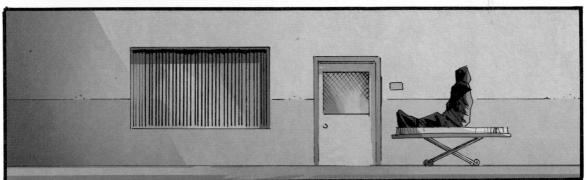

TIME TO
SEE AN OLD
FRIEND.

HELLO,
WARREN.

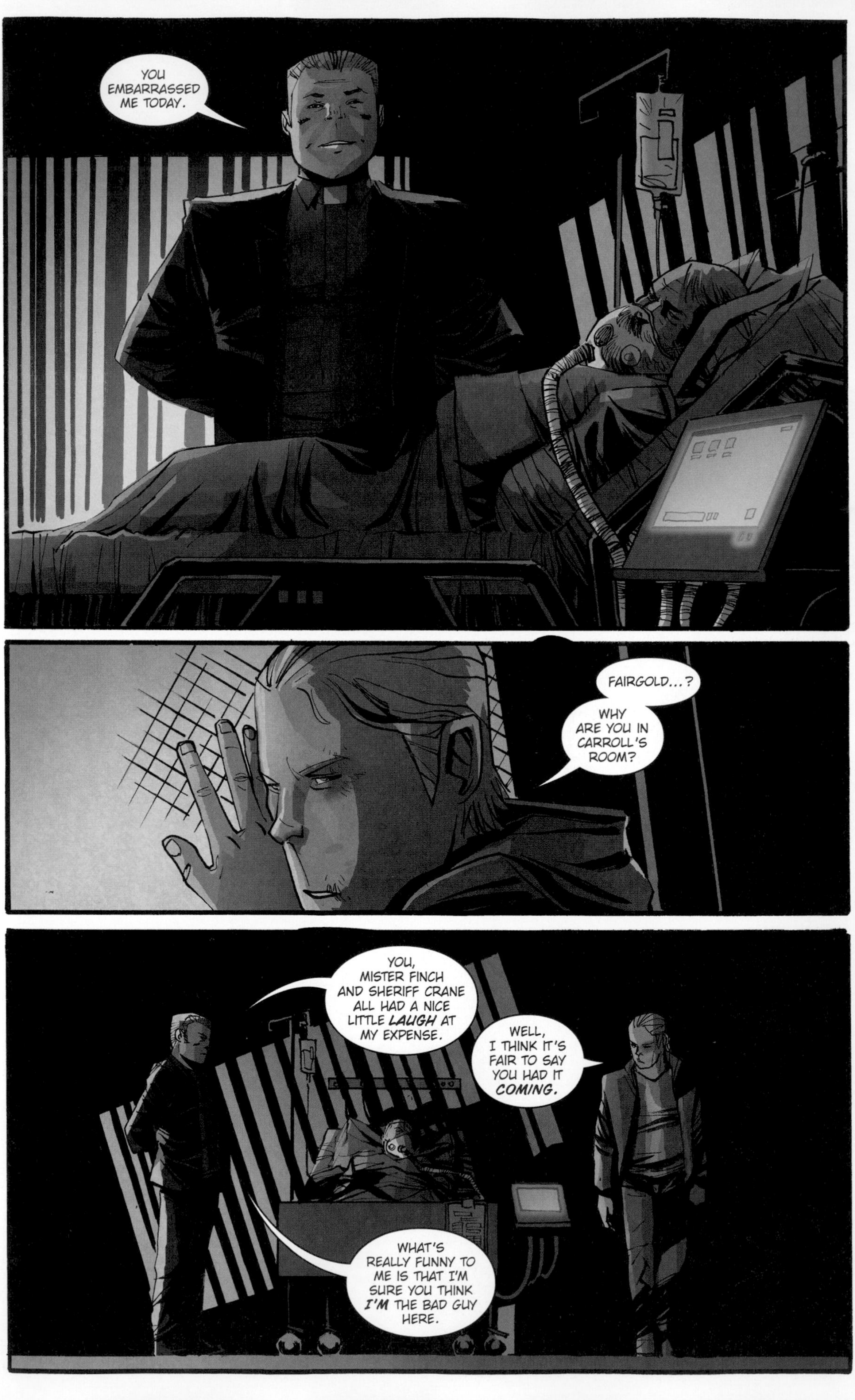
YOU EMBARRASSED ME TODAY.
FAIRGOLD...?
WHY ARE YOU IN CARROLL'S ROOM?
YOU, MISTER FINCH AND SHERIFF CRANE ALL HAD A NICE LITTLE *LAUGH* AT MY EXPENSE.
WELL, I THINK IT'S FAIR TO SAY YOU HAD IT *COMING.*
WHAT'S REALLY FUNNY TO ME IS THAT I'M SURE YOU THINK *I'M* THE BAD GUY HERE.

ALL I WANT TO DO IS TO END THE **EVIL** OF THIS TOWN.

TO FIND OUT WHO KILLED MY SON...

THE SAME MAN WHO CUT OFF YOUR FRIEND HERE'S ARMS AND LEGS.

AND TO MAKE SURE IT **NEVER** HAPPENS AGAIN.

WHAT ARE YOU...?

AND YET... NO ONE SEES A **GRIEVING** FATHER. THEY SEE A MAN **OBSESSED.**

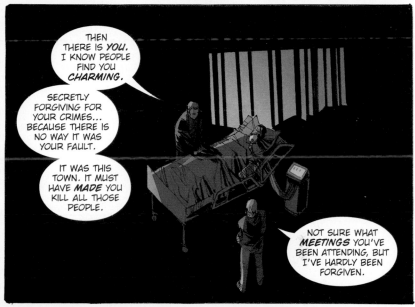

THEN THERE IS **YOU.** I KNOW PEOPLE FIND YOU **CHARMING.**

SECRETLY FORGIVING FOR YOUR CRIMES... BECAUSE THERE IS NO WAY IT WAS YOUR FAULT.

IT WAS THIS TOWN. IT MUST HAVE **MADE** YOU KILL ALL THOSE PEOPLE.

NOT SURE WHAT **MEETINGS** YOU'VE BEEN ATTENDING, BUT I'VE HARDLY BEEN FORGIVEN.

MY **SIN** IS THAT I DON'T UNDERSTAND YOU. I CAN'T **RELATE** TO YOU.

BUT MAYBE CARROLL'S **WOUNDS** CAN HELP ME WITH THAT.

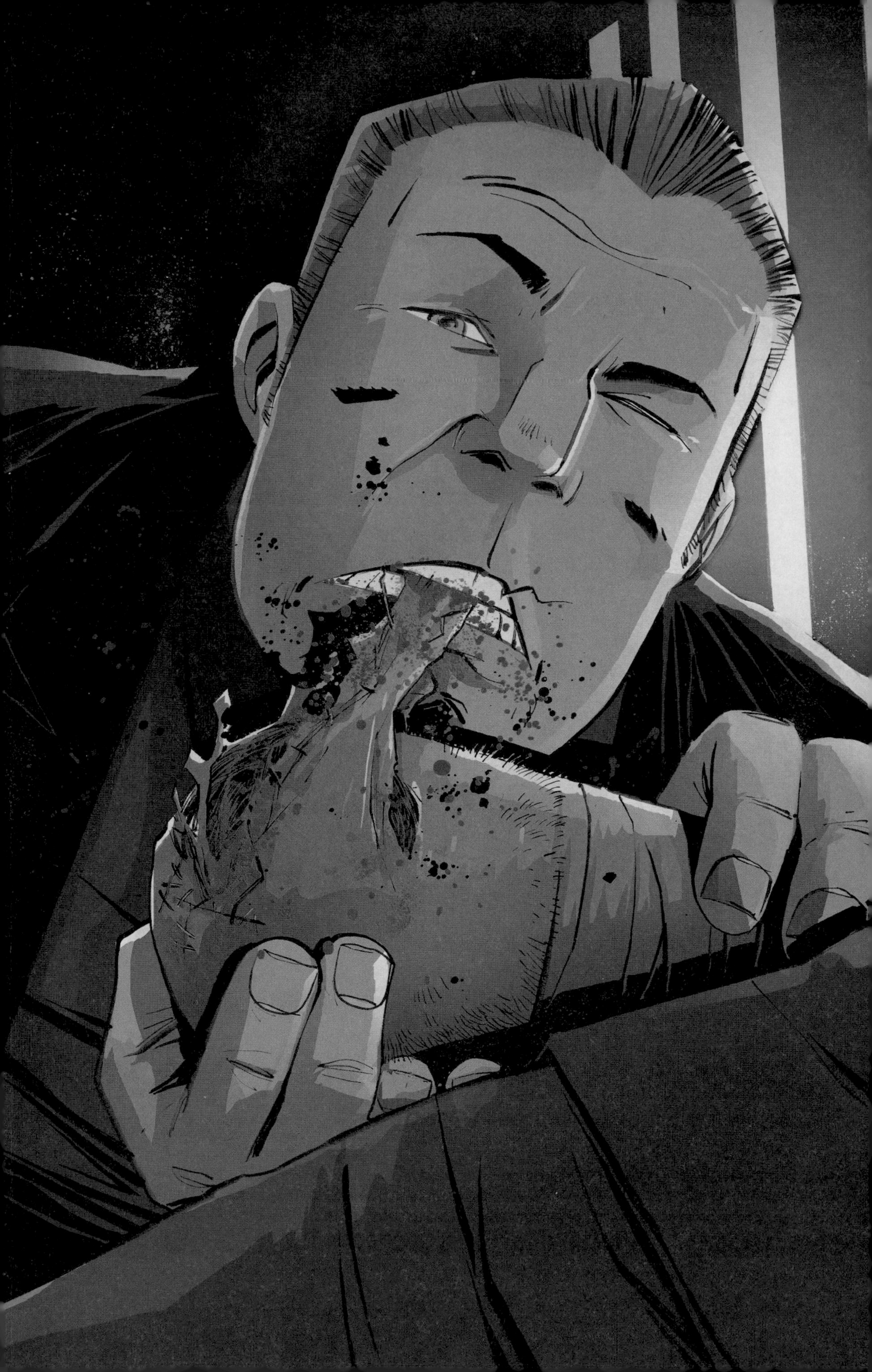

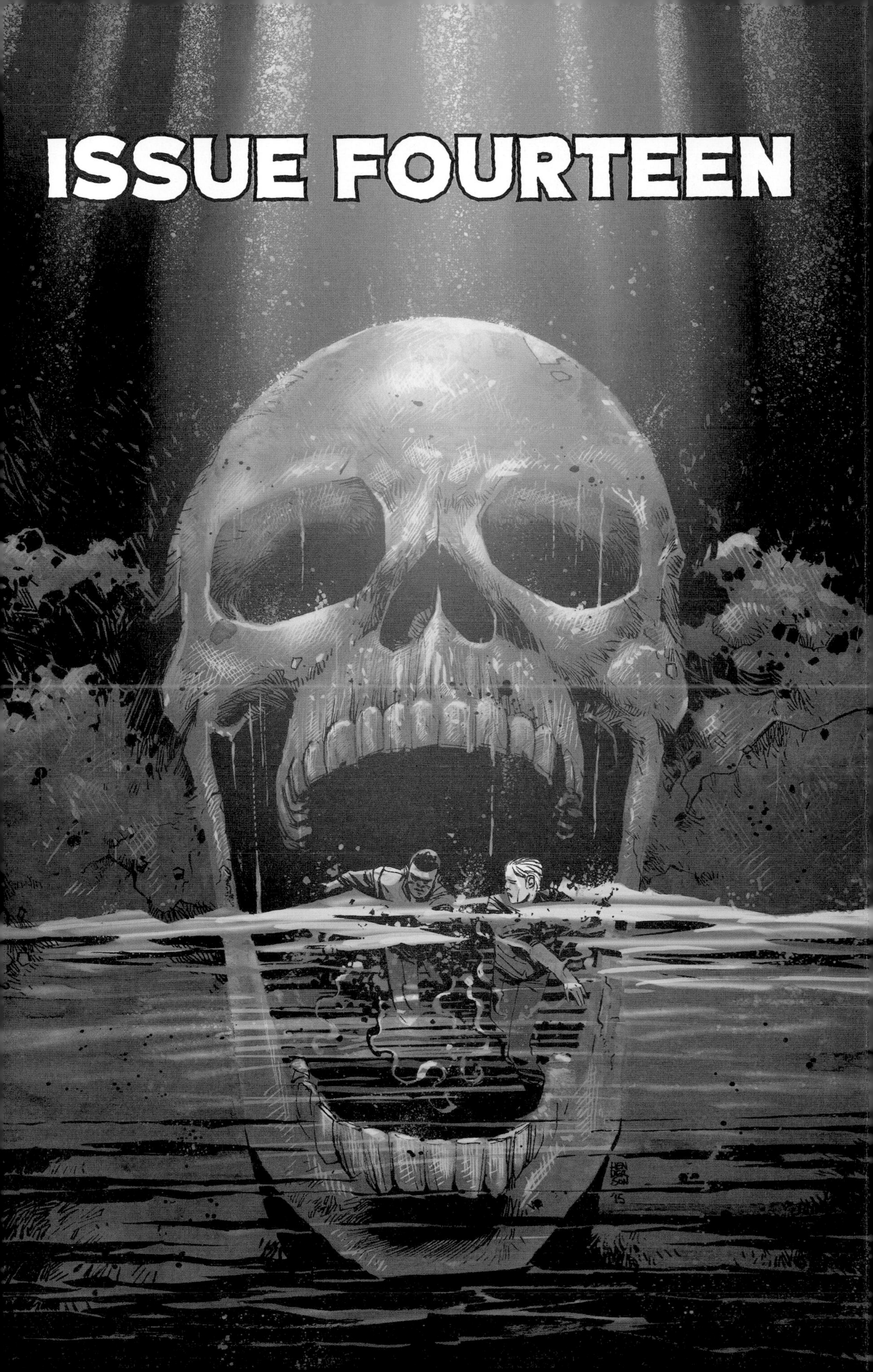
ISSUE FOURTEEN
HENDERSON '15

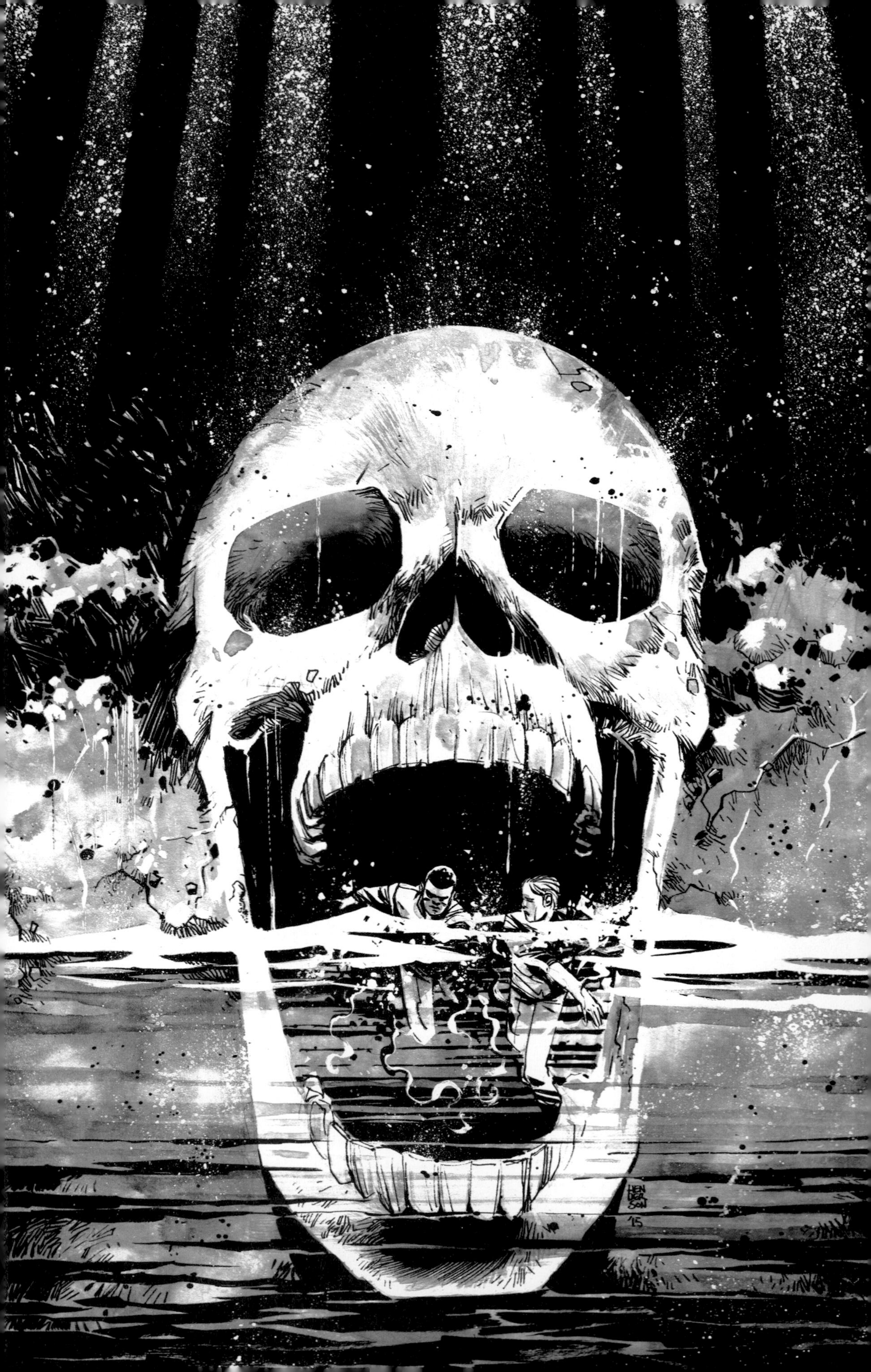
HENDERSON '15

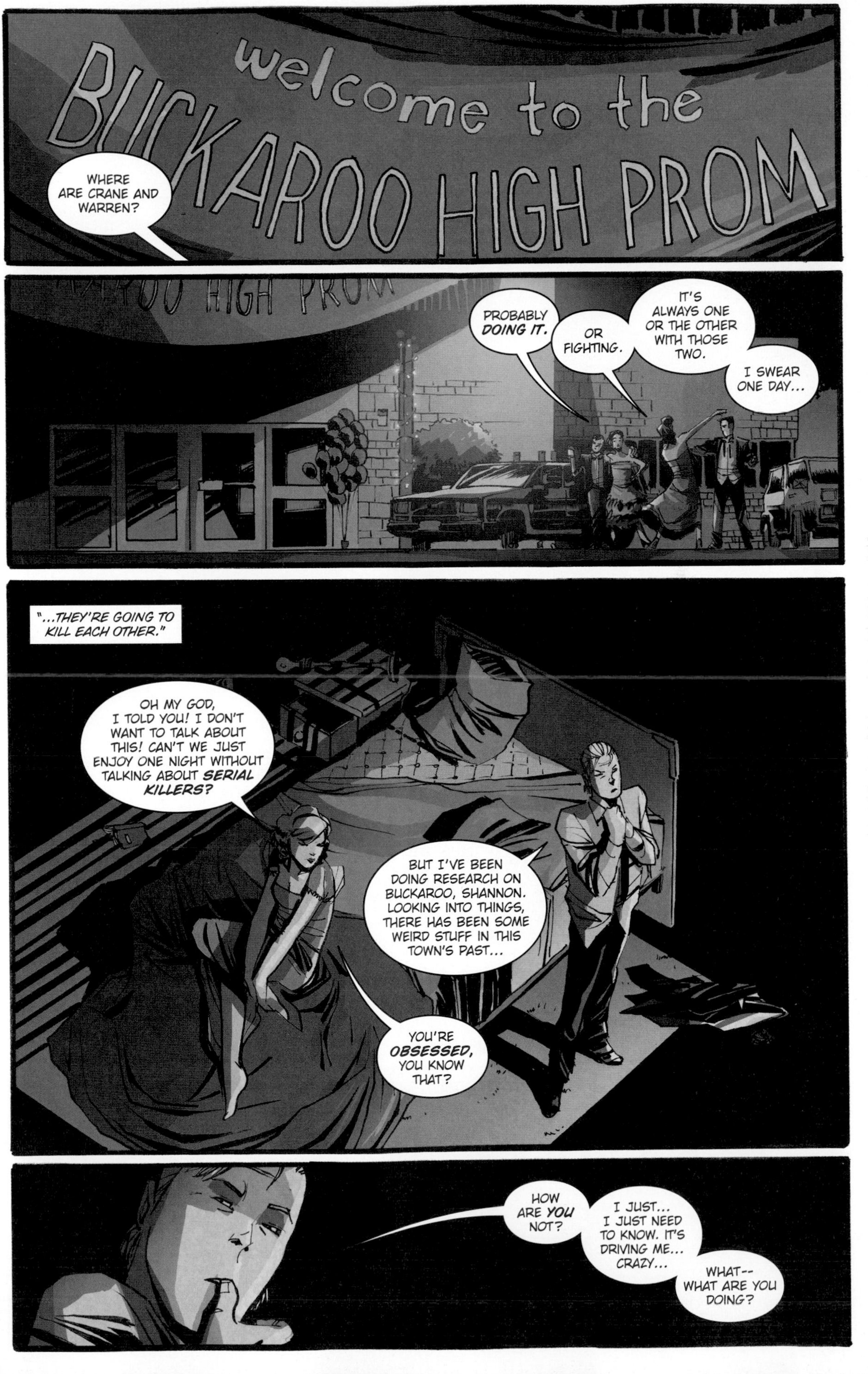
welcome to the BUCKAROO HIGH PROM
WHERE ARE CRANE AND WARREN?
PROBABLY DOING IT.
OR FIGHTING.
IT'S ALWAYS ONE OR THE OTHER WITH THOSE TWO.
I SWEAR ONE DAY...
"...THEY'RE GOING TO KILL EACH OTHER."
OH MY GOD, I TOLD YOU! I DON'T WANT TO TALK ABOUT THIS! CAN'T WE JUST ENJOY ONE NIGHT WITHOUT TALKING ABOUT SERIAL KILLERS?
BUT I'VE BEEN DOING RESEARCH ON BUCKAROO, SHANNON. LOOKING INTO THINGS, THERE HAS BEEN SOME WEIRD STUFF IN THIS TOWN'S PAST...
YOU'RE OBSESSED, YOU KNOW THAT?
HOW ARE YOU NOT?
I JUST... I JUST NEED TO KNOW. IT'S DRIVING ME... CRAZY...
WHAT-- WHAT ARE YOU DOING?

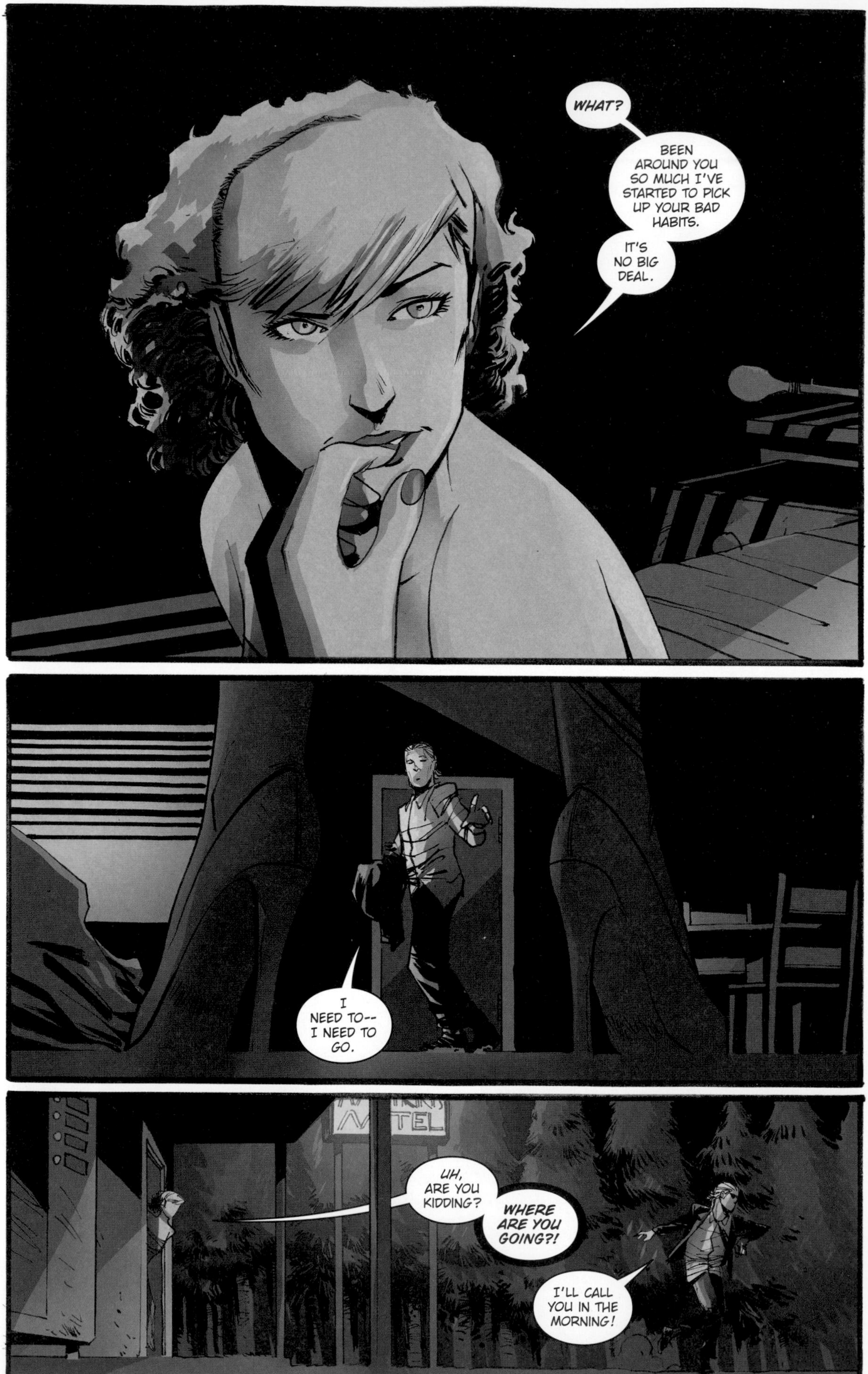
WHAT?
BEEN AROUND YOU SO MUCH I'VE STARTED TO PICK UP YOUR BAD HABITS.
IT'S NO BIG DEAL.
I NEED TO-- I NEED TO GO.
UH, ARE YOU KIDDING?
WHERE ARE YOU GOING?!
I'LL CALL YOU IN THE MORNING!

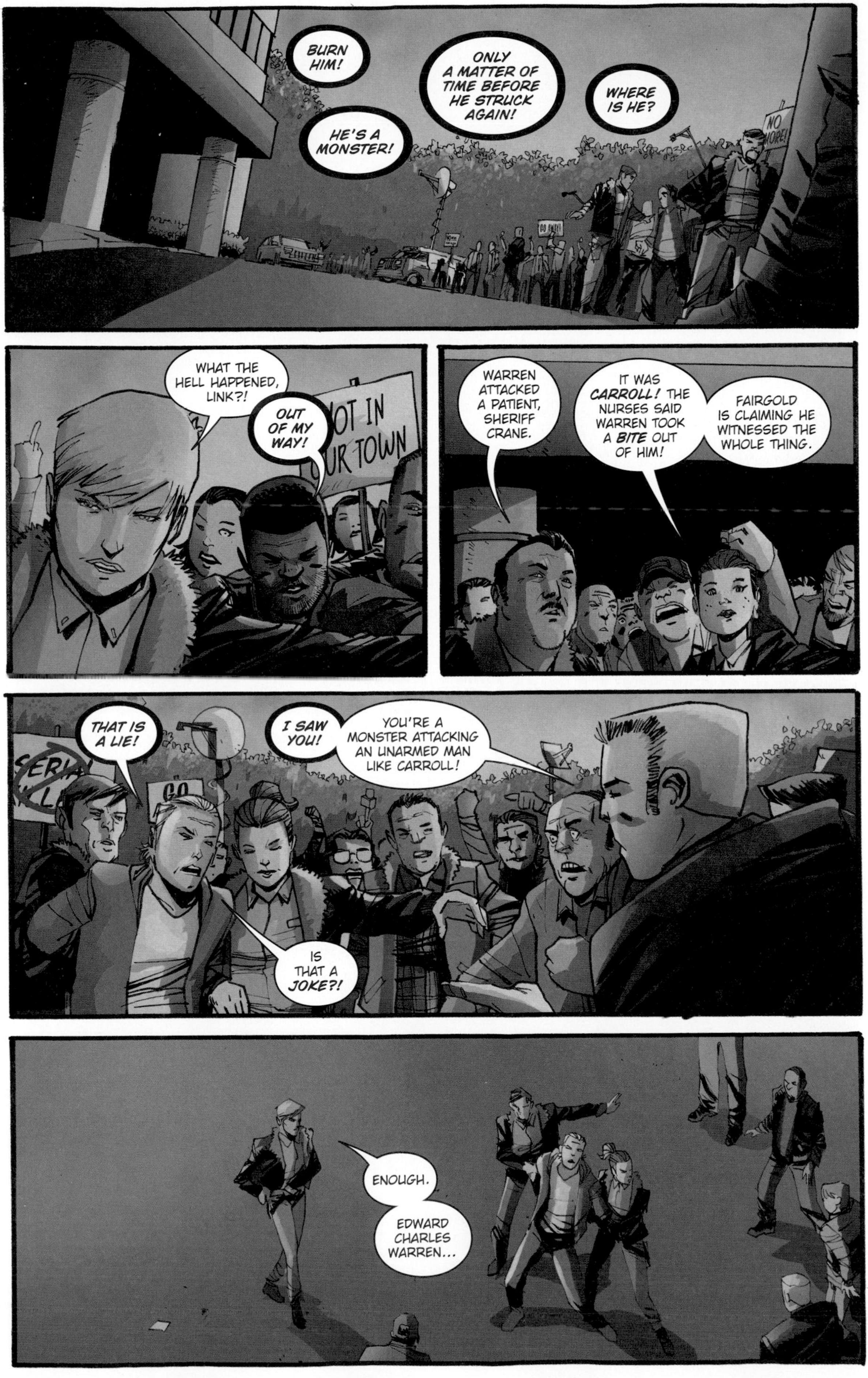
BURN HIM!
HE'S A MONSTER!
ONLY A MATTER OF TIME BEFORE HE STRUCK AGAIN!
WHERE IS HE?
NO MORE!
GO AWAY!
WHAT THE HELL HAPPENED, LINK?!
OUT OF MY WAY!
WARREN ATTACKED A PATIENT, SHERIFF CRANE.
IT WAS CARROLL! THE NURSES SAID WARREN TOOK A BITE OUT OF HIM!
FAIRGOLD IS CLAIMING HE WITNESSED THE WHOLE THING.
THAT IS A LIE!
I SAW YOU!
YOU'RE A MONSTER ATTACKING AN UNARMED MAN LIKE CARROLL!
IS THAT A JOKE?!
ENOUGH.
EDWARD CHARLES WARREN...

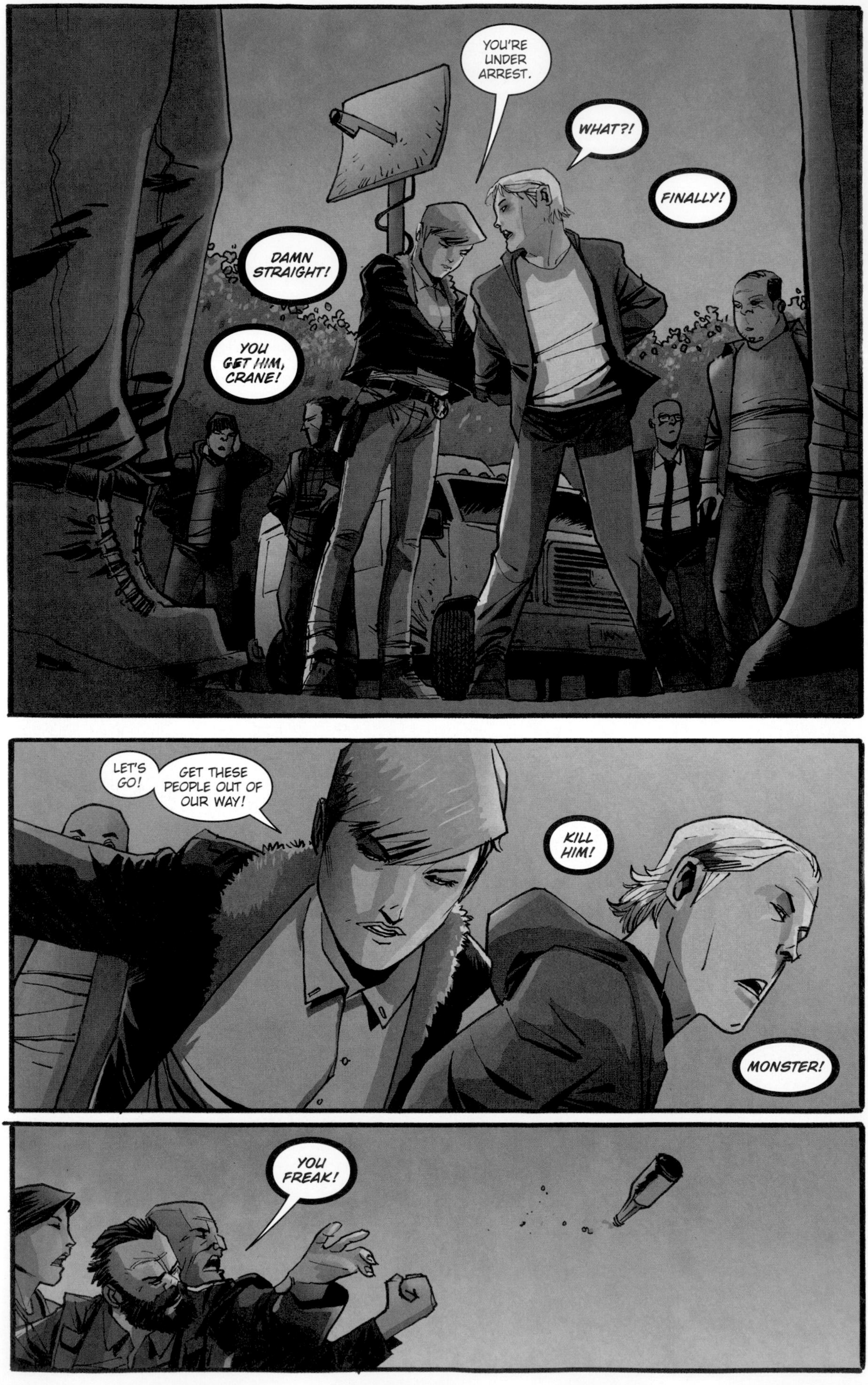
YOU'RE UNDER ARREST.
WHAT?!
FINALLY!
DAMN STRAIGHT!
YOU GET HIM, CRANE!
LET'S GO!
GET THESE PEOPLE OUT OF OUR WAY!
KILL HIM!
MONSTER!
YOU FREAK!

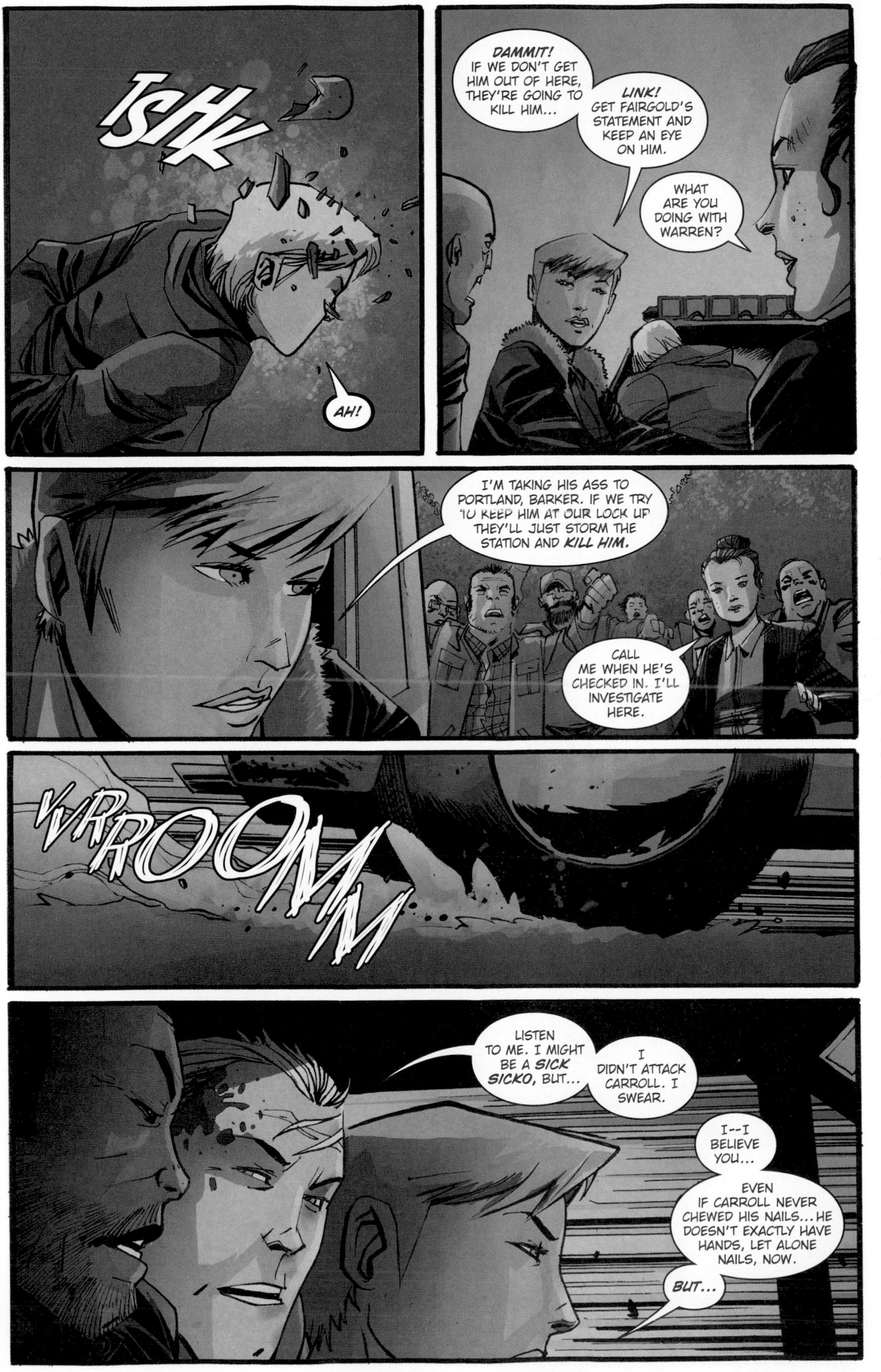
TSHK
AH!
DAMMIT! IF WE DON'T GET HIM OUT OF HERE, THEY'RE GOING TO KILL HIM...
LINK! GET FAIRGOLD'S STATEMENT AND KEEP AN EYE ON HIM.
WHAT ARE YOU DOING WITH WARREN?
I'M TAKING HIS ASS TO PORTLAND, BARKER. IF WE TRY TO KEEP HIM AT OUR LOCK UP THEY'LL JUST STORM THE STATION AND KILL HIM.
CALL ME WHEN HE'S CHECKED IN. I'LL INVESTIGATE HERE.
VVRROOMM
LISTEN TO ME. I MIGHT BE A SICK SICKO, BUT...
I DIDN'T ATTACK CARROLL. I SWEAR.
I--I BELIEVE YOU...
EVEN IF CARROLL NEVER CHEWED HIS NAILS... HE DOESN'T EXACTLY HAVE HANDS, LET ALONE NAILS, NOW.
BUT...

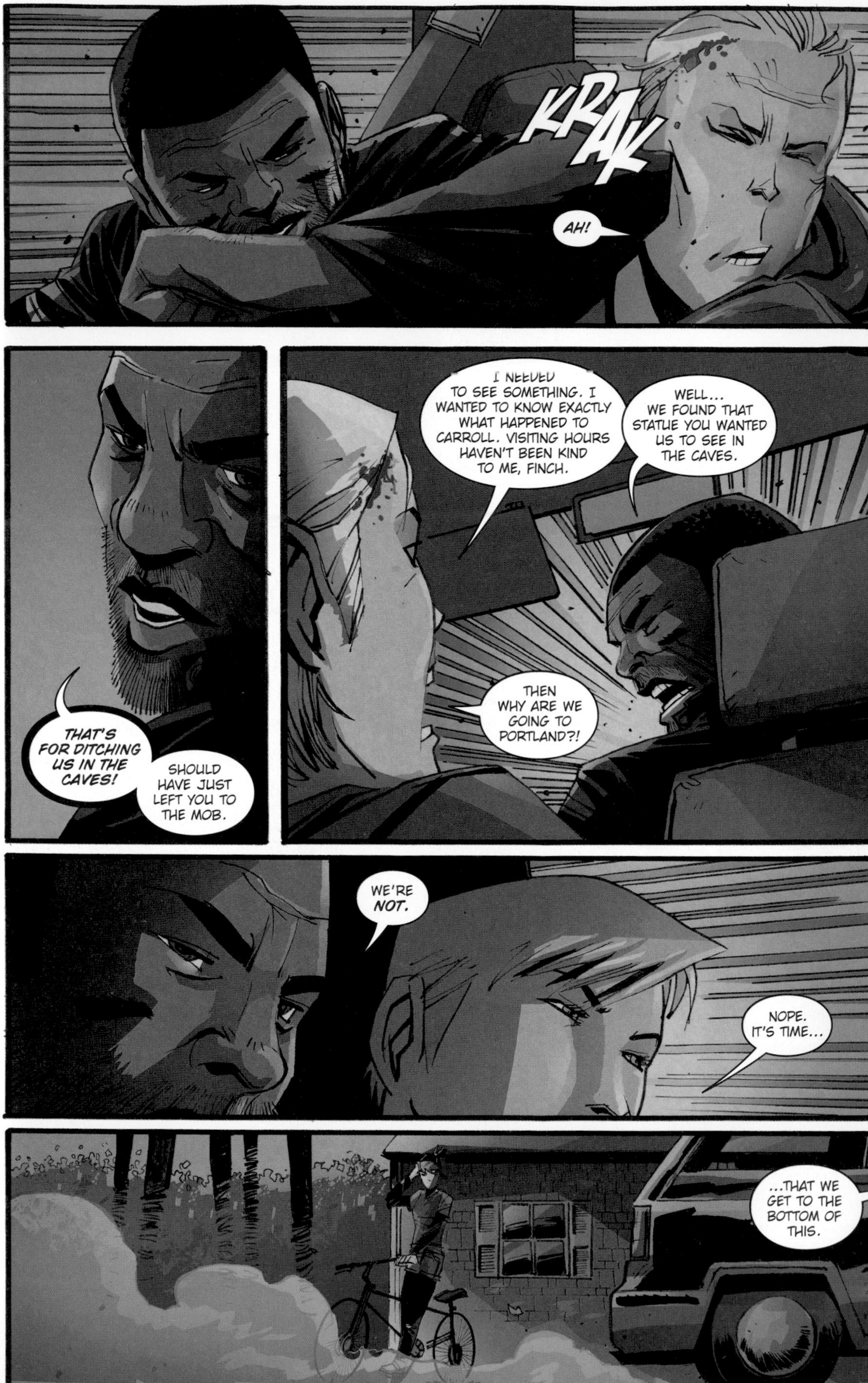
KRAK
AH!
THAT'S FOR DITCHING US IN THE CAVES!
SHOULD HAVE JUST LEFT YOU TO THE MOB.
I NEEDED TO SEE SOMETHING. I WANTED TO KNOW EXACTLY WHAT HAPPENED TO CARROLL. VISITING HOURS HAVEN'T BEEN KIND TO ME, FINCH.
WELL... WE FOUND THAT STATUE YOU WANTED US TO SEE IN THE CAVES.
THEN WHY ARE WE GOING TO PORTLAND?!
WE'RE NOT.
NOPE. IT'S TIME...
...THAT WE GET TO THE BOTTOM OF THIS.

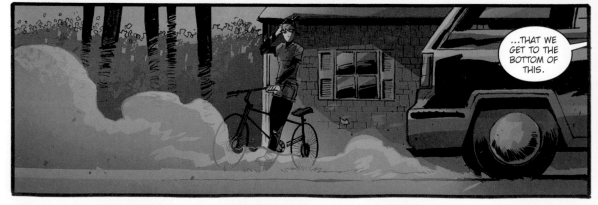

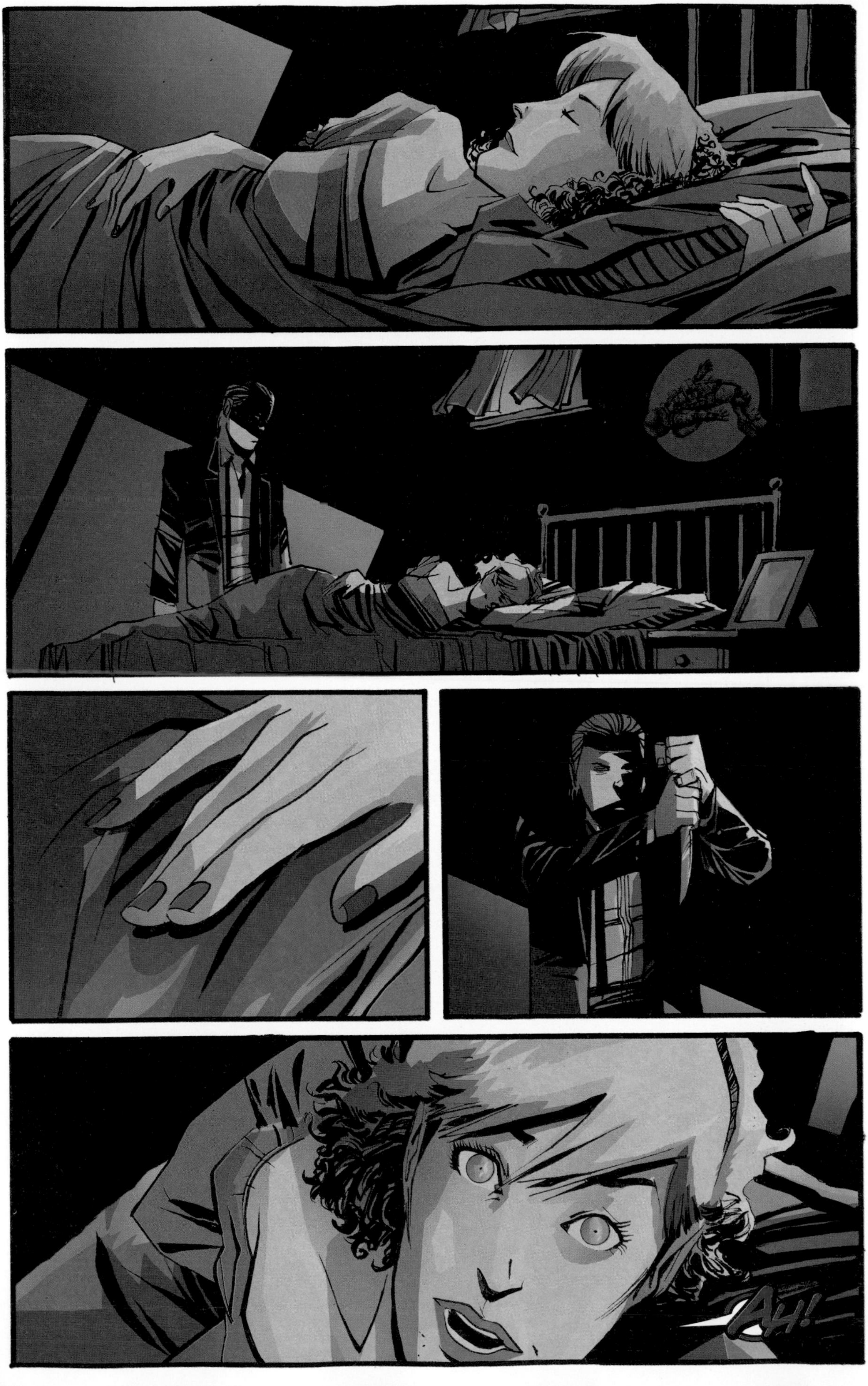
AH!

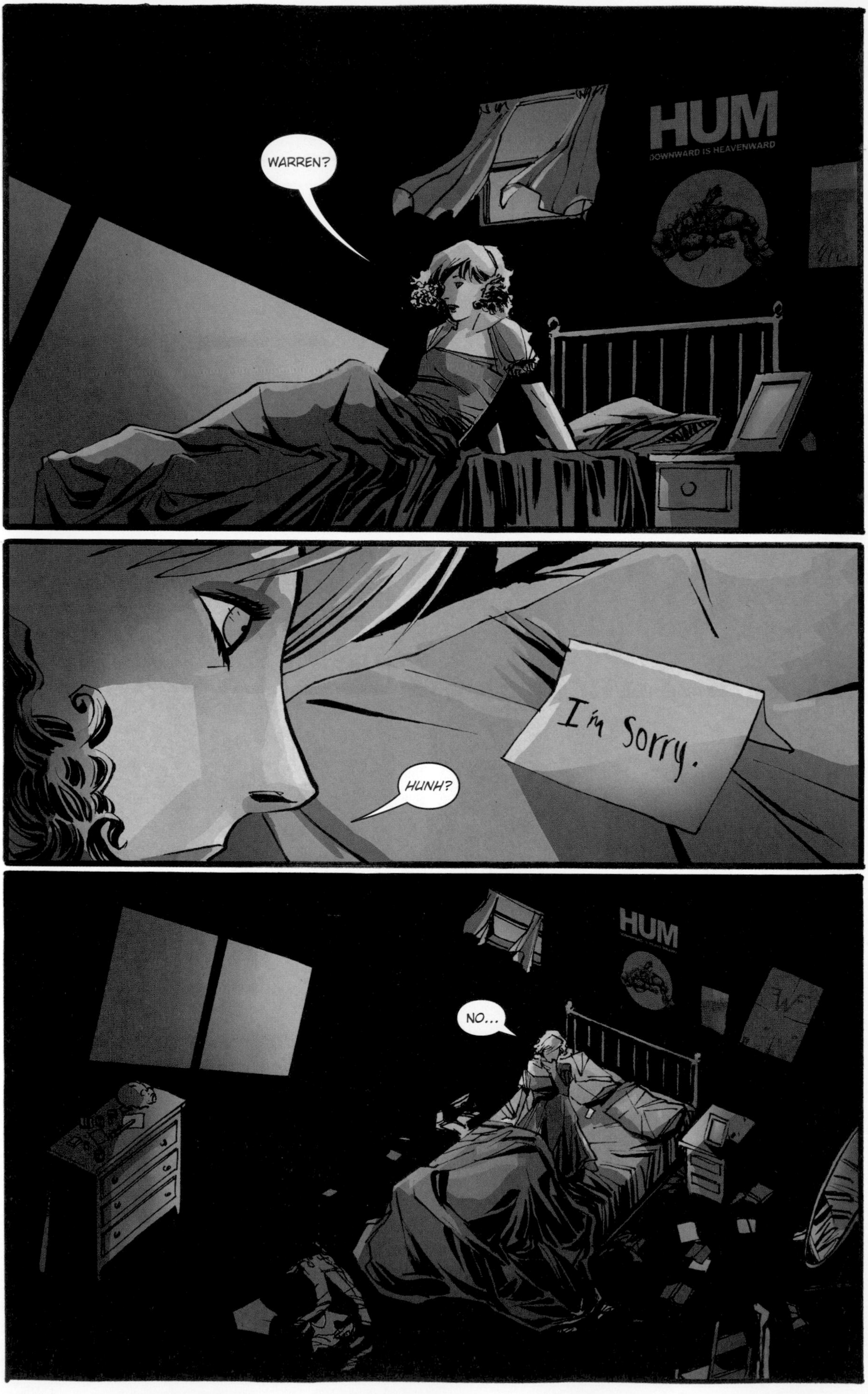
HUM
DOWNWARD IS HEAVENWARD
WARREN?
I'm Sorry.
HUNH?
HUM
NO...

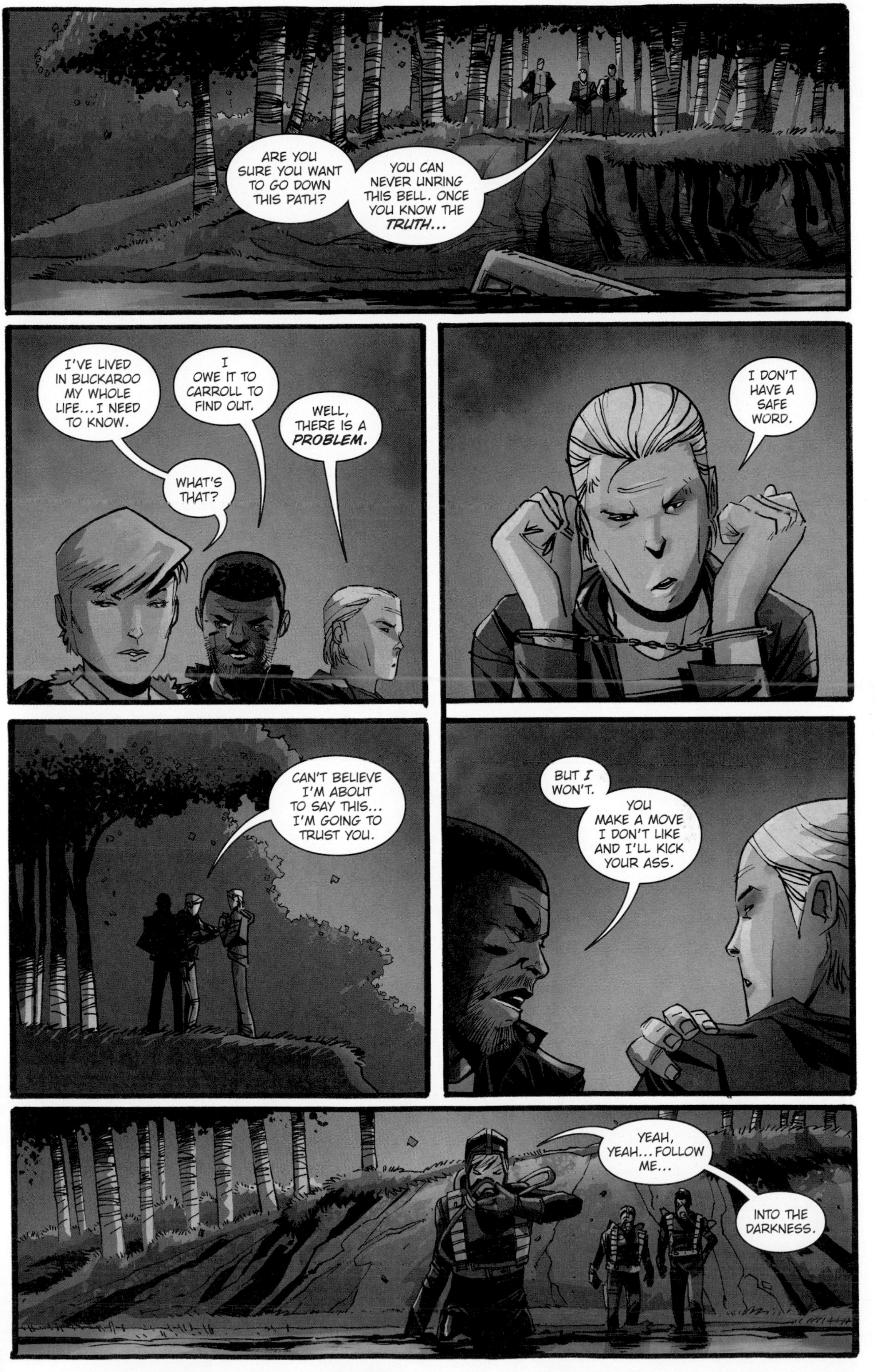
ARE YOU SURE YOU WANT TO GO DOWN THIS PATH?
YOU CAN NEVER UNRING THIS BELL. ONCE YOU KNOW THE TRUTH...
I'VE LIVED IN BUCKAROO MY WHOLE LIFE... I NEED TO KNOW.
I OWE IT TO CARROLL TO FIND OUT.
WELL, THERE IS A PROBLEM.
WHAT'S THAT?
I DON'T HAVE A SAFE WORD.
CAN'T BELIEVE I'M ABOUT TO SAY THIS... I'M GOING TO TRUST YOU.
BUT I WON'T.
YOU MAKE A MOVE I DON'T LIKE AND I'LL KICK YOUR ASS.
YEAH, YEAH... FOLLOW ME...
INTO THE DARKNESS.

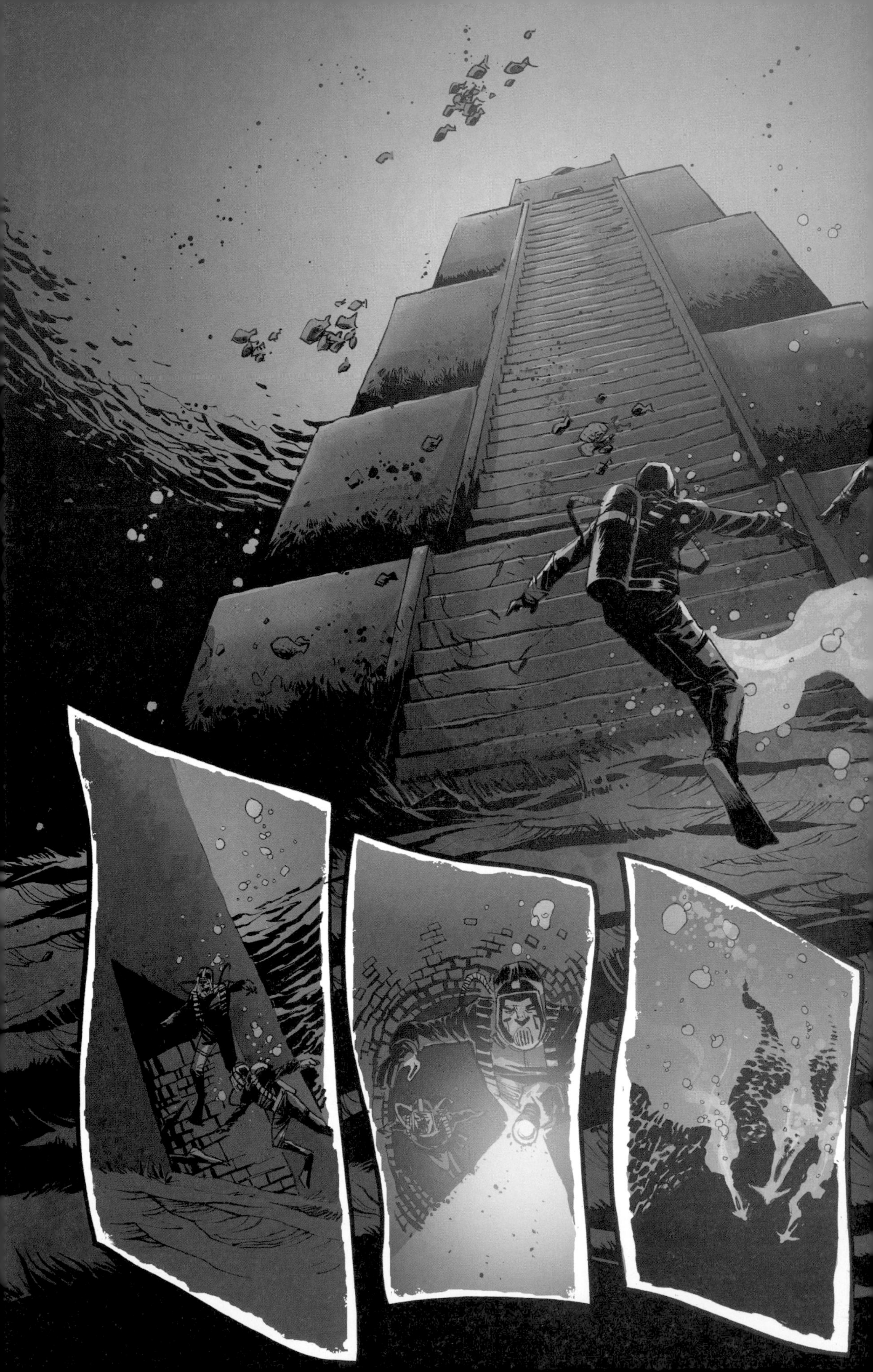

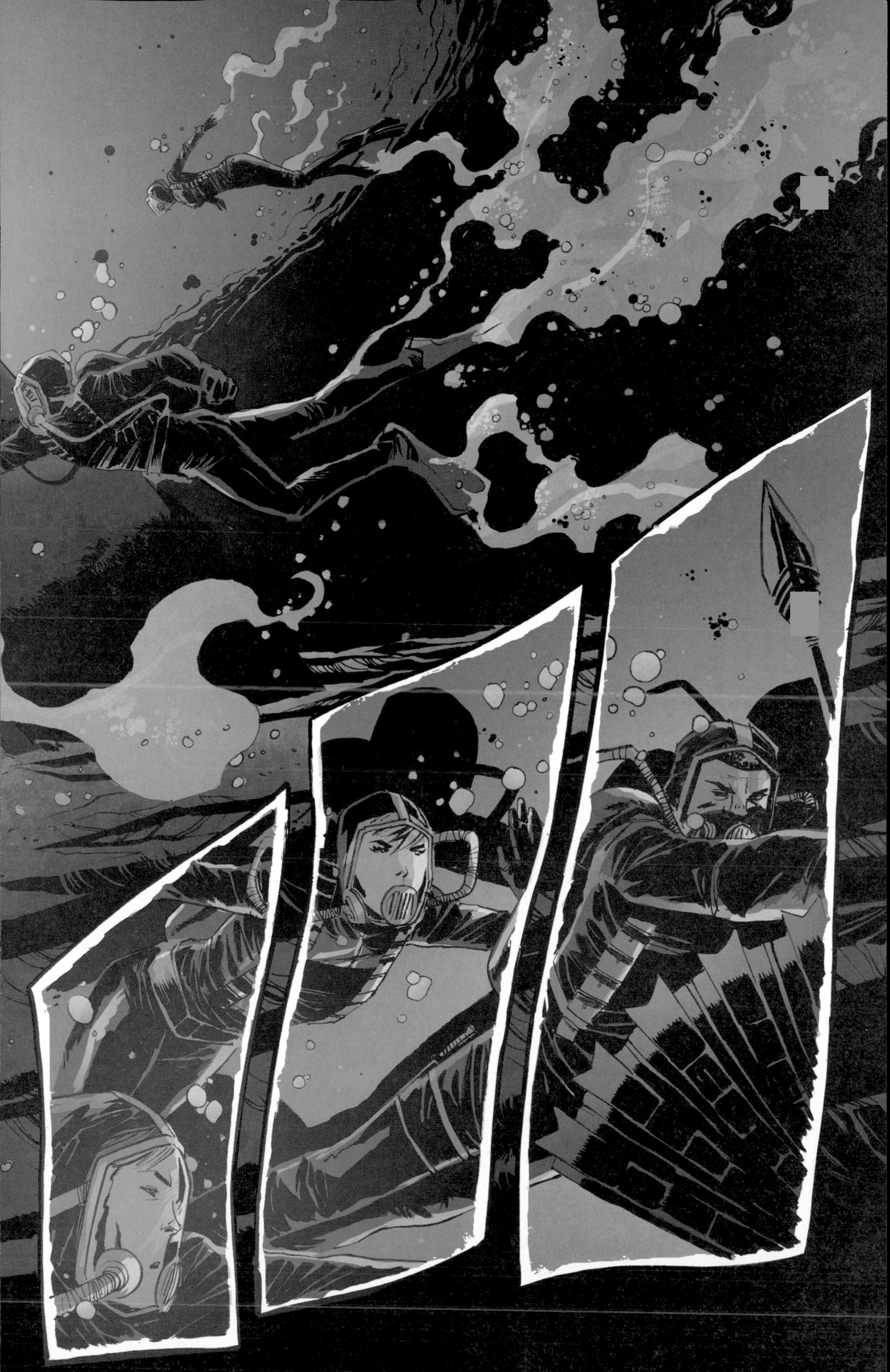

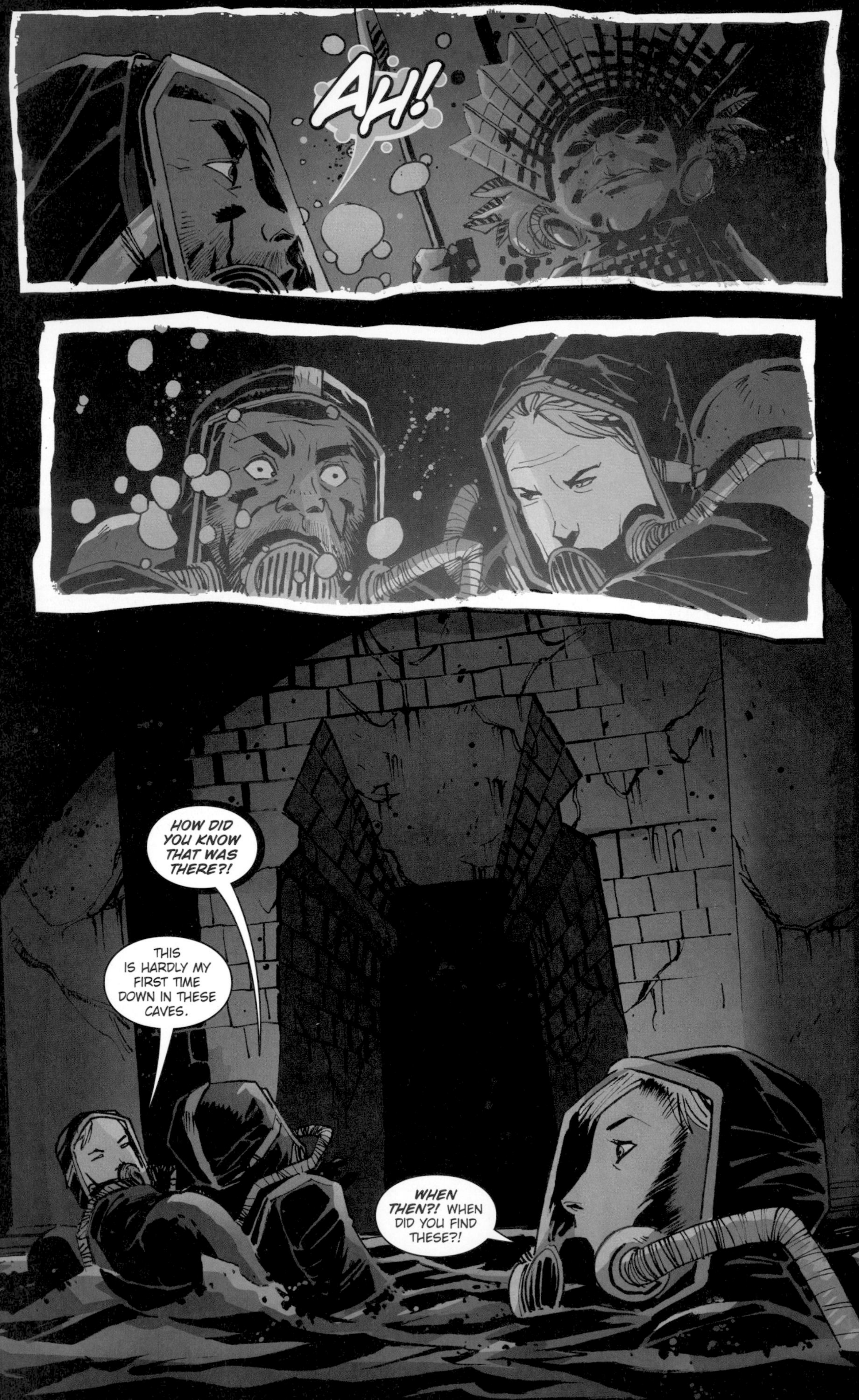
AH!
HOW DID YOU KNOW THAT WAS THERE?!
THIS IS HARDLY MY FIRST TIME DOWN IN THESE CAVES.
WHEN THEN?! WHEN DID YOU FIND THESE?!

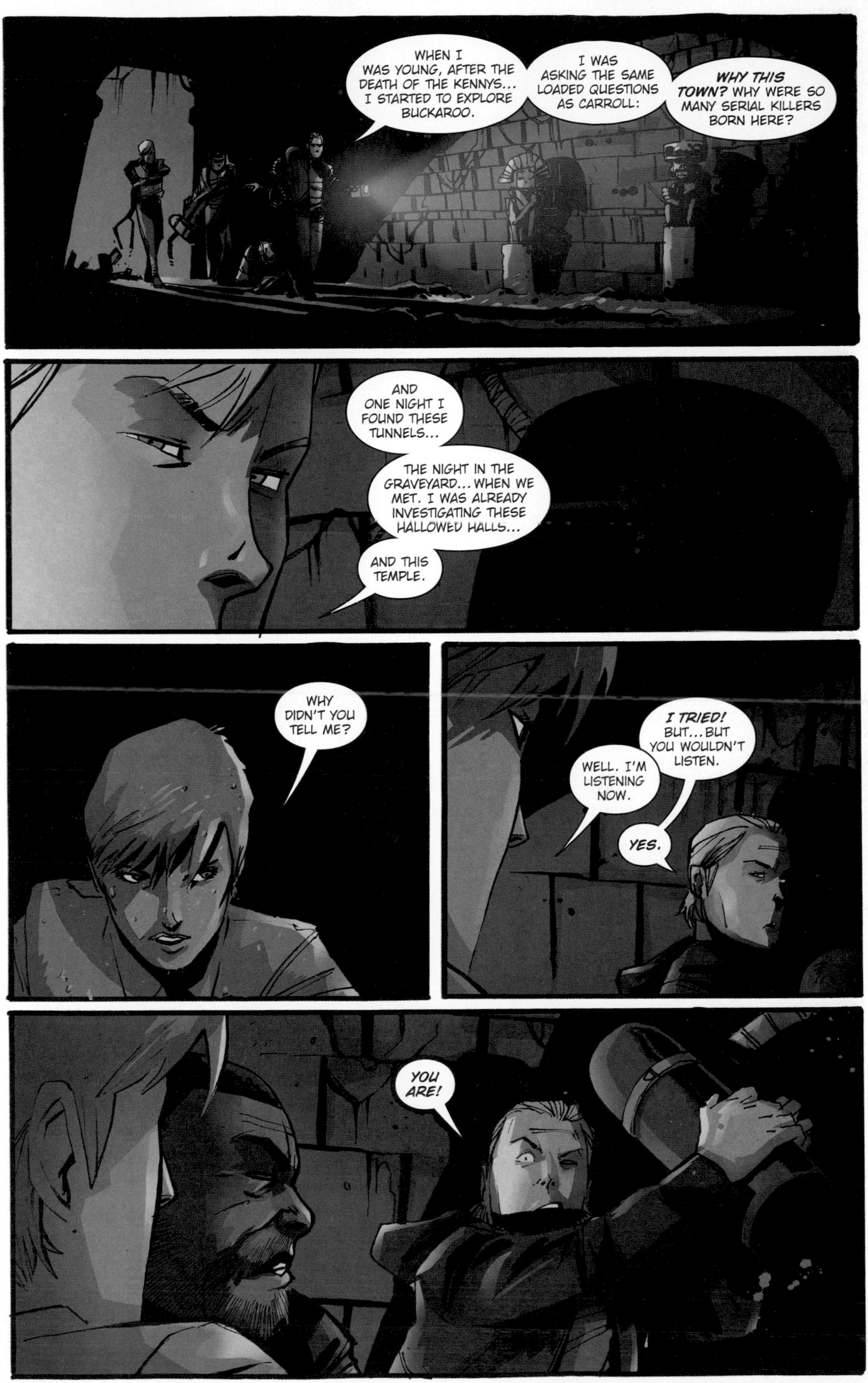
WHEN I WAS YOUNG, AFTER THE DEATH OF THE KENNYS... I STARTED TO EXPLORE BUCKAROO.
I WAS ASKING THE SAME LOADED QUESTIONS AS CARROLL:
WHY THIS TOWN? WHY WERE SO MANY SERIAL KILLERS BORN HERE?
AND ONE NIGHT I FOUND THESE TUNNELS...
THE NIGHT IN THE GRAVEYARD... WHEN WE MET. I WAS ALREADY INVESTIGATING THESE HALLOWED HALLS...
AND THIS TEMPLE.
WHY DIDN'T YOU TELL ME?
I TRIED! BUT... BUT YOU WOULDN'T LISTEN.
WELL. I'M LISTENING NOW.
YES.
YOU ARE!

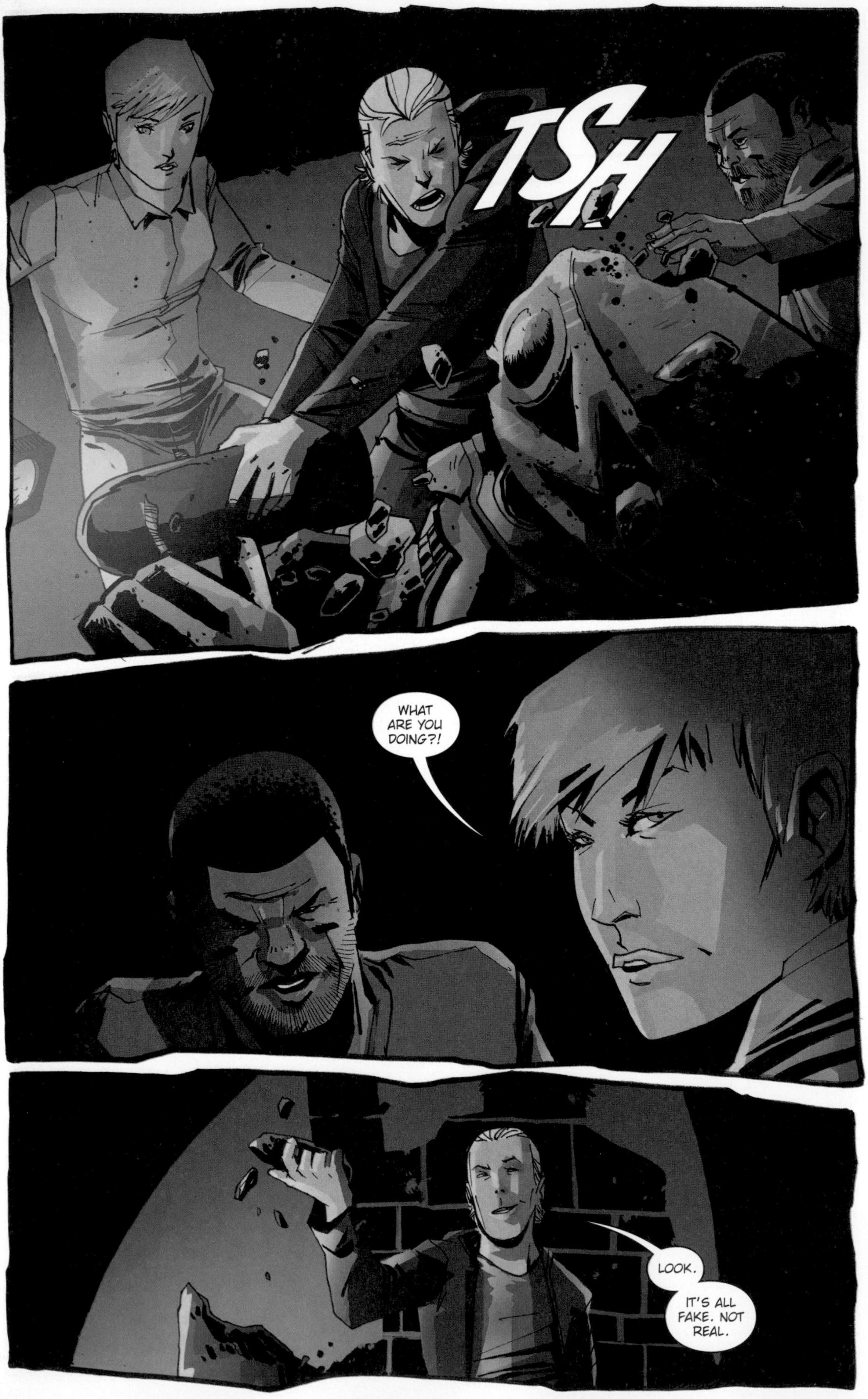
TSH
WHAT ARE YOU DOING?!
LOOK.
IT'S ALL FAKE. NOT REAL.

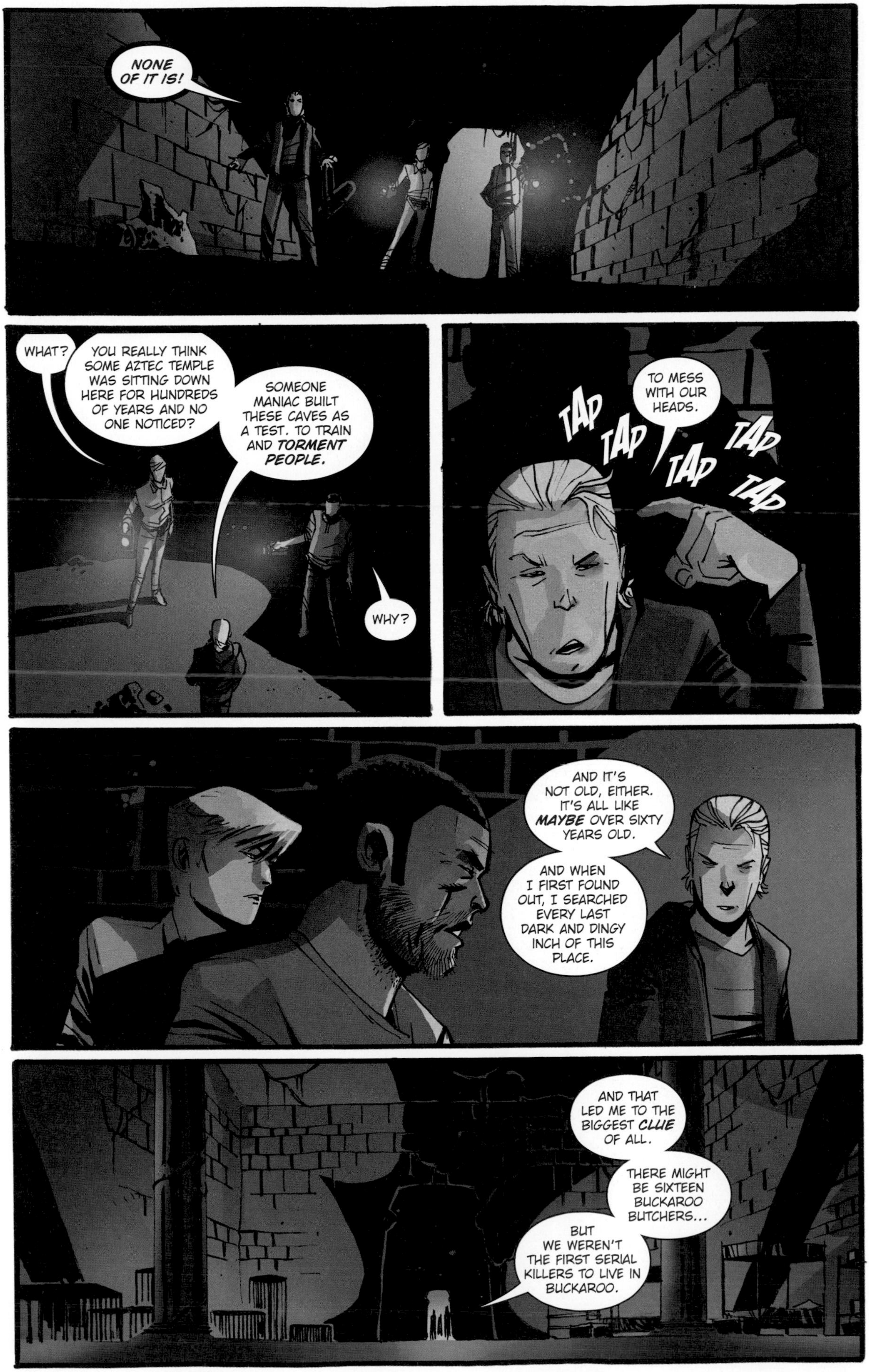
NONE OF IT IS!
WHAT?
YOU REALLY THINK SOME AZTEC TEMPLE WAS SITTING DOWN HERE FOR HUNDREDS OF YEARS AND NO ONE NOTICED?
SOMEONE MANIAC BUILT THESE CAVES AS A TEST. TO TRAIN AND TORMENT PEOPLE.
WHY?
TAP TAP
TO MESS WITH OUR HEADS.
TAP TAP TAP
AND IT'S NOT OLD, EITHER. IT'S ALL LIKE MAYBE OVER SIXTY YEARS OLD.
AND WHEN I FIRST FOUND OUT, I SEARCHED EVERY LAST DARK AND DINGY INCH OF THIS PLACE.
AND THAT LED ME TO THE BIGGEST CLUE OF ALL.
THERE MIGHT BE SIXTEEN BUCKAROO BUTCHERS...
BUT WE WEREN'T THE FIRST SERIAL KILLERS TO LIVE IN BUCKAROO.

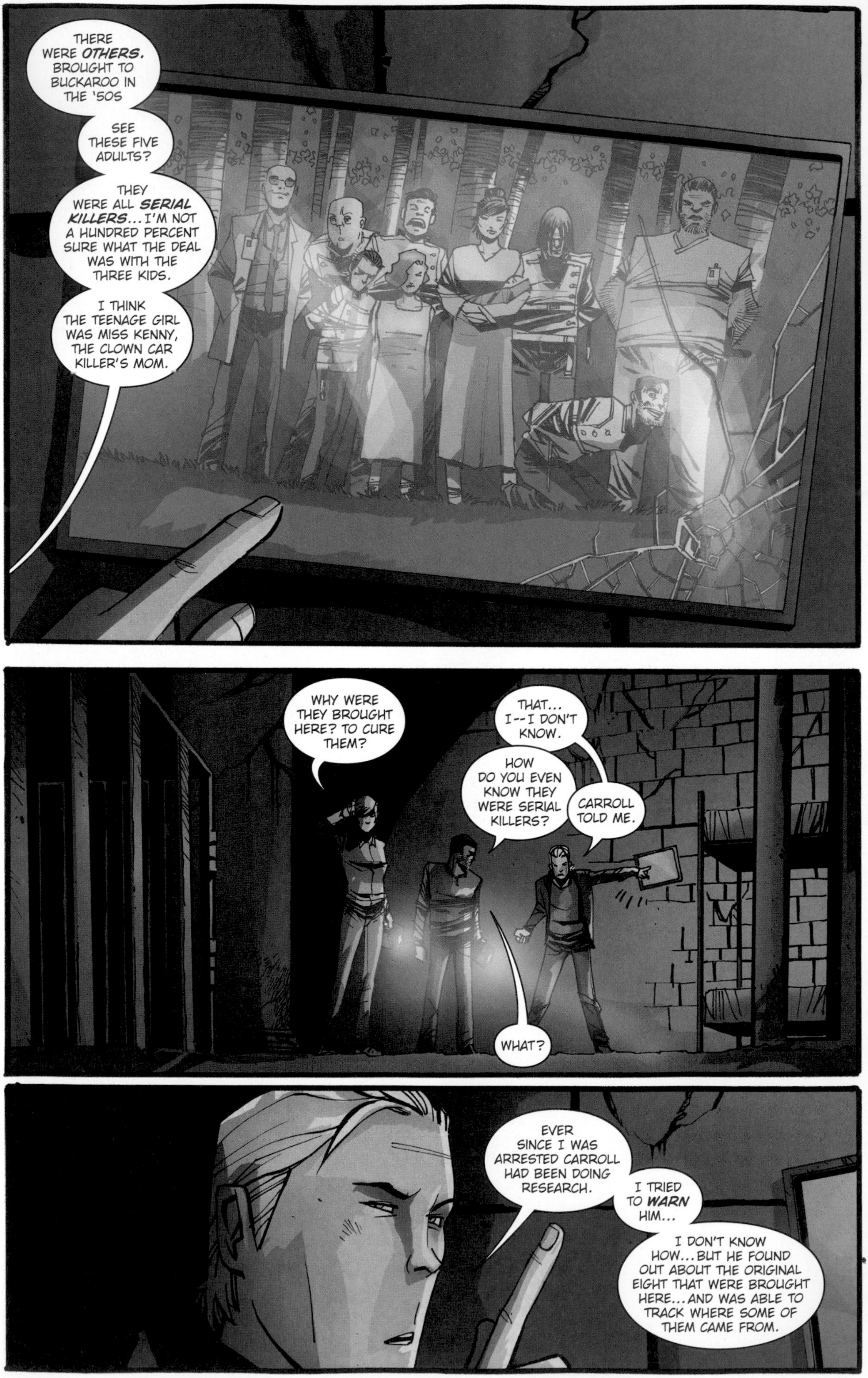
THERE WERE OTHERS. BROUGHT TO BUCKAROO IN THE '50s
SEE THESE FIVE ADULTS?
THEY WERE ALL SERIAL KILLERS... I'M NOT A HUNDRED PERCENT SURE WHAT THE DEAL WAS WITH THE THREE KIDS.
I THINK THE TEENAGE GIRL WAS MISS KENNY, THE CLOWN CAR KILLER'S MOM.
WHY WERE THEY BROUGHT HERE? TO CURE THEM?
THAT... I--I DON'T KNOW.
HOW DO YOU EVEN KNOW THEY WERE SERIAL KILLERS?
CARROLL TOLD ME.
WHAT?
EVER SINCE I WAS ARRESTED CARROLL HAD BEEN DOING RESEARCH.
I TRIED TO WARN HIM...
I DON'T KNOW HOW... BUT HE FOUND OUT ABOUT THE ORIGINAL EIGHT THAT WERE BROUGHT HERE... AND WAS ABLE TO TRACK WHERE SOME OF THEM CAME FROM.

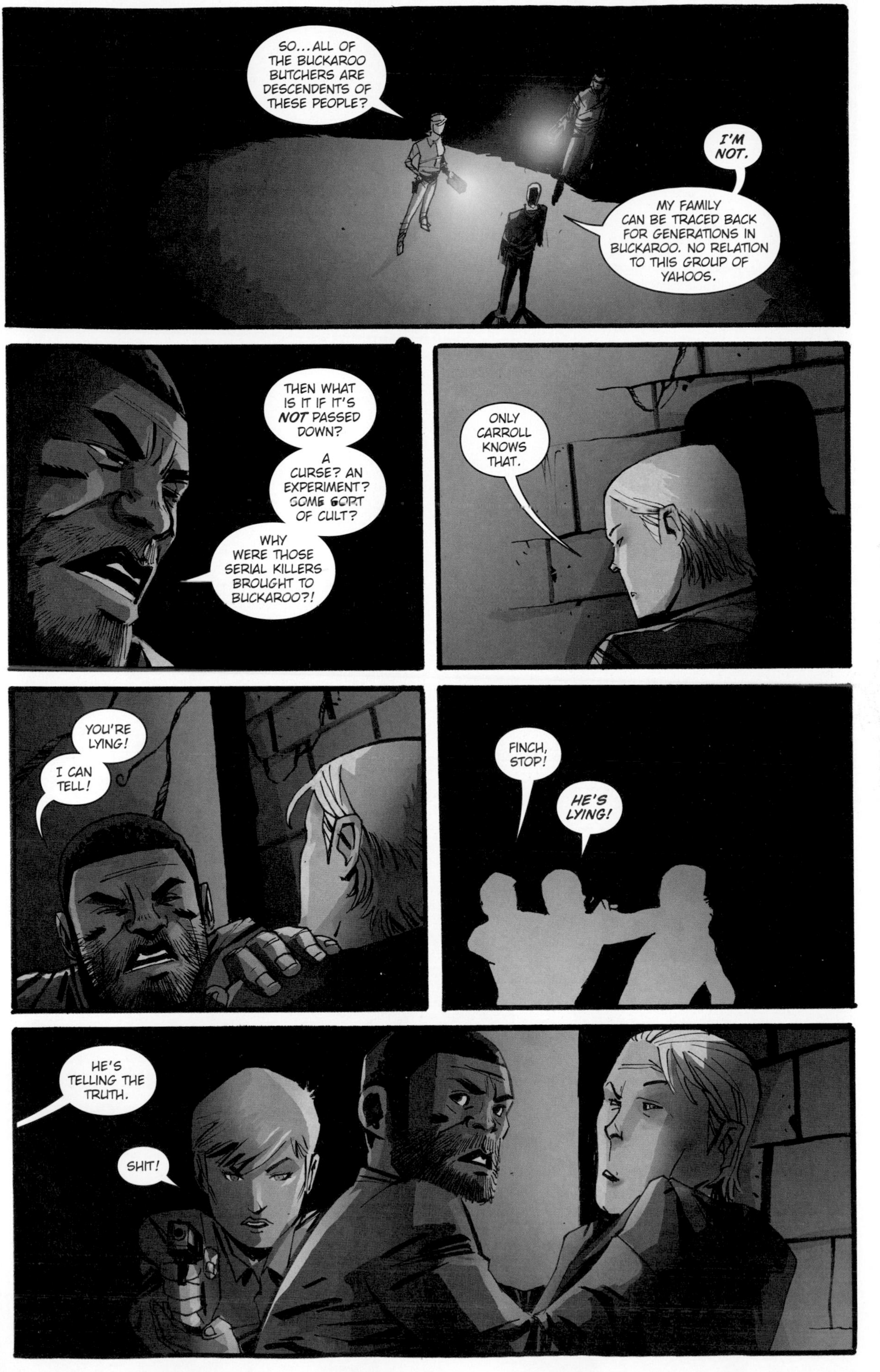
SO... ALL OF THE BUCKAROO BUTCHERS ARE DESCENDENTS OF THESE PEOPLE?
I'M NOT.
MY FAMILY CAN BE TRACED BACK FOR GENERATIONS IN BUCKAROO. NO RELATION TO THIS GROUP OF YAHOOS.
THEN WHAT IS IT IF IT'S NOT PASSED DOWN?
A CURSE? AN EXPERIMENT? SOME SORT OF CULT?
WHY WERE THOSE SERIAL KILLERS BROUGHT TO BUCKAROO?!
ONLY CARROLL KNOWS THAT.
YOU'RE LYING!
I CAN TELL!
FINCH, STOP!
HE'S LYING!
HE'S TELLING THE TRUTH.
SHIT!

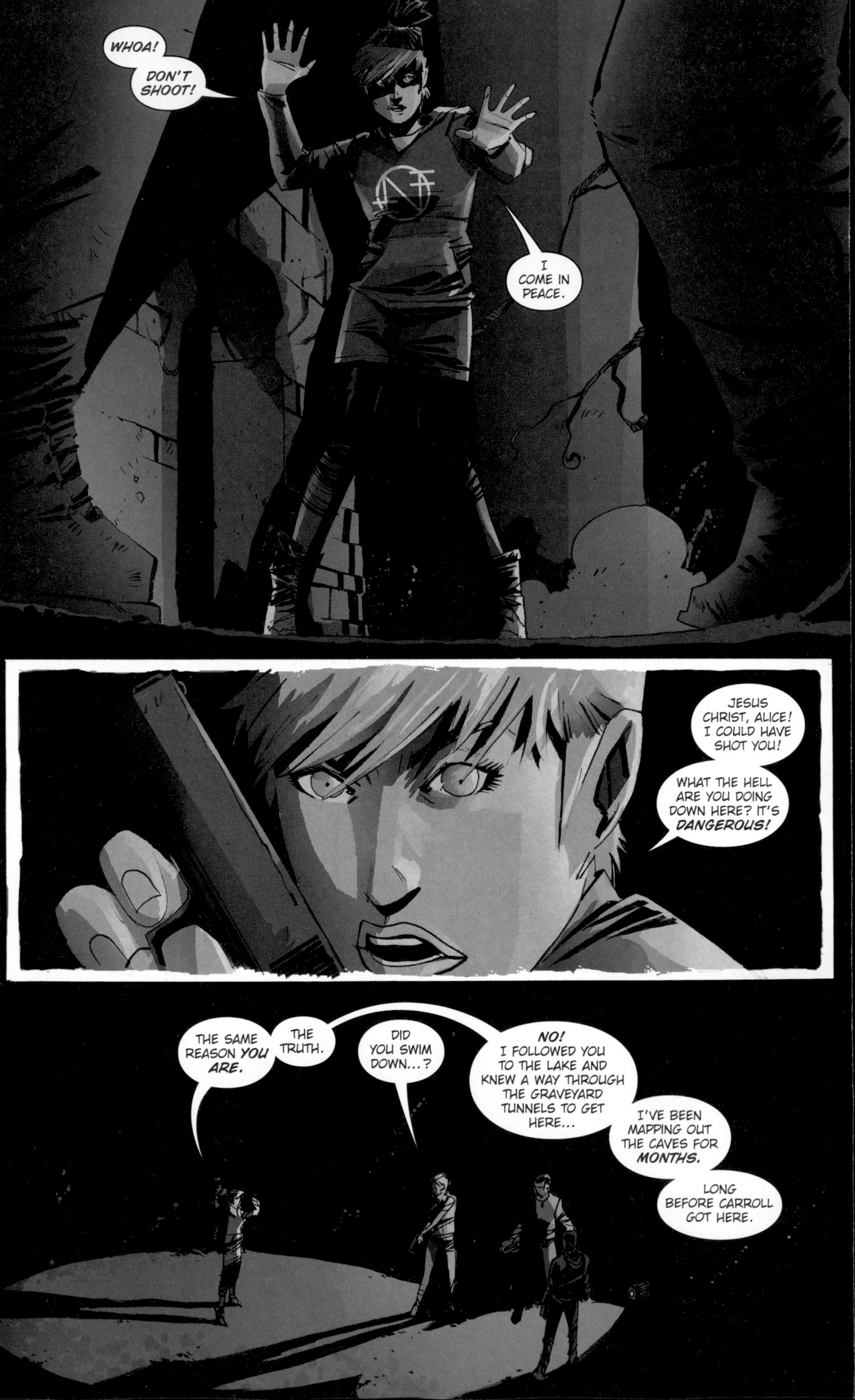
WHOA!
DON'T SHOOT!
I COME IN PEACE.
JESUS CHRIST, ALICE! I COULD HAVE SHOT YOU!
WHAT THE HELL ARE YOU DOING DOWN HERE? IT'S DANGEROUS!
THE SAME REASON YOU ARE.
THE TRUTH.
DID YOU SWIM DOWN...?
NO! I FOLLOWED YOU TO THE LAKE AND KNEW A WAY THROUGH THE GRAVEYARD TUNNELS TO GET HERE...
I'VE BEEN MAPPING OUT THE CAVES FOR MONTHS.
LONG BEFORE CARROLL GOT HERE.

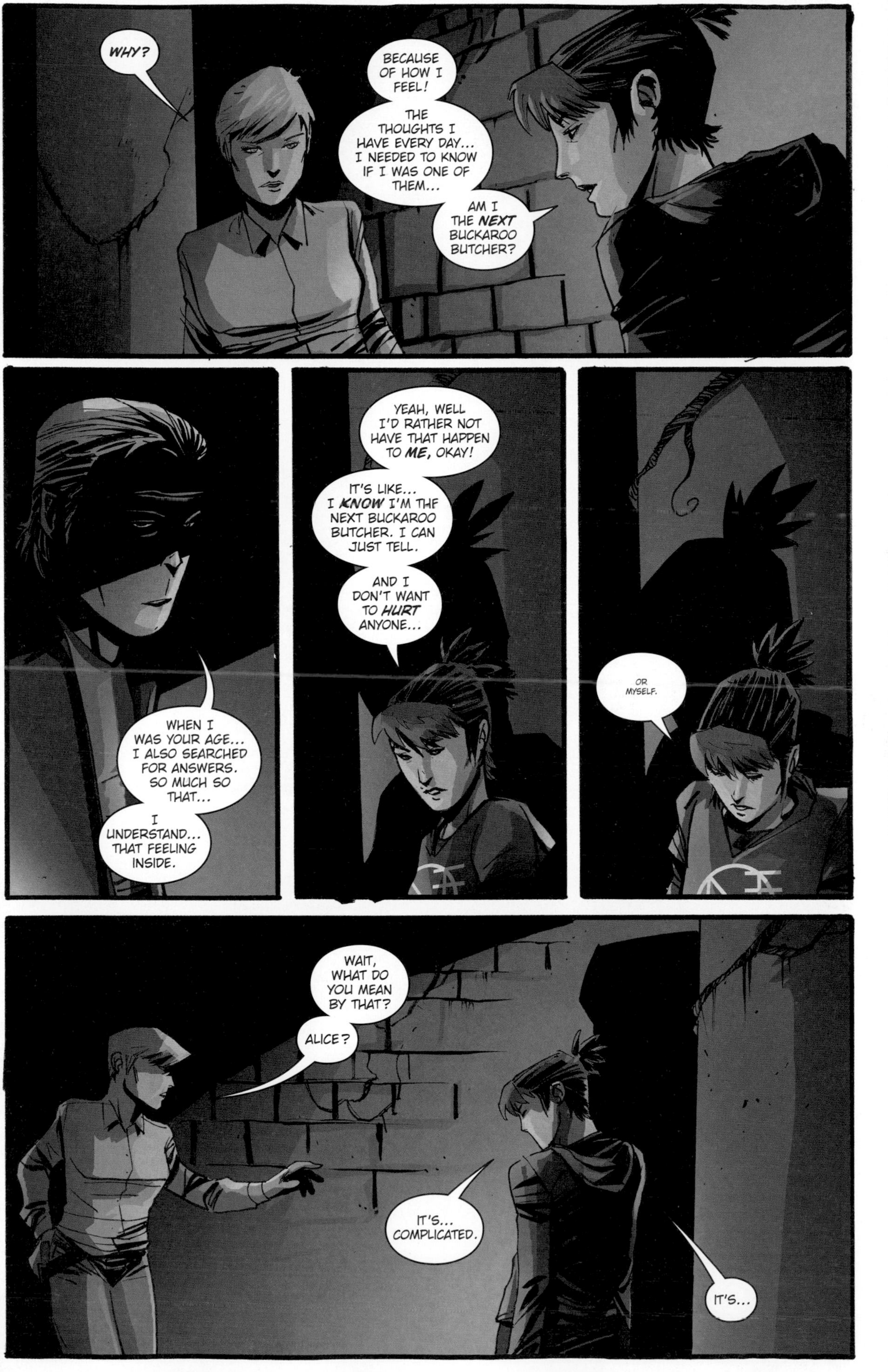
WHY?
BECAUSE OF HOW I FEEL!
THE THOUGHTS I HAVE EVERY DAY... I NEEDED TO KNOW IF I WAS ONE OF THEM...
AM I THE NEXT BUCKAROO BUTCHER?
WHEN I WAS YOUR AGE... I ALSO SEARCHED FOR ANSWERS. SO MUCH SO THAT...
I UNDERSTAND... THAT FEELING INSIDE.
YEAH, WELL I'D RATHER NOT HAVE THAT HAPPEN TO ME, OKAY!
IT'S LIKE... I KNOW I'M THE NEXT BUCKAROO BUTCHER. I CAN JUST TELL.
AND I DON'T WANT TO HURT ANYONE...
OR MYSELF.
WAIT, WHAT DO YOU MEAN BY THAT?
ALICE?
IT'S... COMPLICATED.
IT'S...

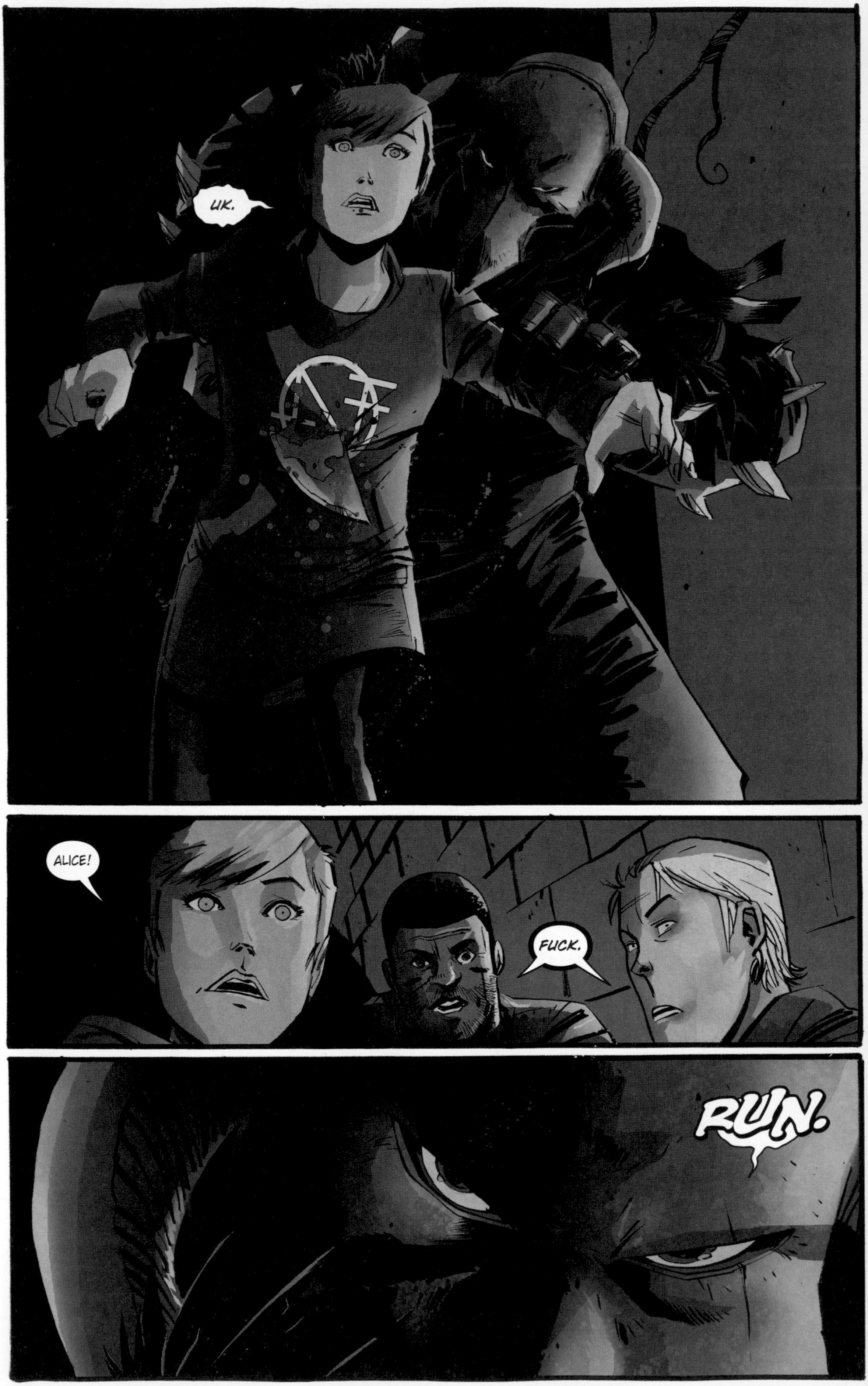
UK.
ALICE!
FUCK.
RUN.

ISSUE FIFTEEN

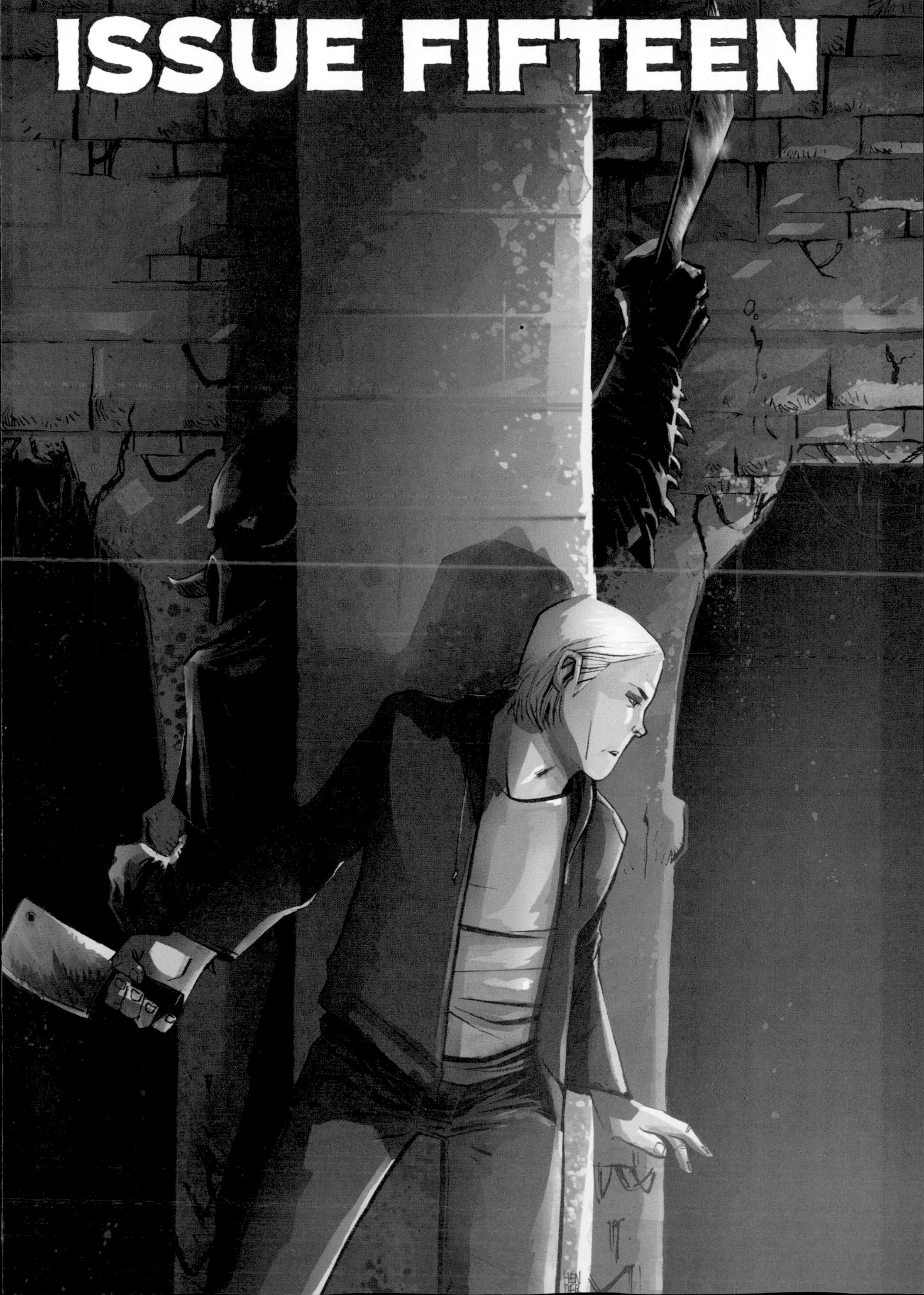

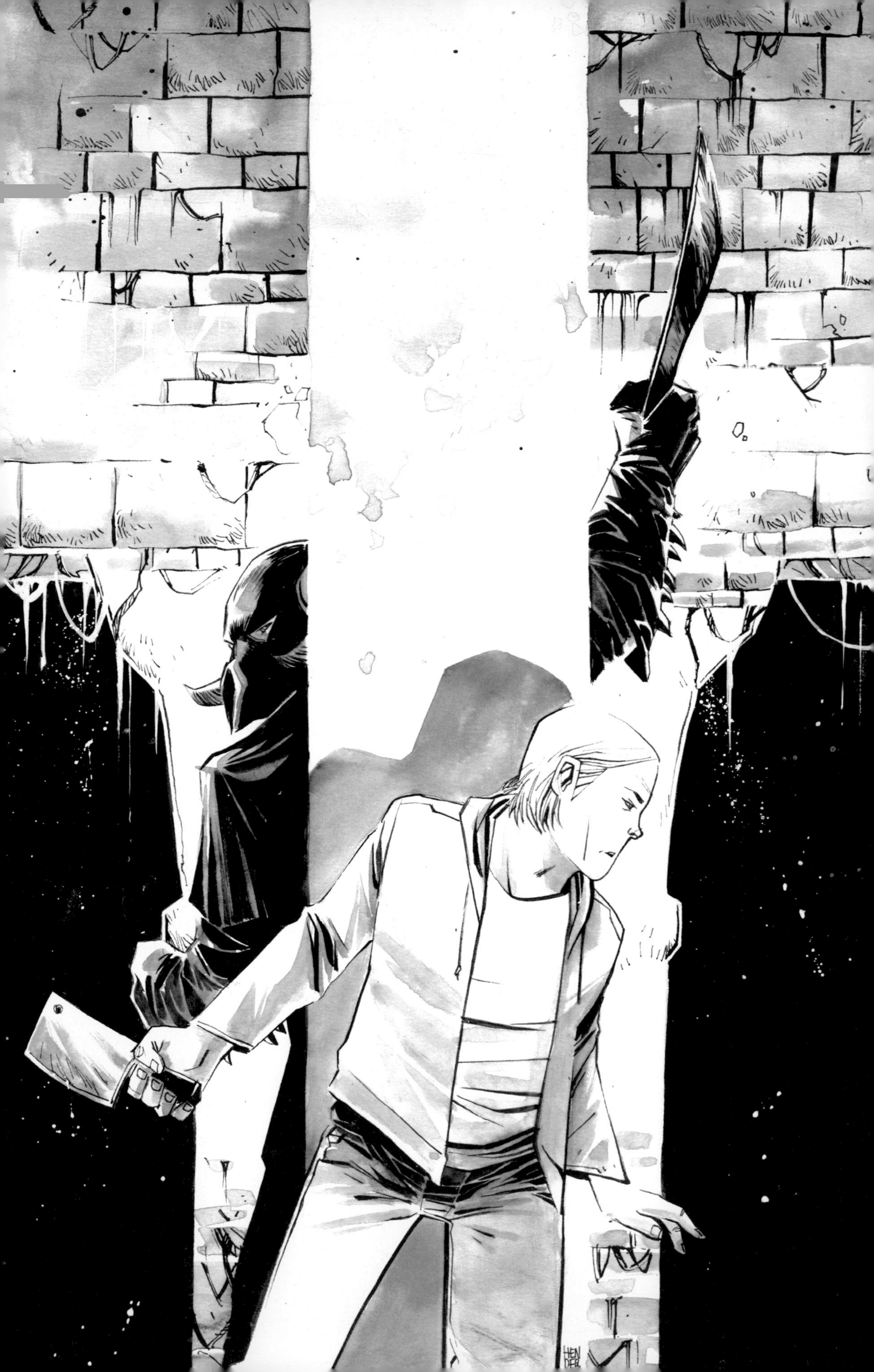

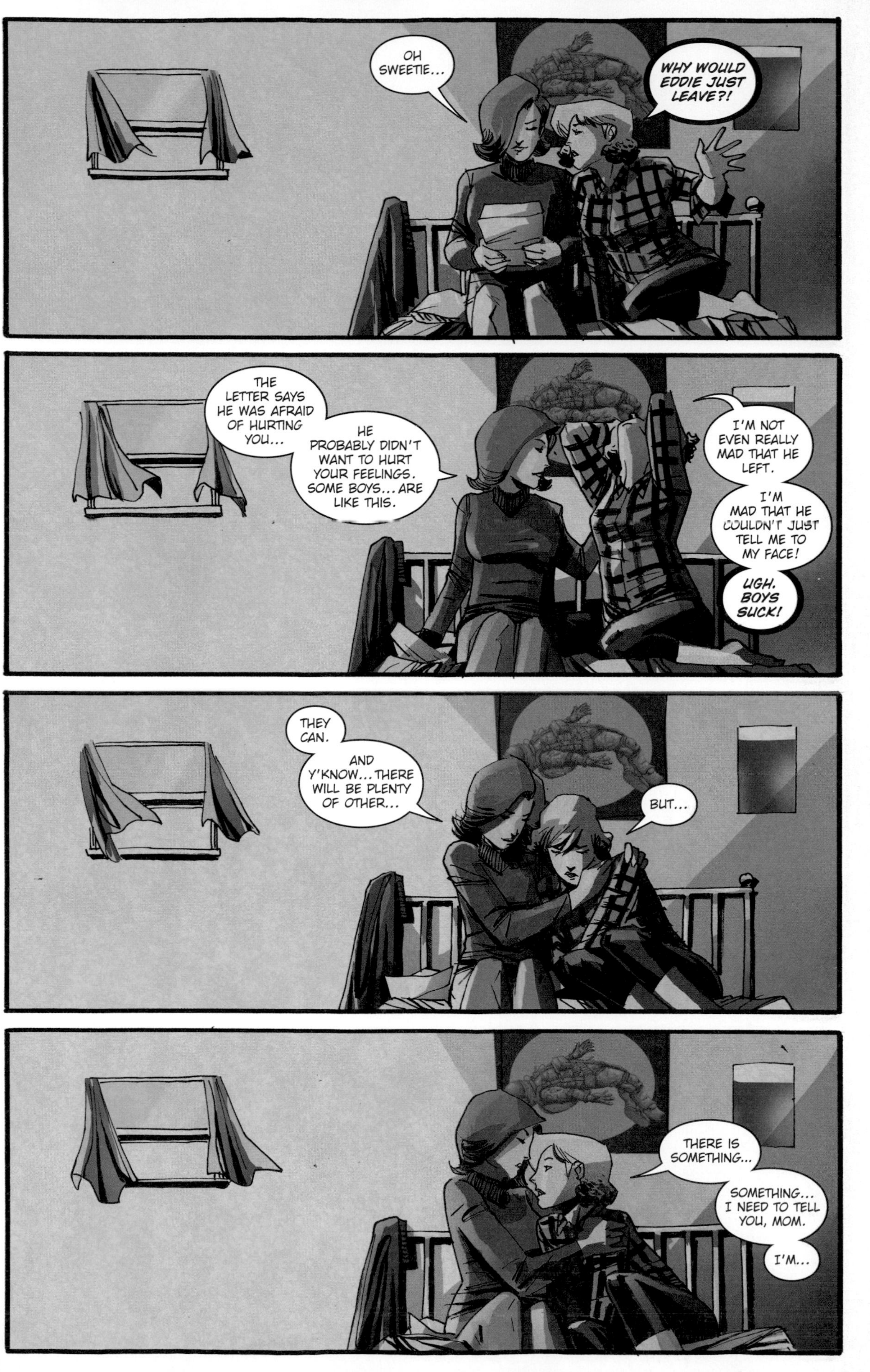
OH SWEETIE...
WHY WOULD EDDIE JUST LEAVE?!
THE LETTER SAYS HE WAS AFRAID OF HURTING YOU...
HE PROBABLY DIDN'T WANT TO HURT YOUR FEELINGS. SOME BOYS... ARE LIKE THIS.
I'M NOT EVEN REALLY MAD THAT HE LEFT.
I'M MAD THAT HE COULDN'T JUST TELL ME TO MY FACE!
UGH. BOYS SUCK!
THEY CAN.
AND Y'KNOW... THERE WILL BE PLENTY OF OTHER...
BUT...
THERE IS SOMETHING...
SOMETHING... I NEED TO TELL YOU, MOM.
I'M...

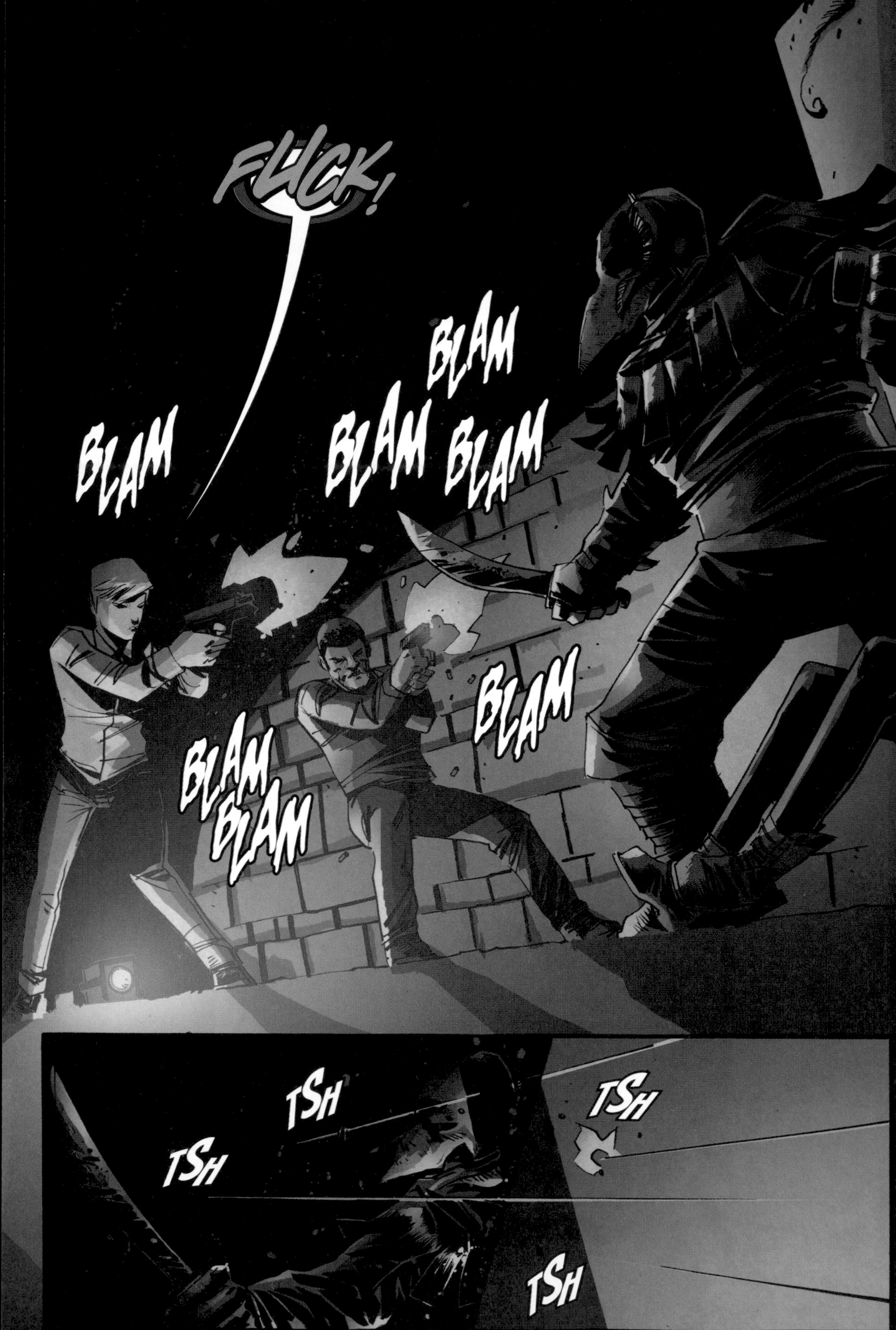
FUCK!
BLAM
BLAM
BLAM
BLAM
BLAM
BLAM BLAM
TSH
TSH
TSH
TSH

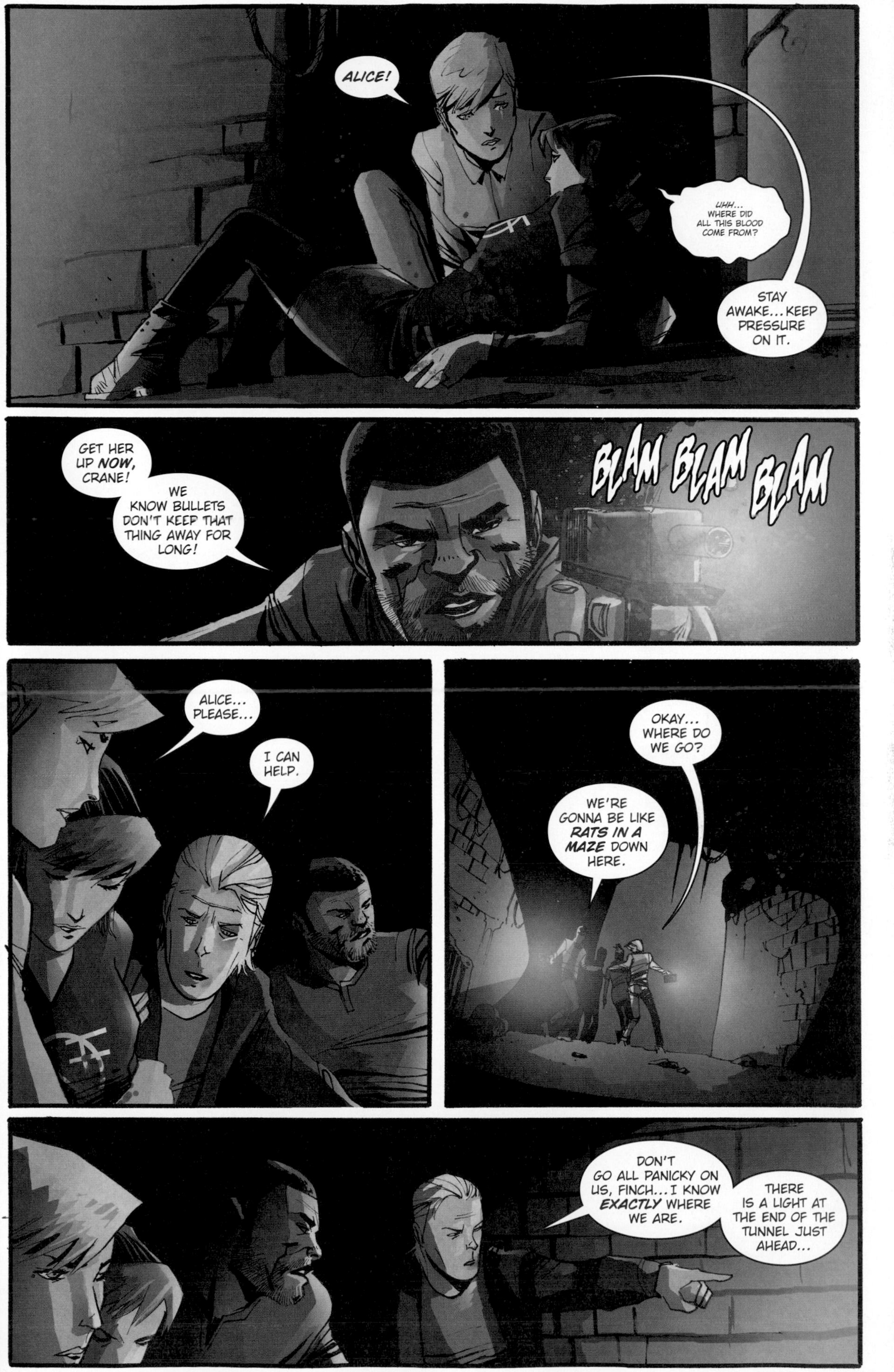

ALICE!
UHH... WHERE DID ALL THIS BLOOD COME FROM?
STAY AWAKE... KEEP PRESSURE ON IT.
GET HER UP NOW, CRANE!
WE KNOW BULLETS DON'T KEEP THAT THING AWAY FOR LONG!
BLAM BLAM BLAM
ALICE... PLEASE...
I CAN HELP.
OKAY... WHERE DO WE GO?
WE'RE GONNA BE LIKE RATS IN A MAZE DOWN HERE.
DON'T GO ALL PANICKY ON US, FINCH... I KNOW EXACTLY WHERE WE ARE.
THERE IS A LIGHT AT THE END OF THE TUNNEL JUST AHEAD...

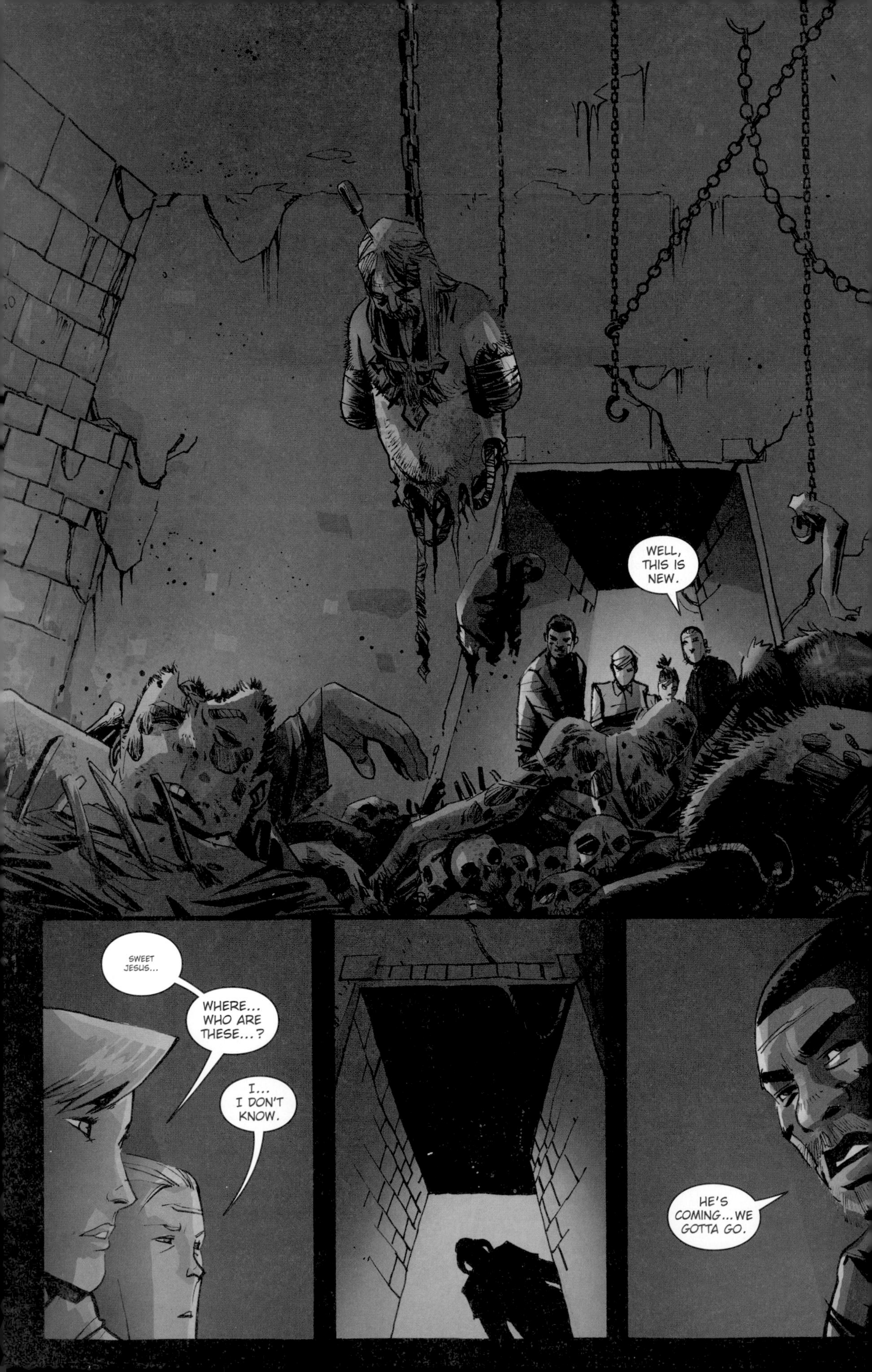
WELL, THIS IS NEW.
SWEET JESUS...
WHERE... WHO ARE THESE...?
I... I DON'T KNOW.
HE'S COMING...WE GOTTA GO.

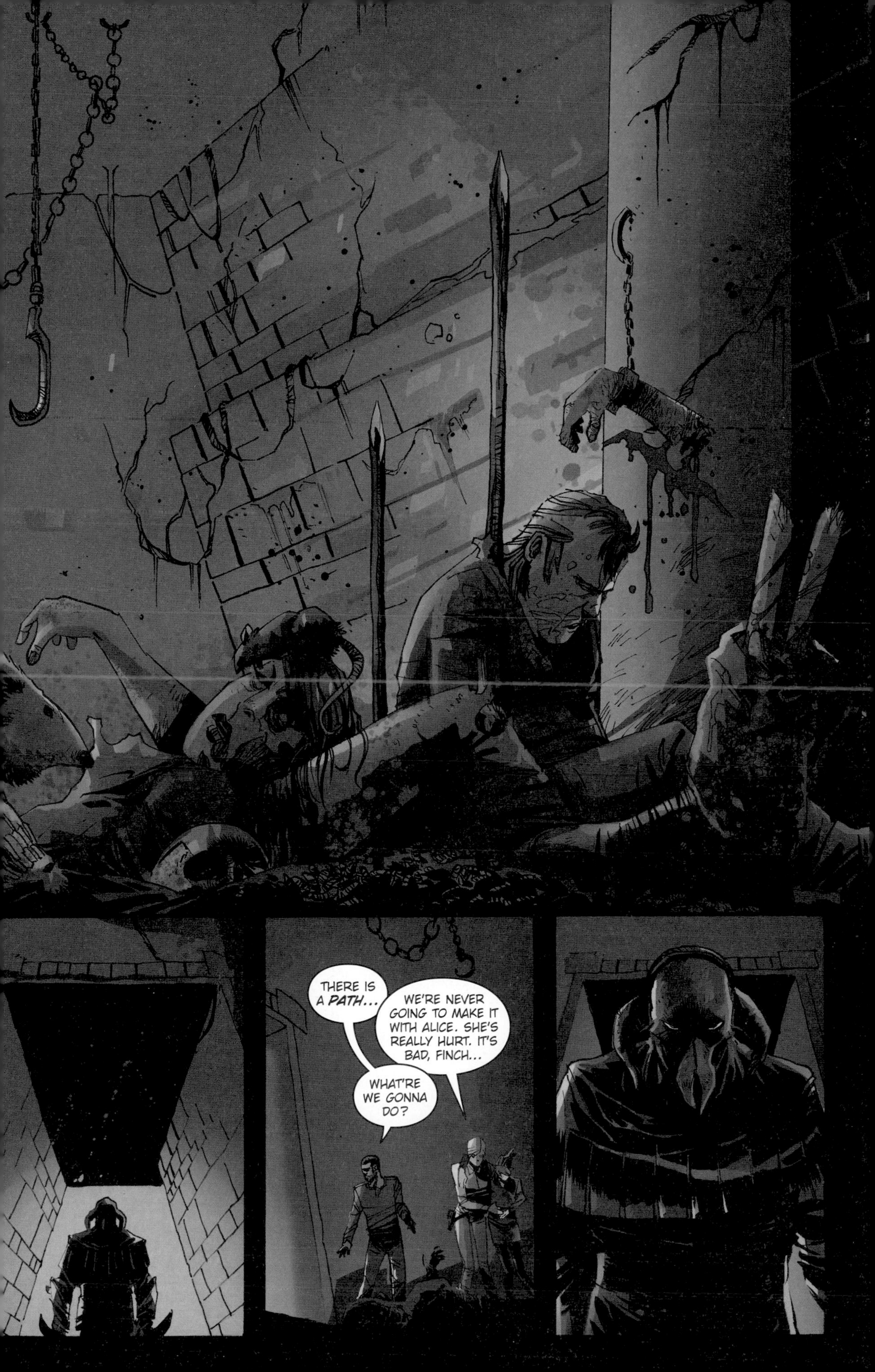
THERE IS A *PATH*...
WE'RE NEVER GOING TO MAKE IT WITH ALICE. SHE'S REALLY HURT. IT'S BAD, FINCH...
WHAT'RE WE GONNA DO?

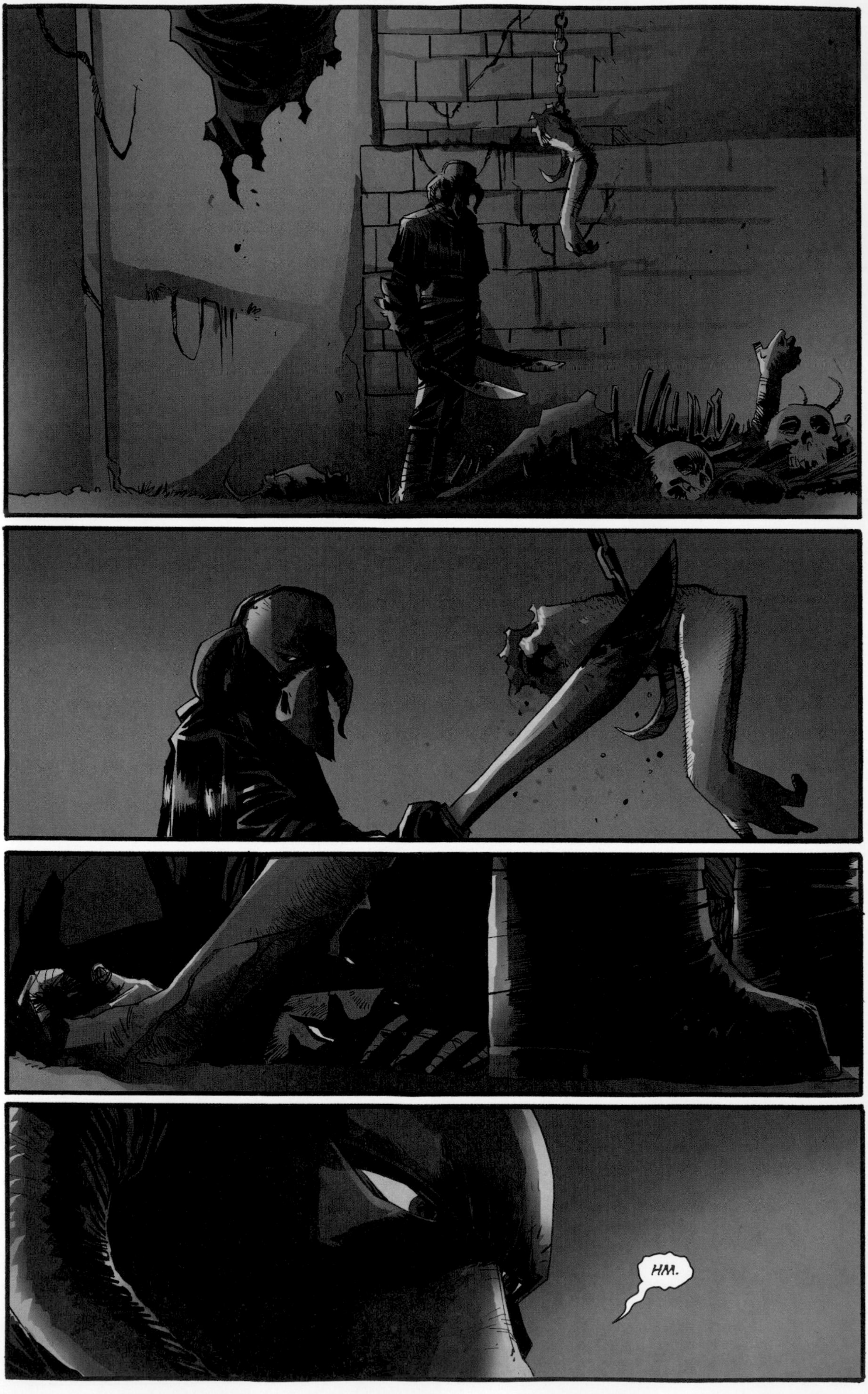
HM.

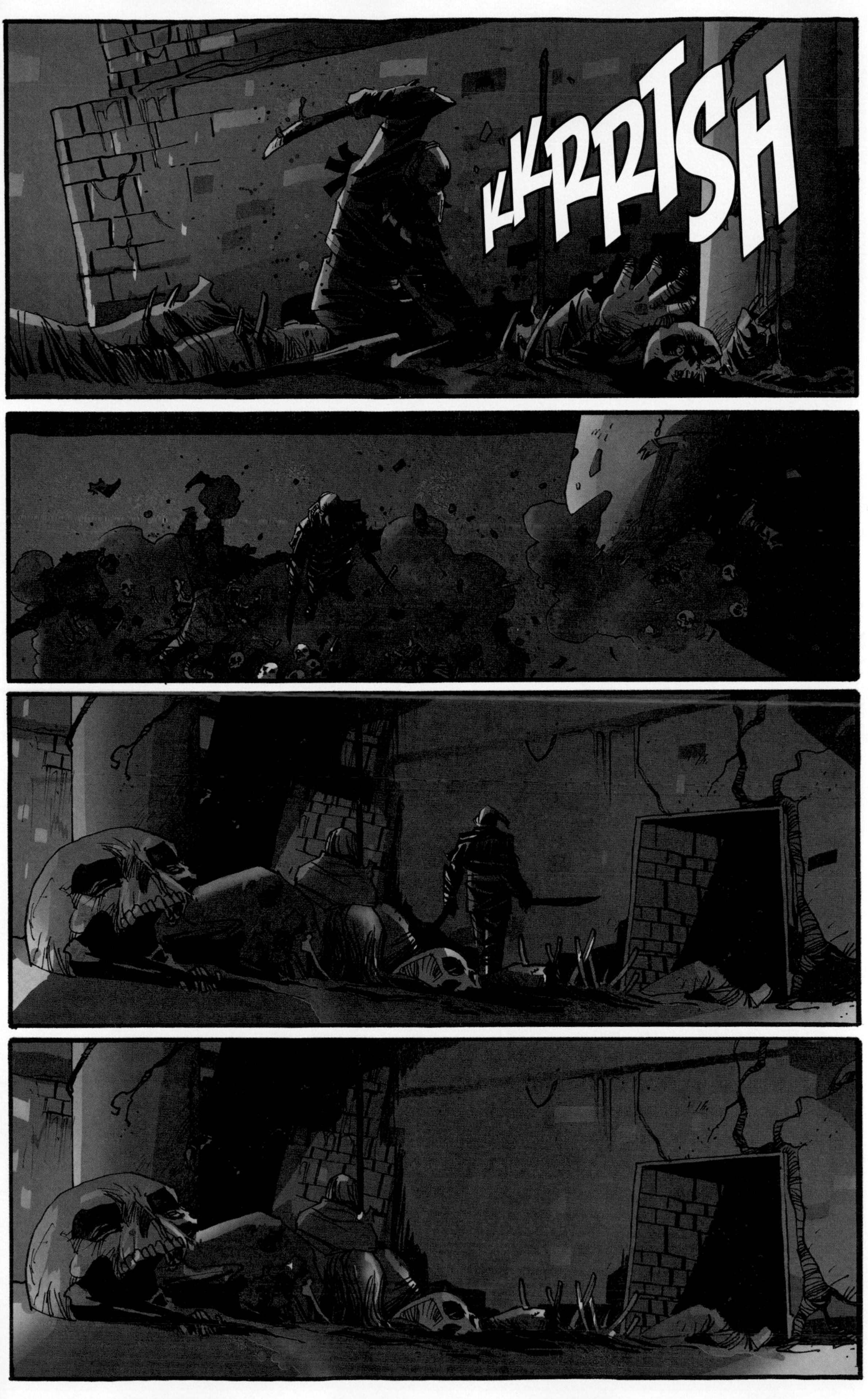
KKRRTSH

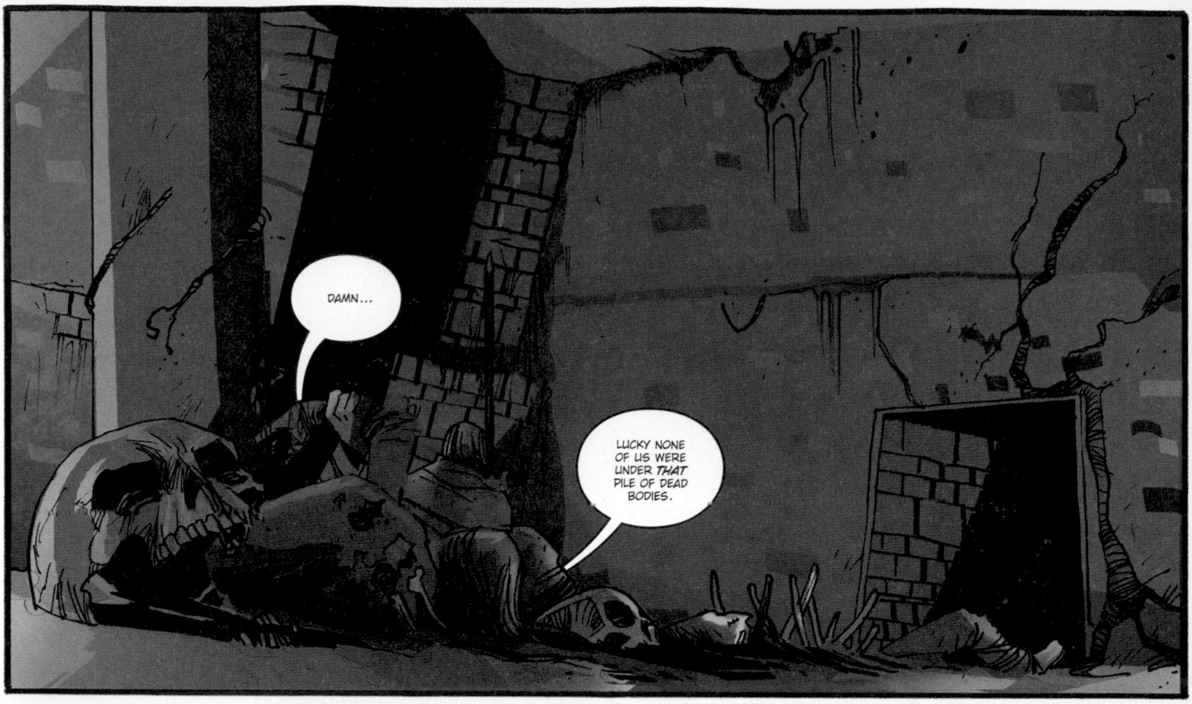
DAMN...
LUCKY NONE OF US WERE UNDER *THAT* PILE OF DEAD BODIES.

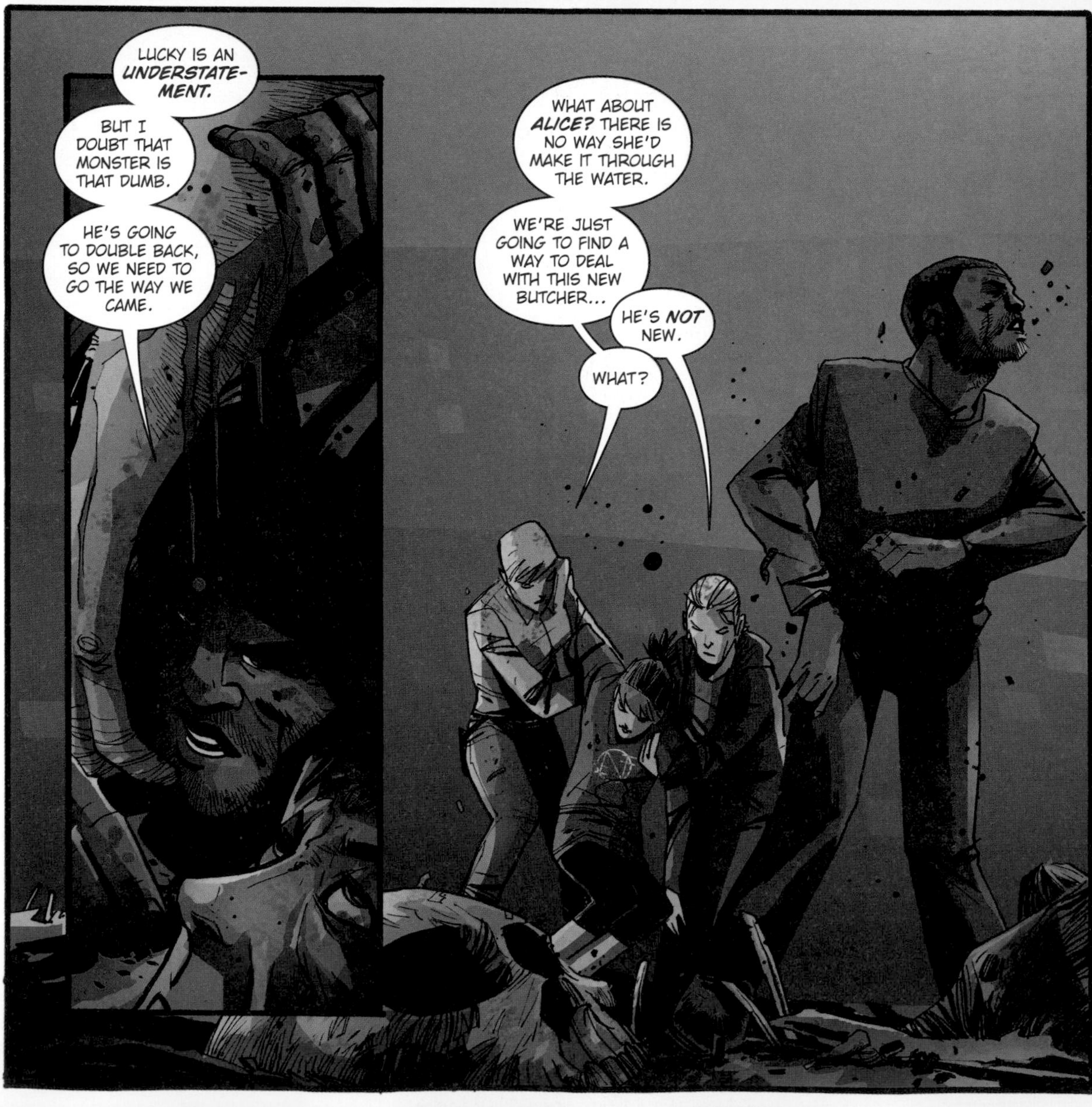
LUCKY IS AN ***UNDERSTATE-MENT.***
BUT I DOUBT THAT MONSTER IS THAT DUMB.
HE'S GOING TO DOUBLE BACK, SO WE NEED TO GO THE WAY WE CAME.
WHAT ABOUT ***ALICE?*** THERE IS NO WAY SHE'D MAKE IT THROUGH THE WATER.
WE'RE JUST GOING TO FIND A WAY TO DEAL WITH THIS NEW BUTCHER...
HE'S ***NOT*** NEW.
WHAT?

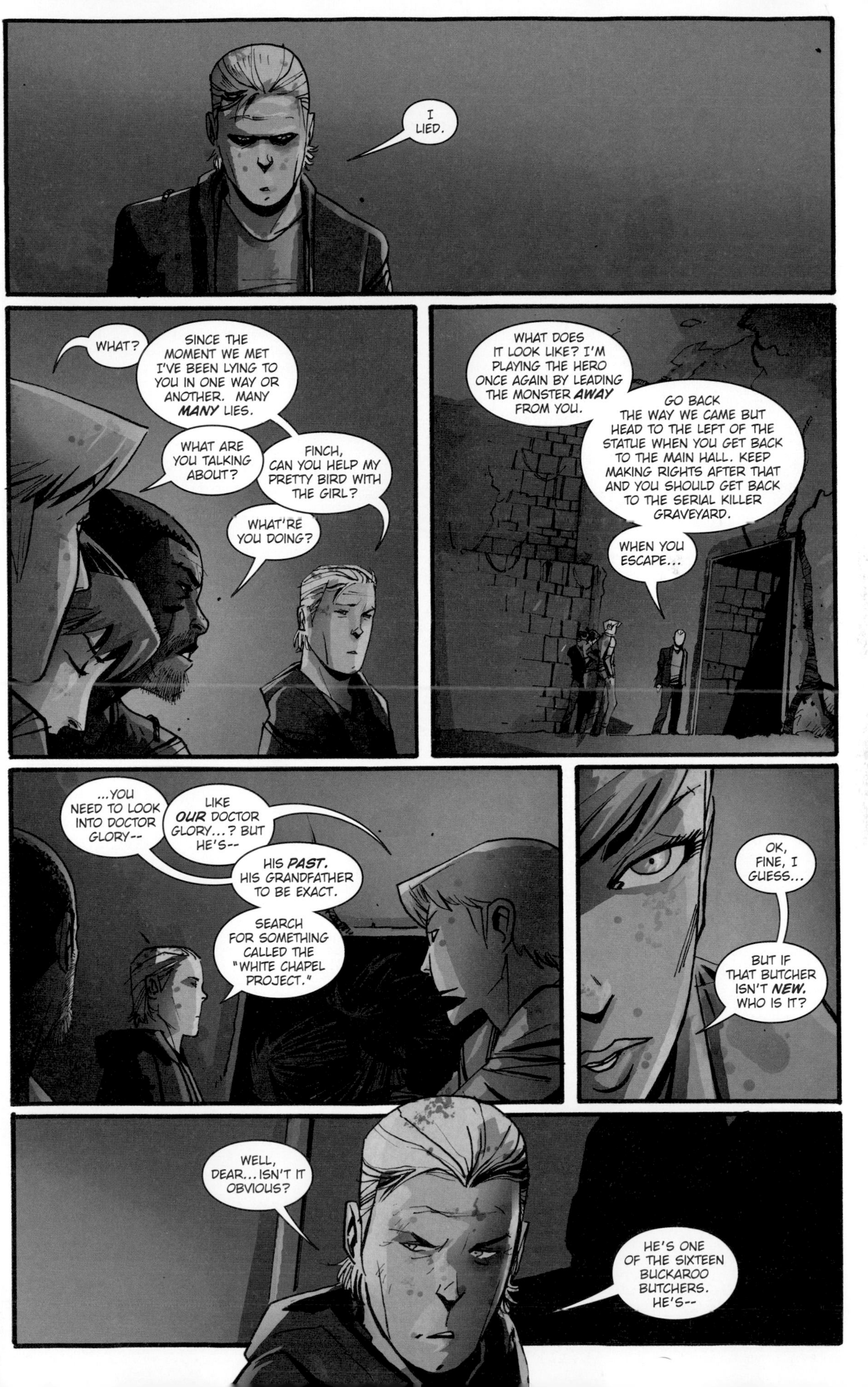
I LIED.
WHAT?
SINCE THE MOMENT WE MET I'VE BEEN LYING TO YOU IN ONE WAY OR ANOTHER. MANY *MANY* LIES.
WHAT ARE YOU TALKING ABOUT?
FINCH, CAN YOU HELP MY PRETTY BIRD WITH THE GIRL?
WHAT'RE YOU DOING?
WHAT DOES IT LOOK LIKE? I'M PLAYING THE HERO ONCE AGAIN BY LEADING THE MONSTER *AWAY* FROM YOU.
GO BACK THE WAY WE CAME BUT HEAD TO THE LEFT OF THE STATUE WHEN YOU GET BACK TO THE MAIN HALL. KEEP MAKING RIGHTS AFTER THAT AND YOU SHOULD GET BACK TO THE SERIAL KILLER GRAVEYARD.
WHEN YOU ESCAPE...
...YOU NEED TO LOOK INTO DOCTOR GLORY--
LIKE *OUR* DOCTOR GLORY...? BUT HE'S--
HIS *PAST.* HIS GRANDFATHER TO BE EXACT.
SEARCH FOR SOMETHING CALLED THE "WHITE CHAPEL PROJECT."
OK, FINE, I GUESS...
BUT IF THAT BUTCHER ISN'T *NEW.* WHO IS IT?
WELL, DEAR... ISN'T IT OBVIOUS?
HE'S ONE OF THE SIXTEEN BUCKAROO BUTCHERS. HE'S--

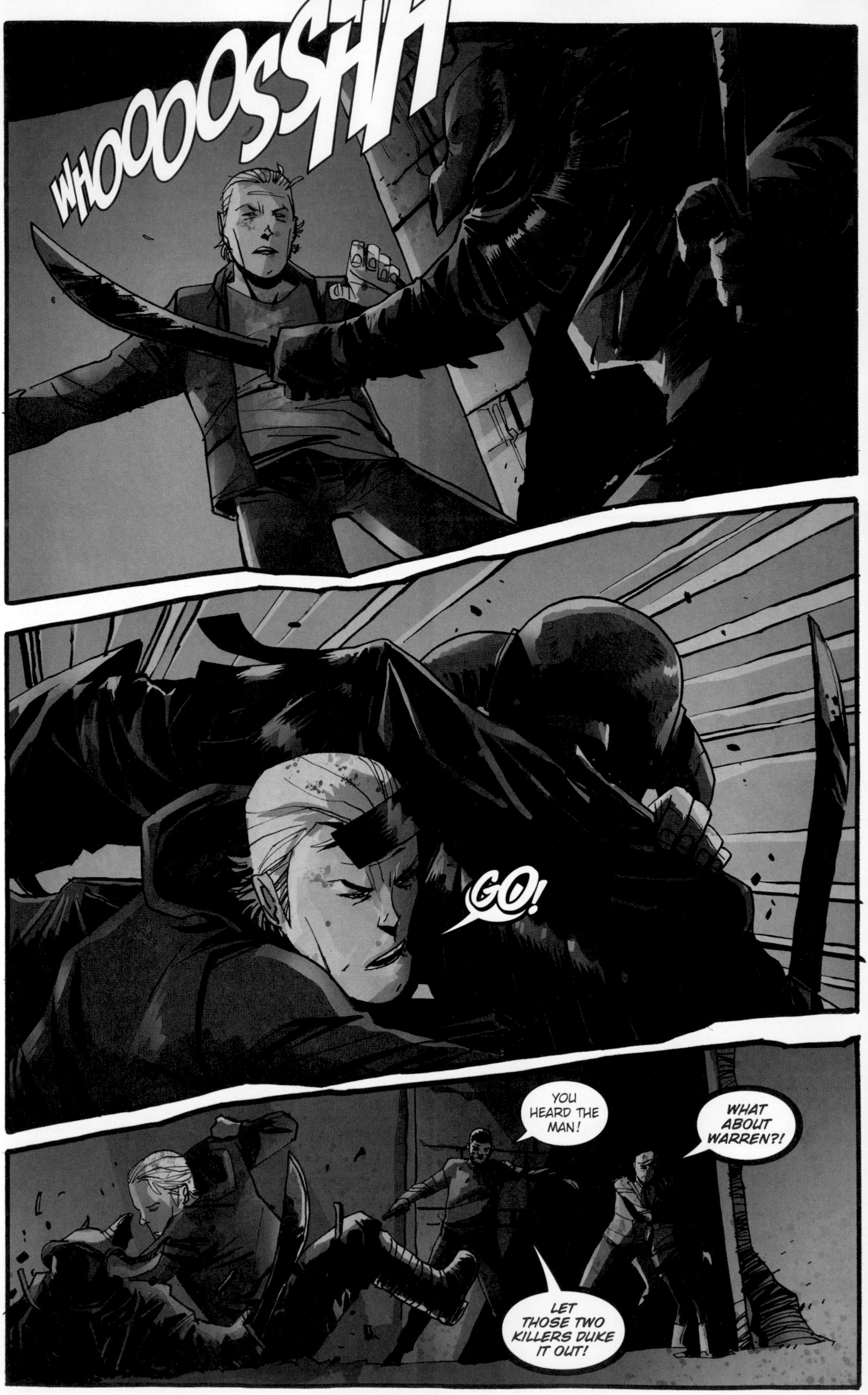
WHOOOOSSHH
GO!
YOU HEARD THE MAN!
WHAT ABOUT WARREN?!
LET THOSE TWO KILLERS DUKE IT OUT!

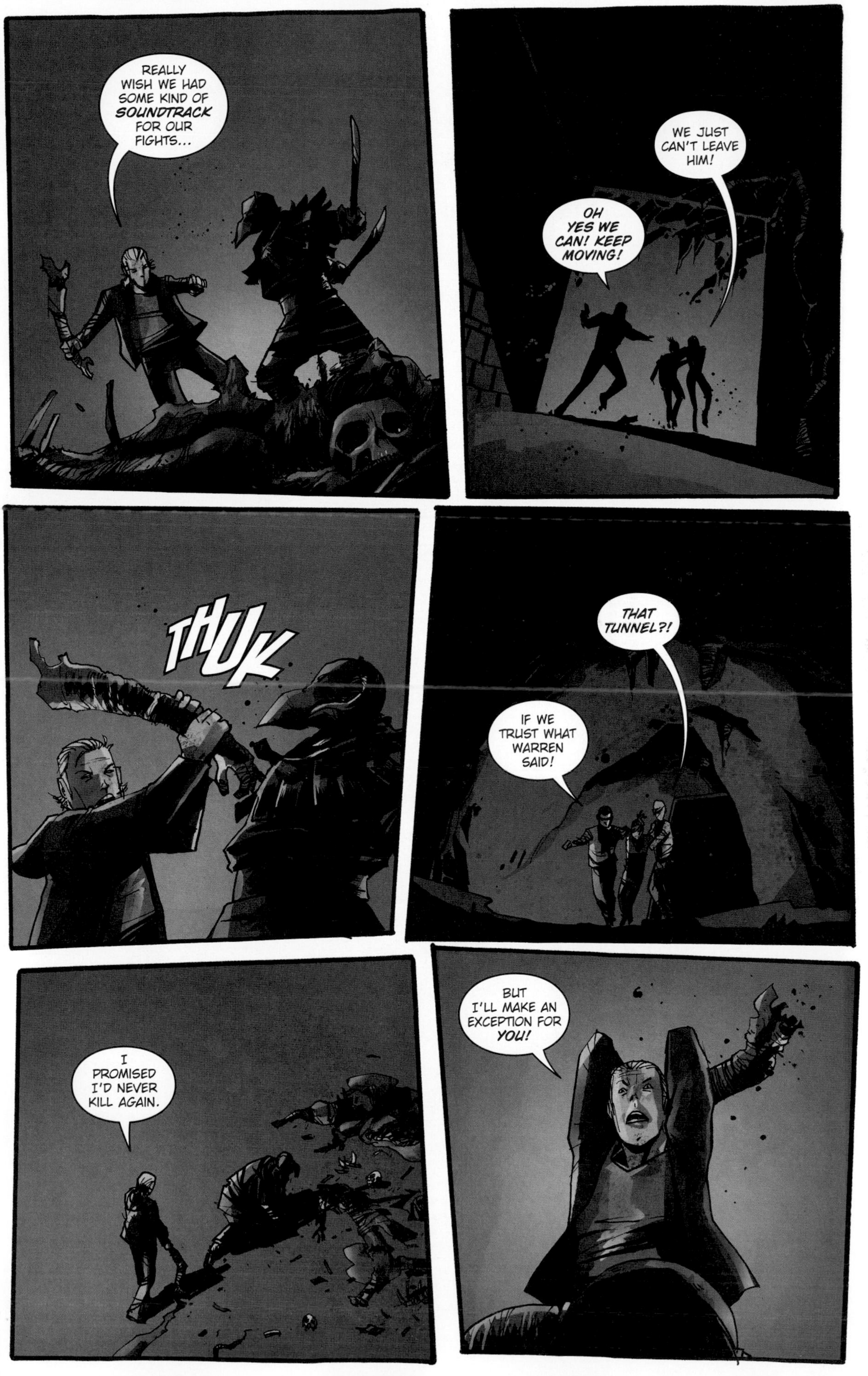
REALLY WISH WE HAD SOME KIND OF SOUNDTRACK FOR OUR FIGHTS...
WE JUST CAN'T LEAVE HIM!
OH YES WE CAN! KEEP MOVING!
THUK
THAT TUNNEL?!
IF WE TRUST WHAT WARREN SAID!
I PROMISED I'D NEVER KILL AGAIN.
BUT I'LL MAKE AN EXCEPTION FOR YOU!

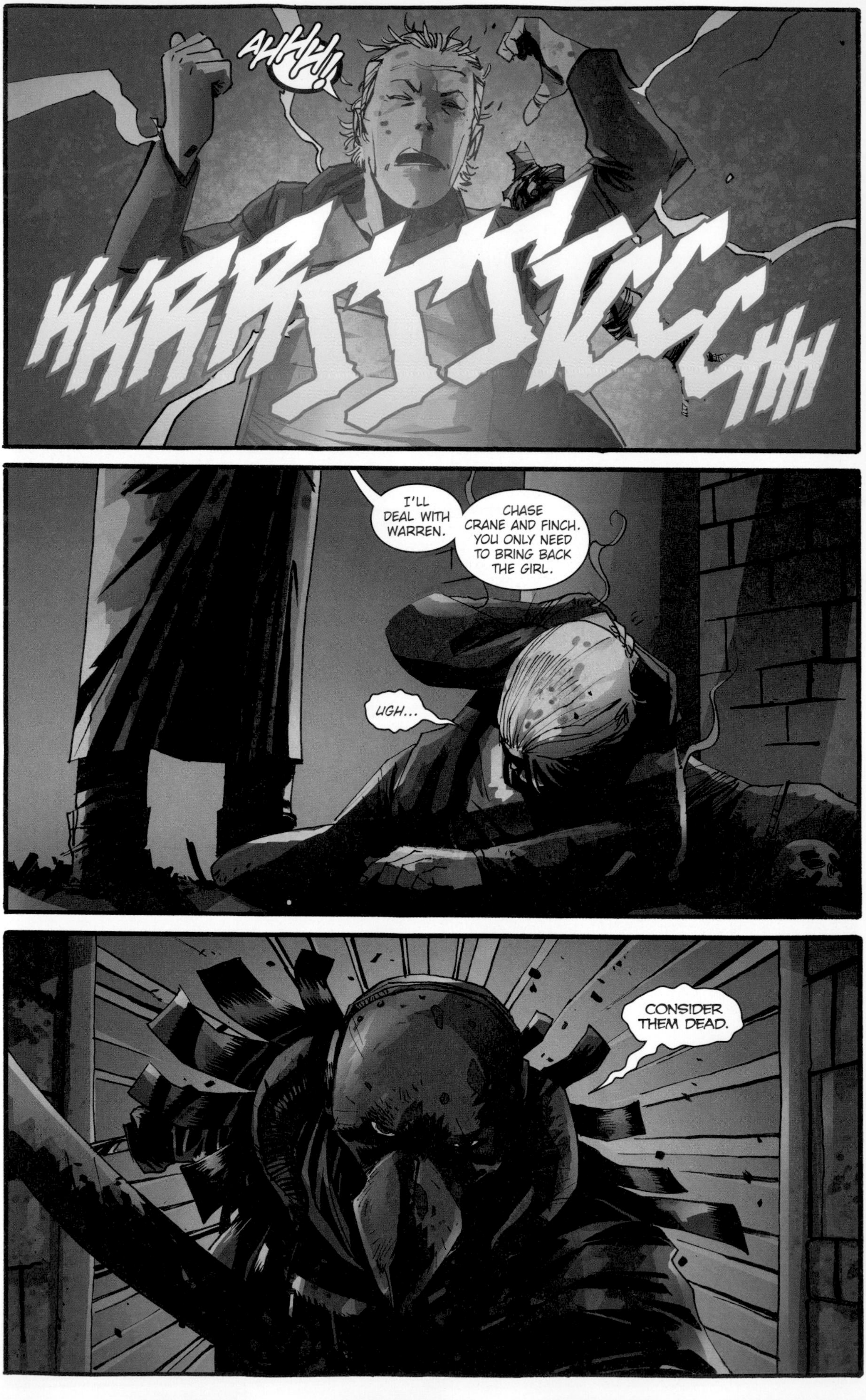
AHHH!!
KKRRSSSCCHH
I'LL DEAL WITH WARREN.
CHASE CRANE AND FINCH. YOU ONLY NEED TO BRING BACK THE GIRL.
UGH...
CONSIDER THEM DEAD.

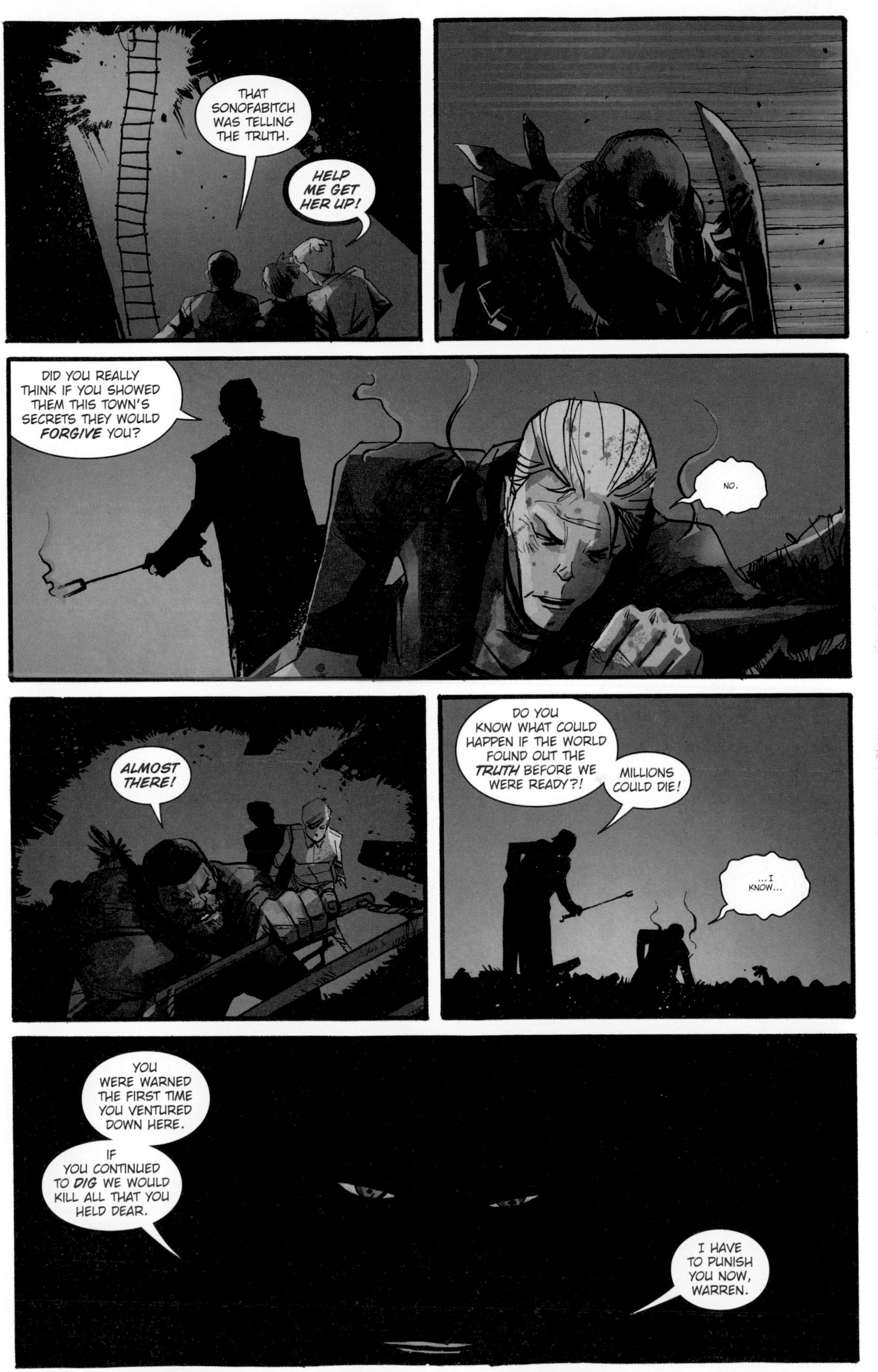
THAT SONOFABITCH WAS TELLING THE TRUTH.
HELP ME GET HER UP!
DID YOU REALLY THINK IF YOU SHOWED THEM THIS TOWN'S SECRETS THEY WOULD FORGIVE YOU?
NO.
ALMOST THERE!
DO YOU KNOW WHAT COULD HAPPEN IF THE WORLD FOUND OUT THE TRUTH BEFORE WE WERE READY?!
MILLIONS COULD DIE!
...I KNOW...
YOU WERE WARNED THE FIRST TIME YOU VENTURED DOWN HERE.
IF YOU CONTINUED TO DIG WE WOULD KILL ALL THAT YOU HELD DEAR.
I HAVE TO PUNISH YOU NOW, WARREN.

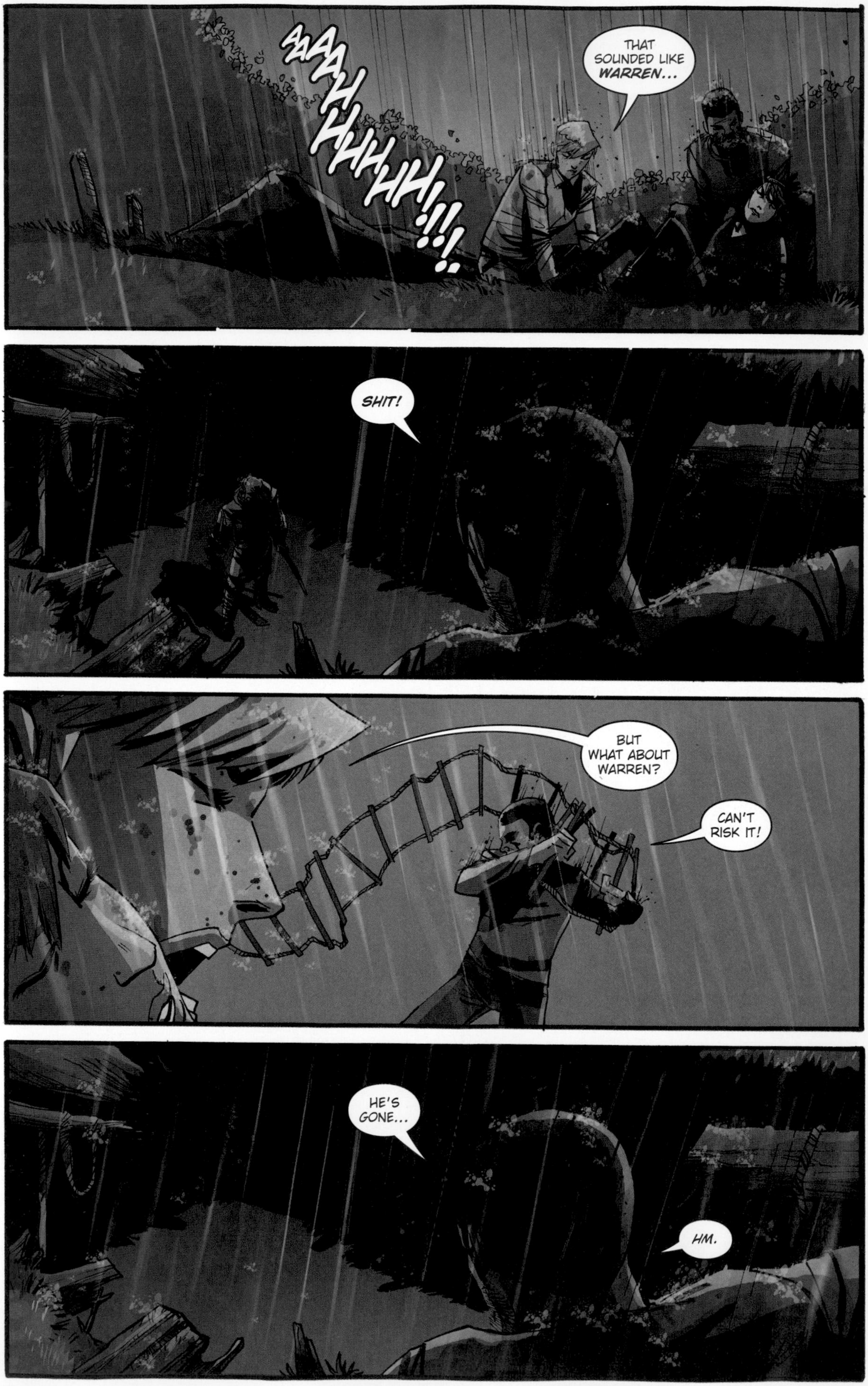
AAAAHHHHHH!!!!
THAT SOUNDED LIKE WARREN...
SHIT!
BUT WHAT ABOUT WARREN?
CAN'T RISK IT!
HE'S GONE...
HM.

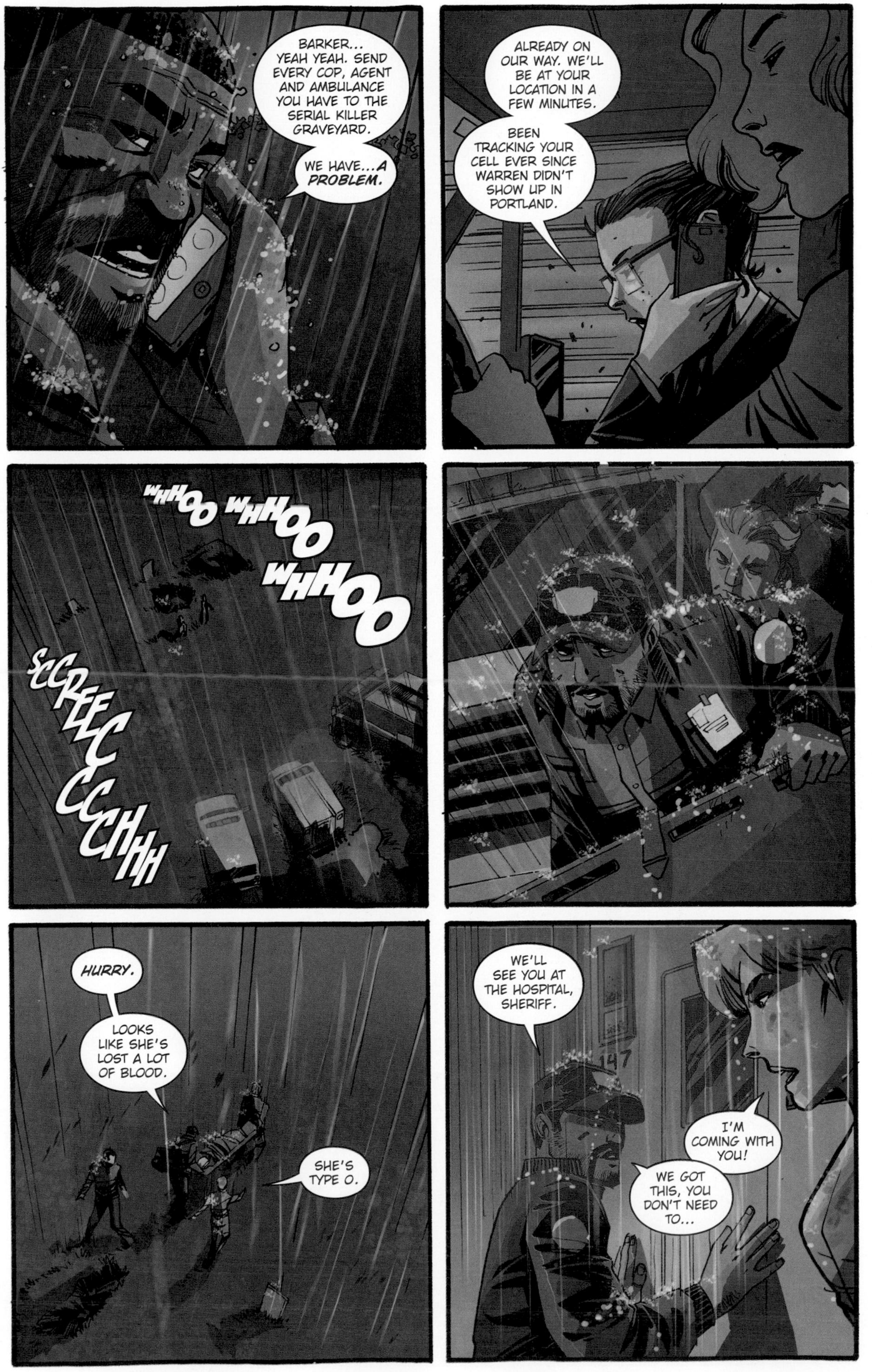
BARKER... YEAH YEAH. SEND EVERY COP, AGENT AND AMBULANCE YOU HAVE TO THE SERIAL KILLER GRAVEYARD.
WE HAVE...A PROBLEM.
ALREADY ON OUR WAY. WE'LL BE AT YOUR LOCATION IN A FEW MINUTES.
BEEN TRACKING YOUR CELL EVER SINCE WARREN DIDN'T SHOW UP IN PORTLAND.
WHHOO WHHOO WHHOO
SCCREECCCCHHH
HURRY.
LOOKS LIKE SHE'S LOST A LOT OF BLOOD.
SHE'S TYPE O.
WE'LL SEE YOU AT THE HOSPITAL, SHERIFF.
I'M COMING WITH YOU!
WE GOT THIS, YOU DON'T NEED TO...

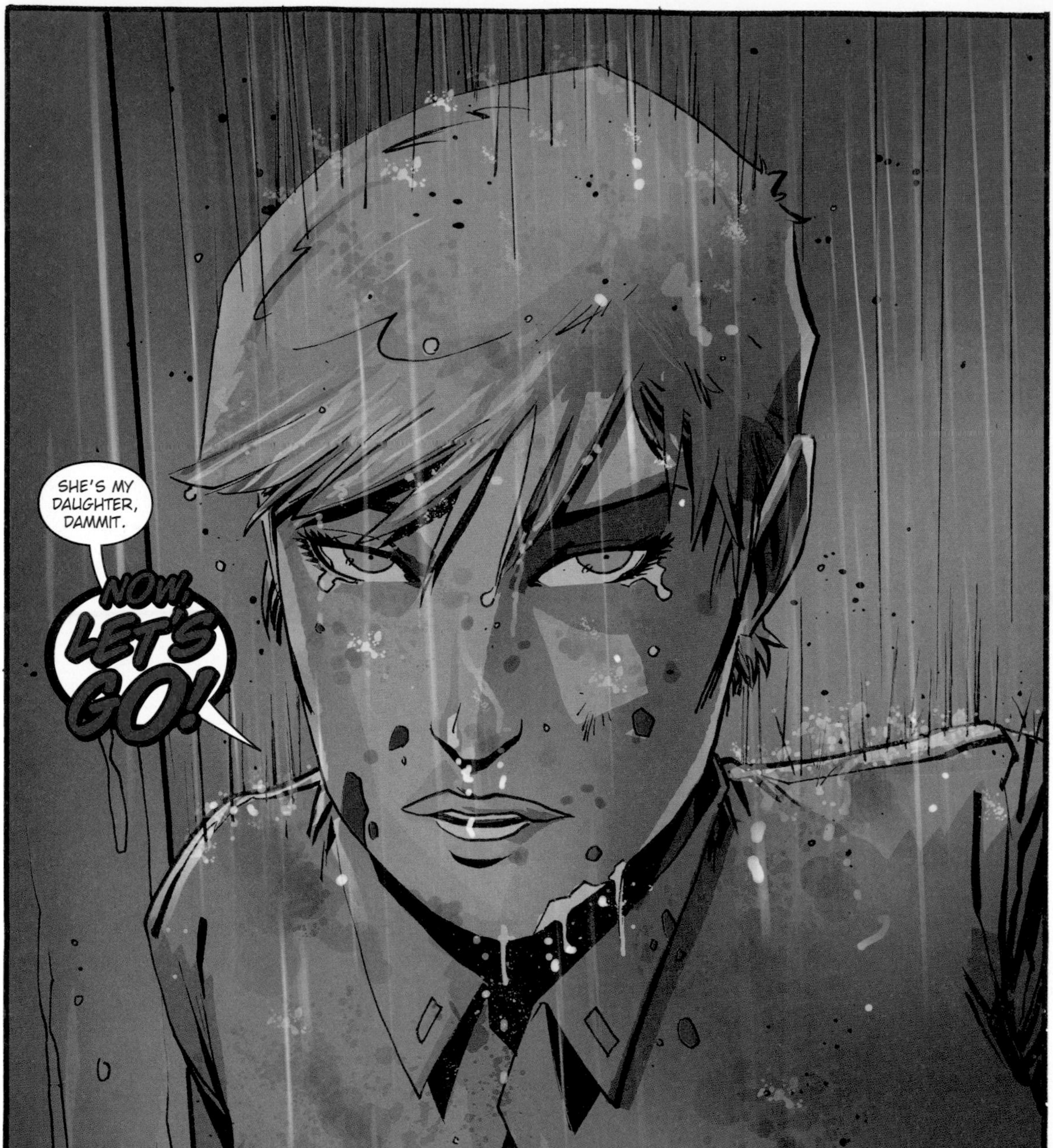
SHE'S MY DAUGHTER, DAMMIT.
NOW. LET'S GO!

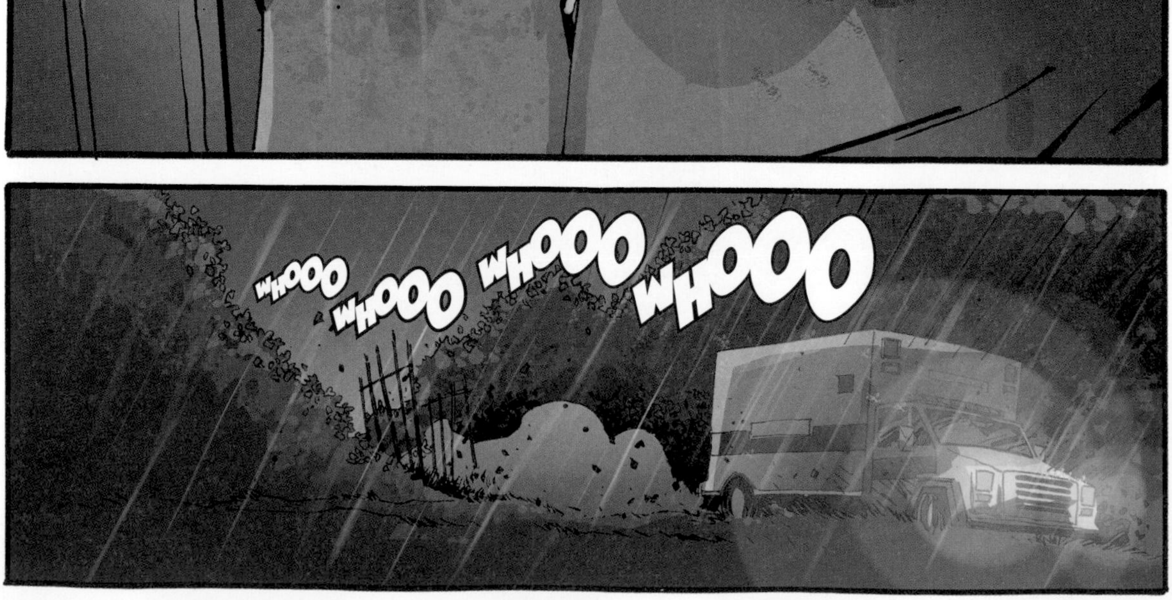
WHOOO WHOOO WHOOO WHOOO

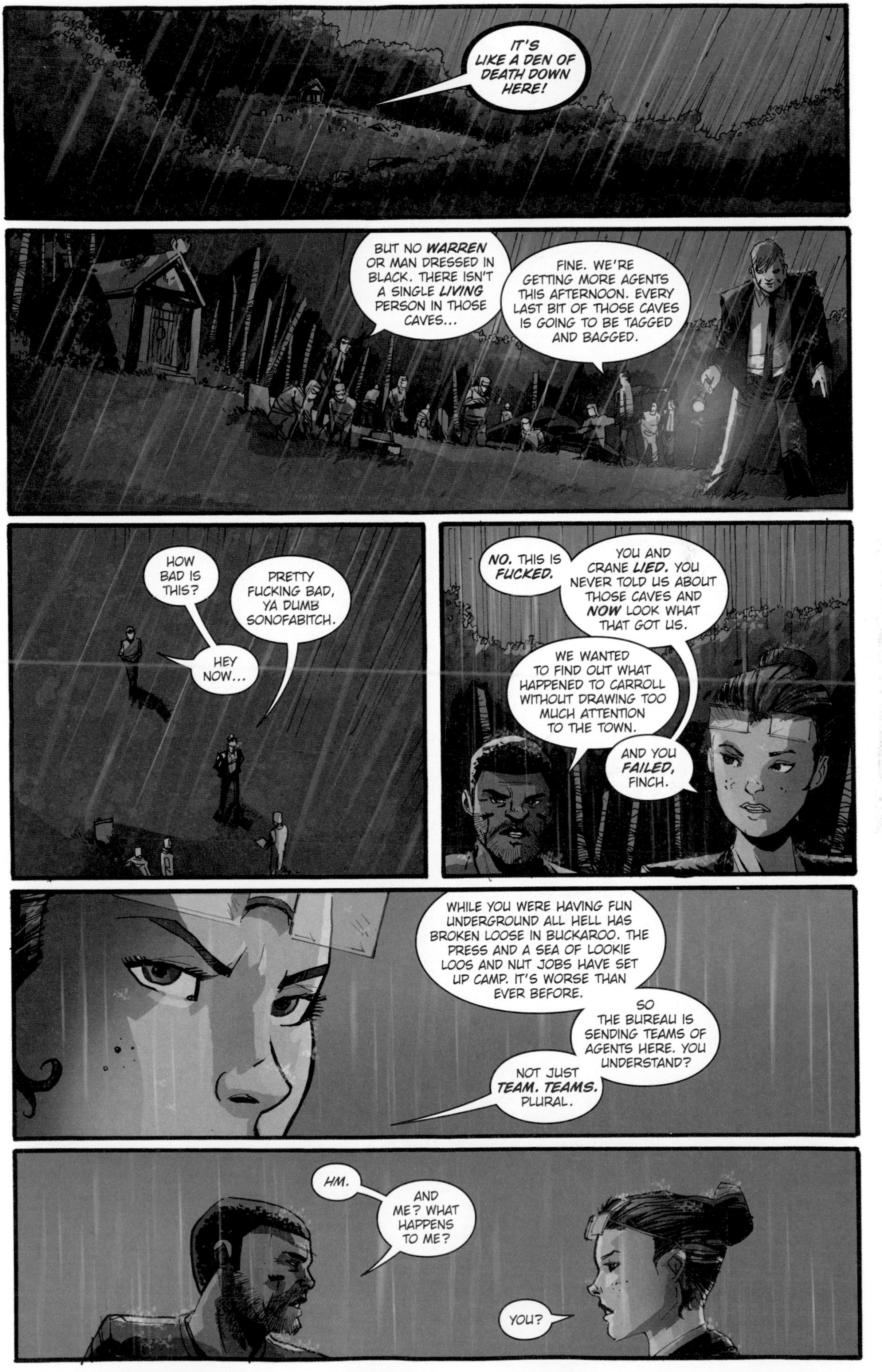
IT'S LIKE A DEN OF DEATH DOWN HERE!
BUT NO WARREN OR MAN DRESSED IN BLACK. THERE ISN'T A SINGLE LIVING PERSON IN THOSE CAVES...
FINE. WE'RE GETTING MORE AGENTS THIS AFTERNOON. EVERY LAST BIT OF THOSE CAVES IS GOING TO BE TAGGED AND BAGGED.
HOW BAD IS THIS?
PRETTY FUCKING BAD, YA DUMB SONOFABITCH.
HEY NOW...
NO. THIS IS FUCKED.
YOU AND CRANE LIED. YOU NEVER TOLD US ABOUT THOSE CAVES AND NOW LOOK WHAT THAT GOT US.
WE WANTED TO FIND OUT WHAT HAPPENED TO CARROLL WITHOUT DRAWING TOO MUCH ATTENTION TO THE TOWN.
AND YOU FAILED, FINCH.
WHILE YOU WERE HAVING FUN UNDERGROUND ALL HELL HAS BROKEN LOOSE IN BUCKAROO. THE PRESS AND A SEA OF LOOKIE LOOS AND NUT JOBS HAVE SET UP CAMP. IT'S WORSE THAN EVER BEFORE.
SO THE BUREAU IS SENDING TEAMS OF AGENTS HERE. YOU UNDERSTAND?
NOT JUST TEAM. TEAMS. PLURAL.
HM.
AND ME? WHAT HAPPENS TO ME?
YOU?

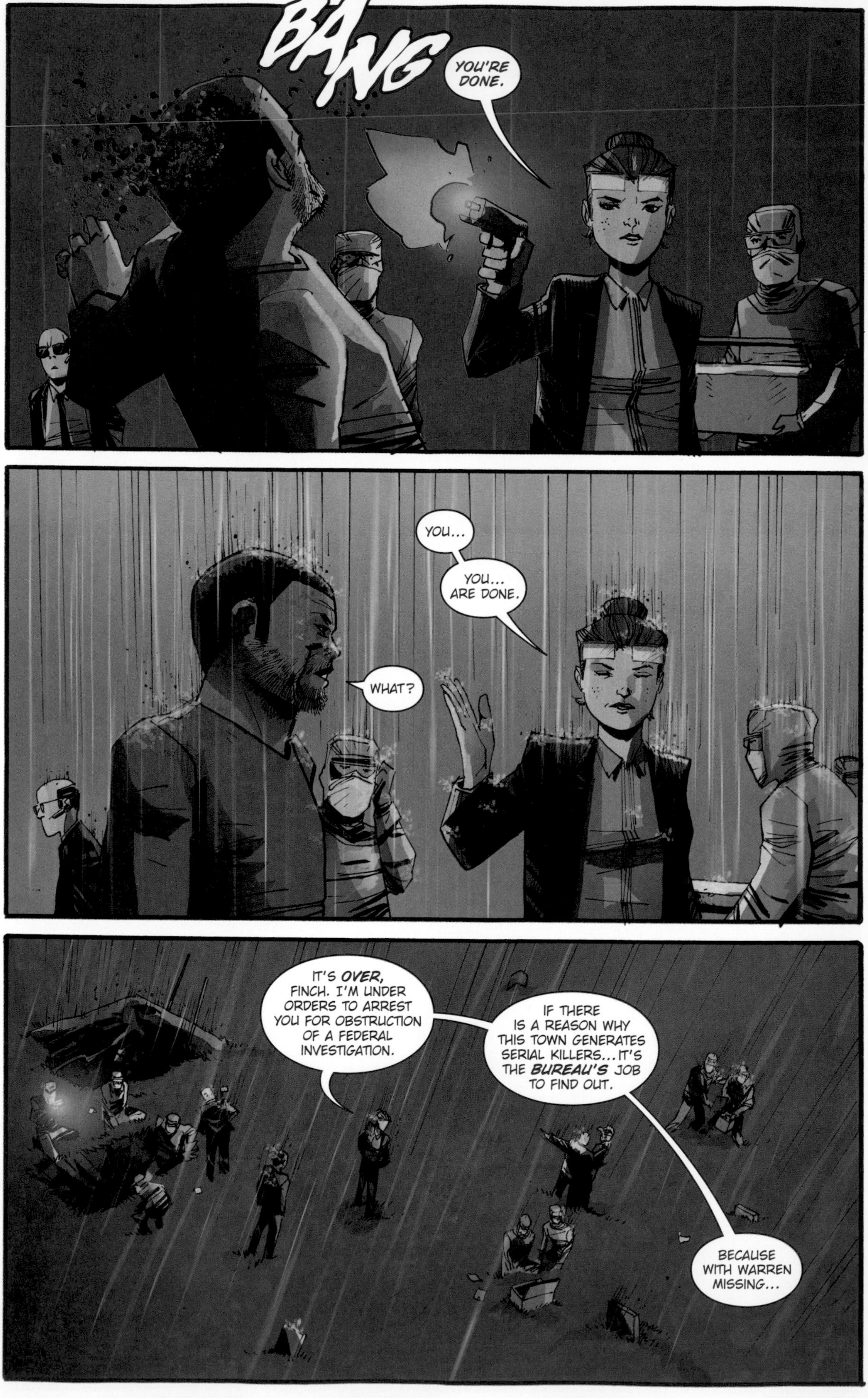
BANG
YOU'RE DONE.
YOU...
YOU... ARE DONE.
WHAT?
IT'S OVER, FINCH. I'M UNDER ORDERS TO ARREST YOU FOR OBSTRUCTION OF A FEDERAL INVESTIGATION.
IF THERE IS A REASON WHY THIS TOWN GENERATES SERIAL KILLERS... IT'S THE BUREAU'S JOB TO FIND OUT.
BECAUSE WITH WARREN MISSING...

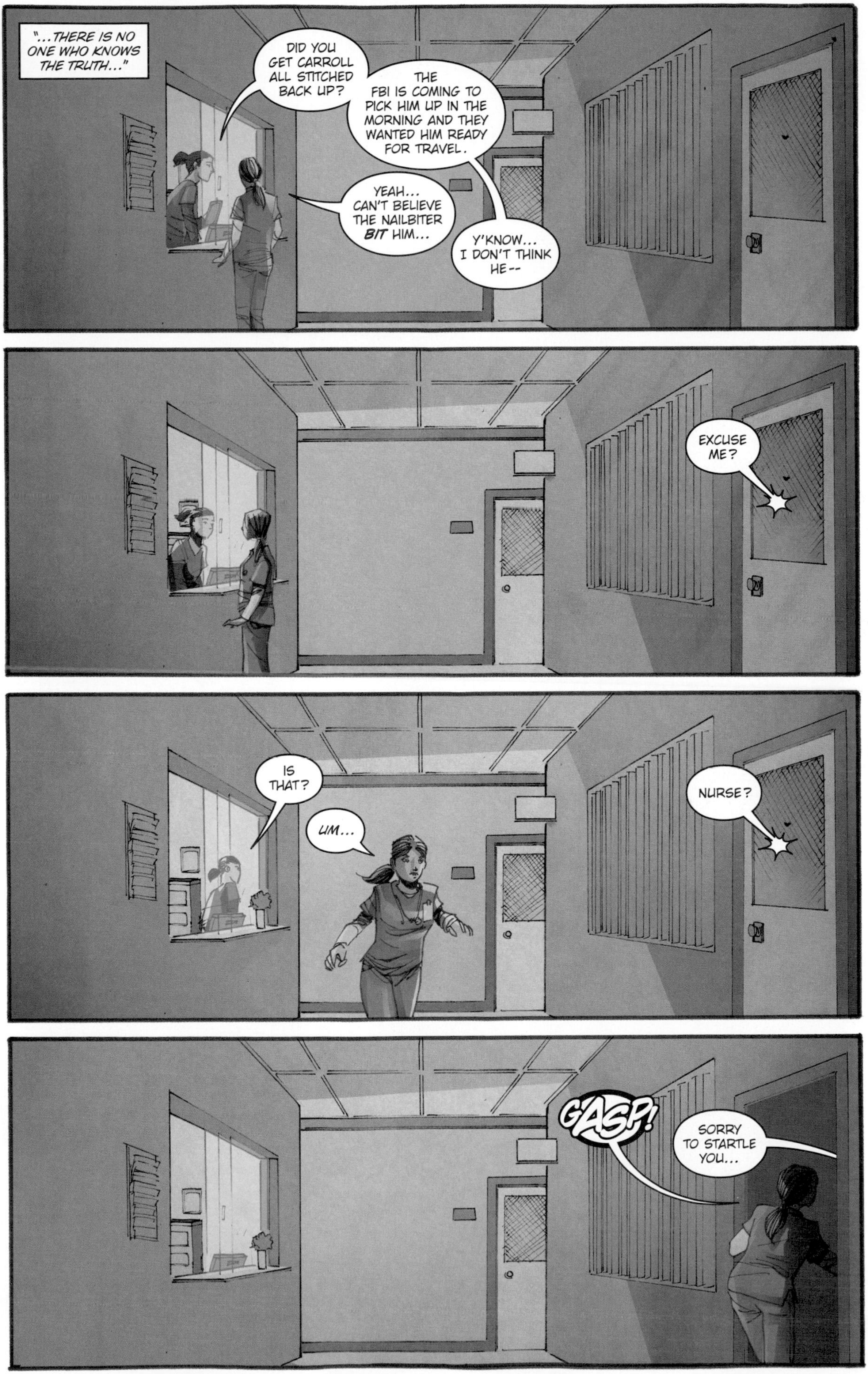
"...THERE IS NO ONE WHO KNOWS THE TRUTH..."
DID YOU GET CARROLL ALL STITCHED BACK UP?
THE FBI IS COMING TO PICK HIM UP IN THE MORNING AND THEY WANTED HIM READY FOR TRAVEL.
YEAH... CAN'T BELIEVE THE NAILBITER *BIT* HIM...
Y'KNOW... I DON'T THINK HE--
EXCUSE ME?
IS THAT?
UM...
NURSE?
GASP!
SORRY TO STARTLE YOU...

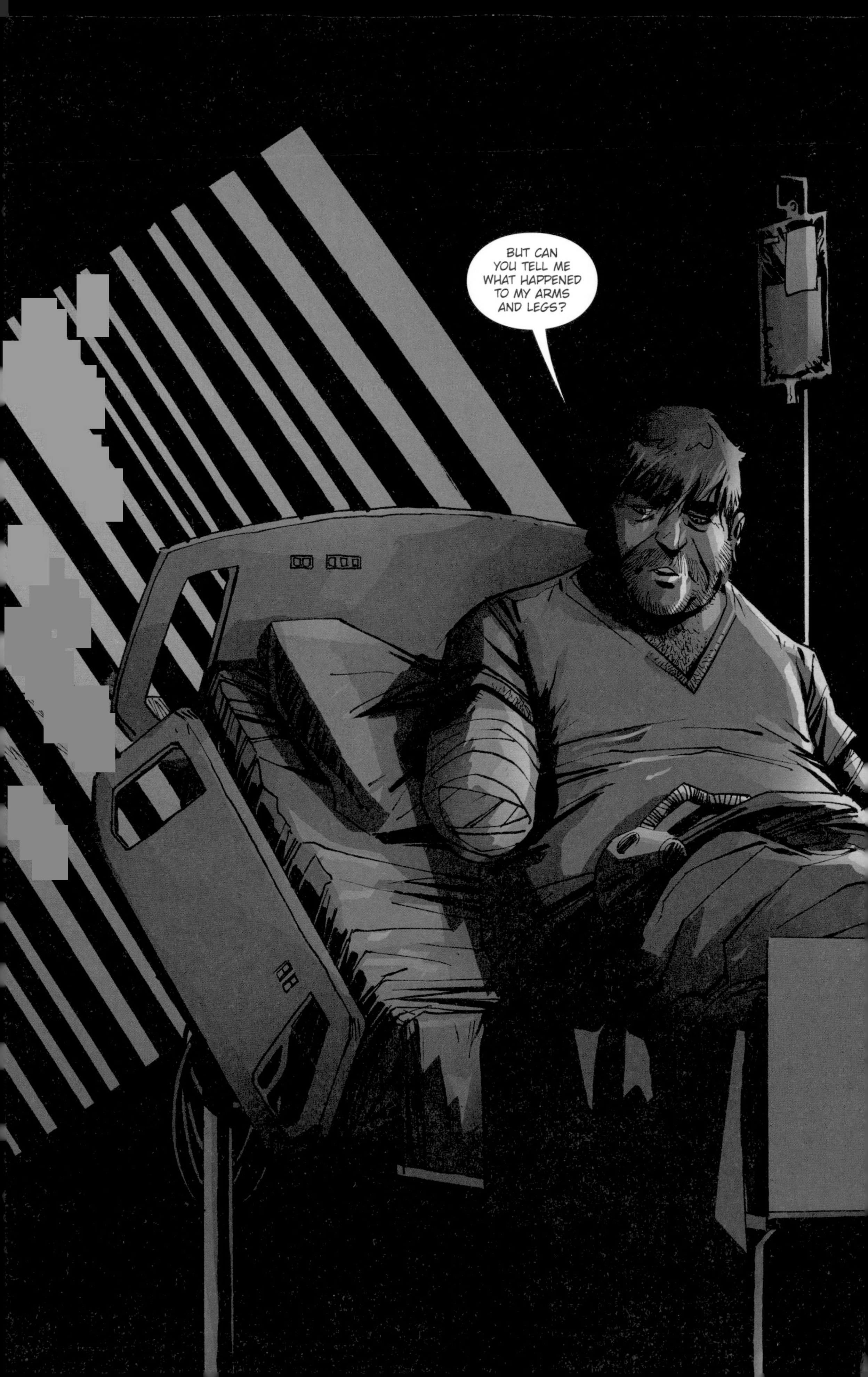
BUT CAN YOU TELL ME WHAT HAPPENED TO MY ARMS AND LEGS?

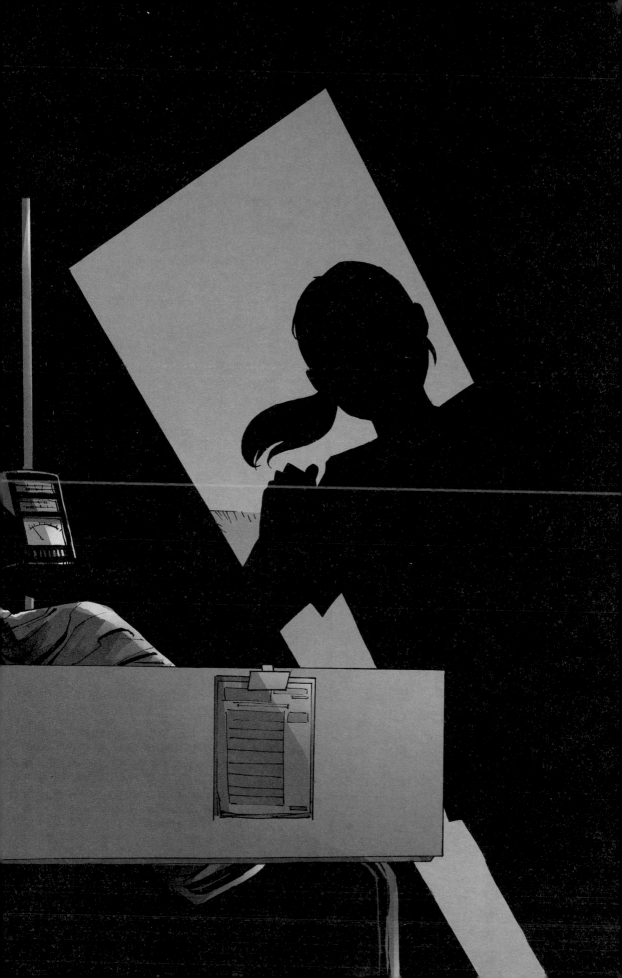

TO

BE

CONTI

NUED.

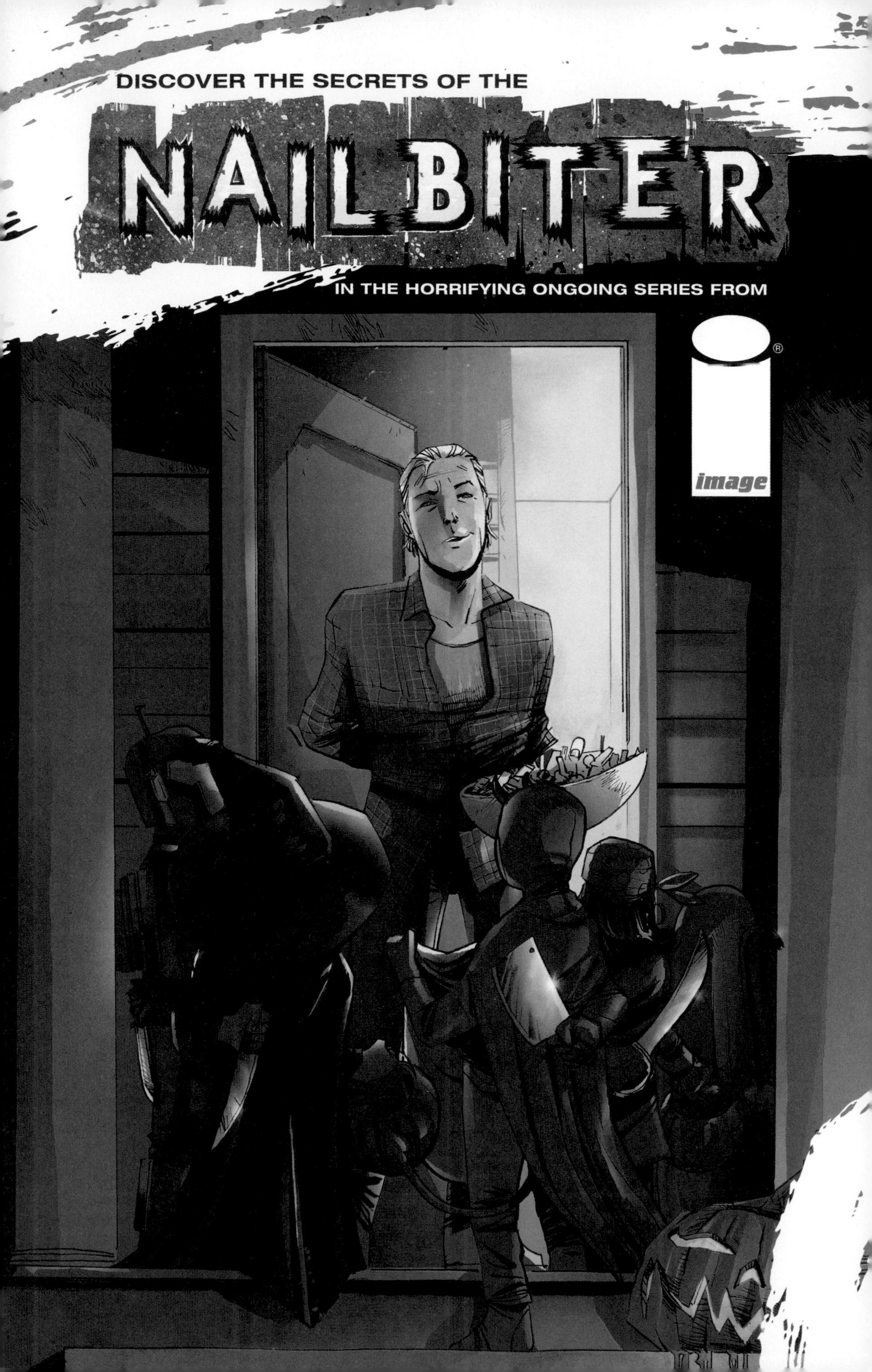

DISCOVER THE SECRETS OF THE
NAILBITER
IN THE HORRIFYING ONGOING SERIES FROM
image

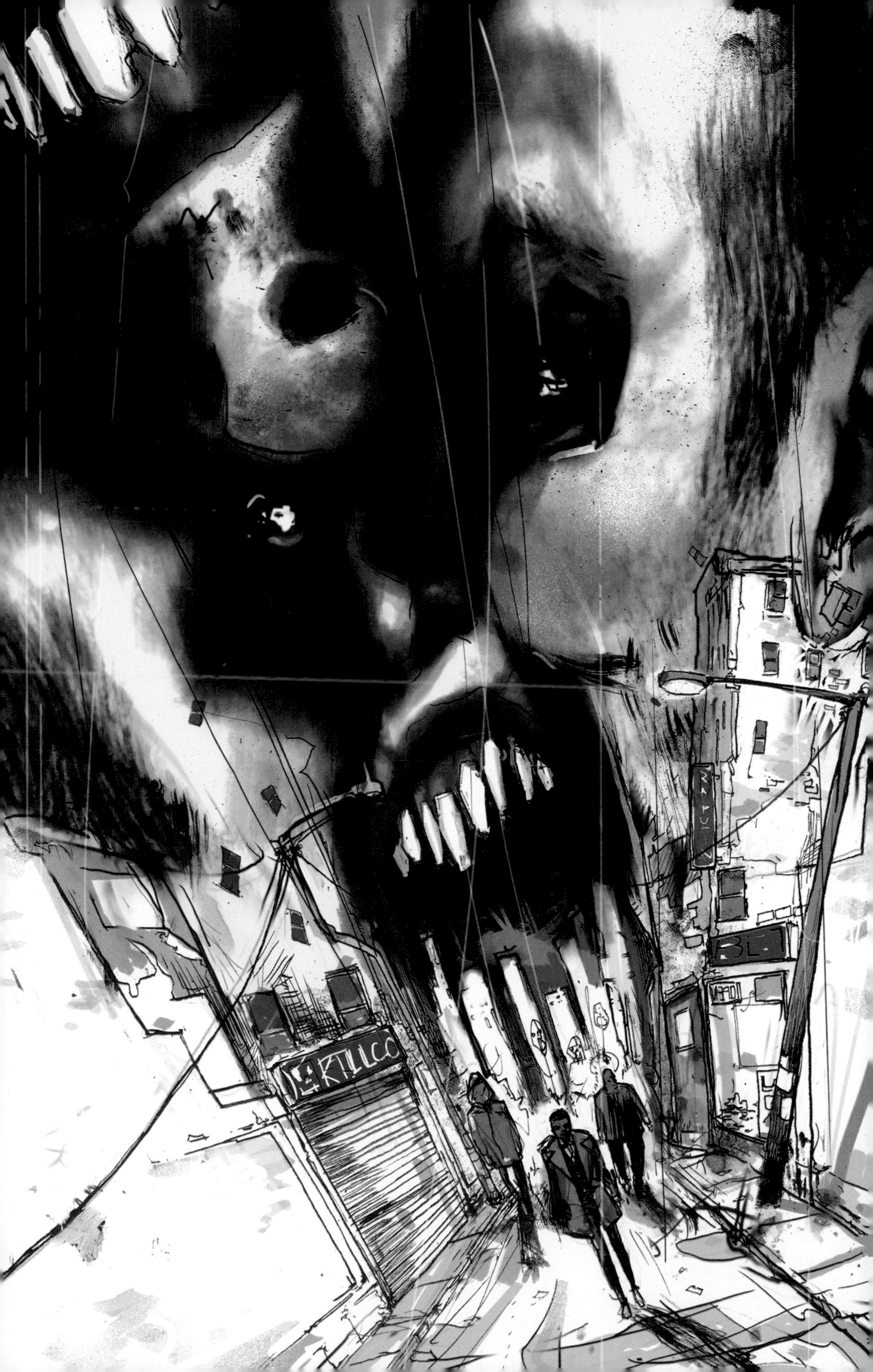

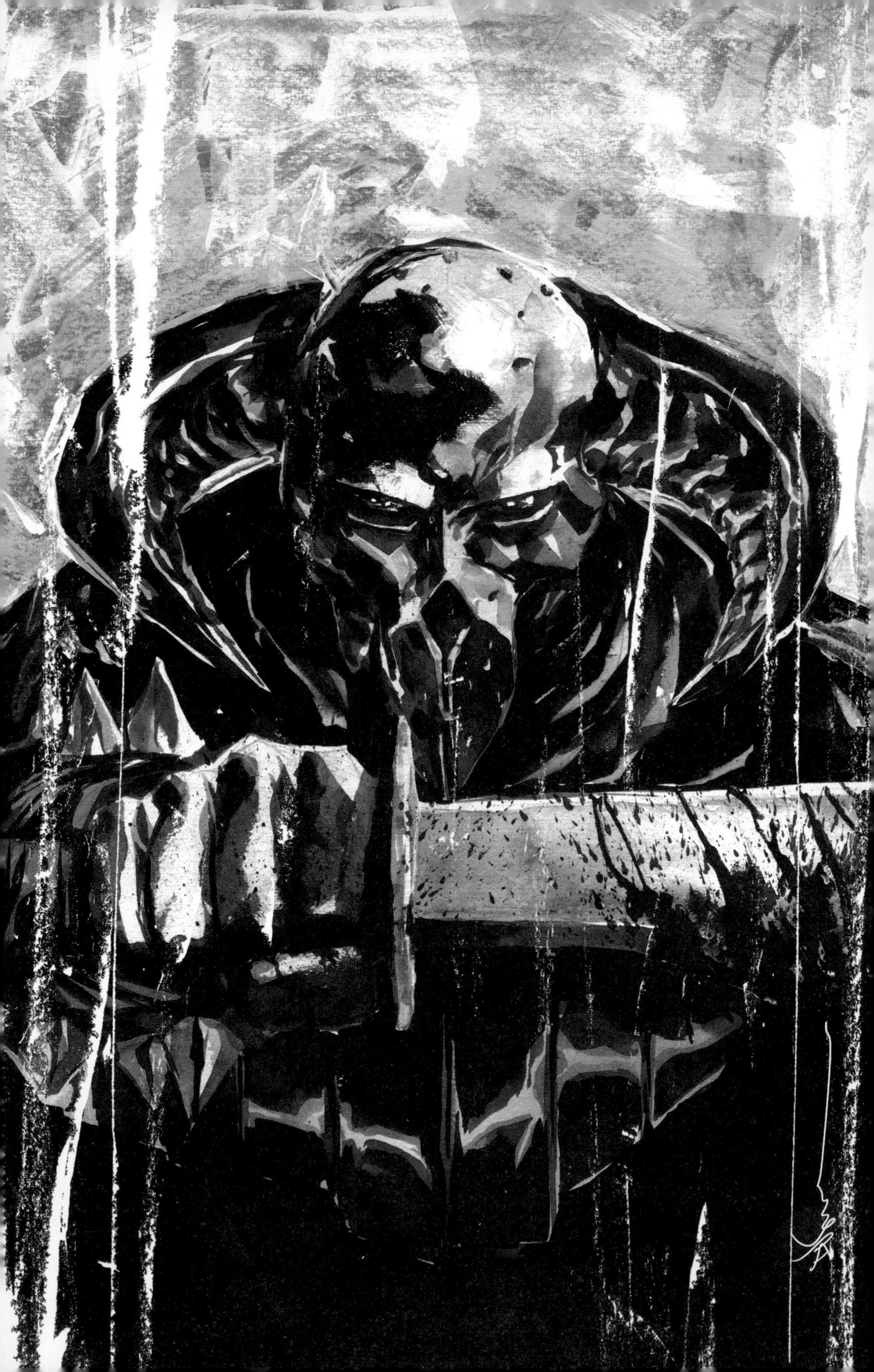

One of my favorite scenes from the third Nailbiter trade was the sequence where the Bee-Man was getting murdered with Barker forced to watch juxtaposed with Warren taunting Finch. So we decided to show the process for those pages here. This isn't my normal script format, but I had to change it up to make it easier on Mike, Adam, John and I. Normally I wouldn't do layouts for comics I work on but here I wanted to make sure my crazy idea would actually work.

PAGE TEN-ELEVEN

Mike, You are going to hate me when you see what I think we should do here.
Yes, I know it's crazy complicated but just imagine how rad it will look. It will really create a LOT of tension.
It's a series of small panels. I already sized them to make sure it can work. And did dialogue tests to make sure it can fit with the dialogue.
There are four things going on with this page.
1) Barker watching the Bee-man get killed.
2) The Beeman getting killed
3) Warren and Finch arguing.
4) Bee-man decapitated body parts.
The body parts will almost seem like they are laid out in order on the table.
Death by gutter as Barker watches the Butcher and the Master kill the Bee-man. We don't really show the death of the Bee-Man, just that he is being dissected. This is going to be super complicated, so I drew an example.

Going from left to right with each layer:

LAYER ONE

1. We see a meat cleaver raised up high. It's shining and clean here. The Butchers's gloved hand is holding it.

2. Barker's face looking confused. Unsure about what is about to happen. We can see her full head here. We'll get closer later.

BARKER (whispering): Oh my god.

3. Warren and Finch. Warren yelling. Same place we left them with Finch threatening Warren.

WARREN: Hurt me, Finch.

4. BLOODY SFX

SFX: CHOP!

5. Severed Left Hand. Belongs to the bee-man.

6. Warren's face yelling

WARREN: Take out all your troubles on me.

7. Barker's face looking scared, getting closer in on her.

8. Warren yelling.

WARREN: You know you want to! Unleash that temper.

LAYER TWO

1. The now bloody cleaver is coming down fast, but we don't see what it hits.

2. Severed Left foot

3. Barker is holding her hands to her mouth and looking scared.

BARKER (whispering): ...no...no...

4. Finch yelling.

FINCH: I WILL!

5. Bloody sound effects.

SFX: CHOP!

6. Warren yelling

WARREN: HURT ME!

7. LEFT SHOULDER

8. Barker looks scared again, but we are much closer in on her.

BAKER (whispering): ... jesus...

LAYER THREE

1. Warren getting angry.

WARREN: I killed people

2 The cleaver comes slamming down again fast.

3 Bloody chop sound effects.

SFX: CHOP! CHOP!

4. Bloody Legs with cuts in them.

5. Warren yelling

WARREN: LOTS of people!

6. TORSO That's been partially open and looks like someone did surgery on it.

7 Bloody chop sound effects.

SFX: CHOP!

8 HEAD- The bee-man's head has been cut off. He is clearly dead. We can see the edge of his neck where his head was cut off.

LAYER FOUR

1. Warren yelling

WARREN: And it was GREAT.

2. RIGHT FOOT

3. Bloody chop!

SFX: CHOP!

4. Warren yelling

WARREN: The time of my life.

5. The bloody cleaver raised up in the air.

6. Finch yelling! Just him. Angry.

FINCH: SHUT UP!

7. RIGHT SHOULDER

8. BLOODY CHOP!

SFX: CHOP!

LAYER FIVE

1. The meat cleaver is really bloody now. Just lots and lots of blood flying into the air.

2. Barker eyes full of terror. Maybe we can even see a hint of the meat cleaver in the reflection of her eye. You can go in super close on the eye so we can see it.

3. Warren yelling!

WARREN: And I got away with it.

4 Bloody Chop! Over taking the panel. Cropped within the panel.

SFX: CHOP! CHOP! CHOP! CHOP! CHOP!

5. RIGHT HAND- Severed.

6. FINCH YELLING About to put the pliers into Warren's mouth.

FINCH: You're going to pay!

7. Warren yelling.

WARREN: DO IT.

8. WARREN REALLY YELLING!

WARREN (LOUD): DO ITTTT!!

This is the layout I did to make sure the idea worked.

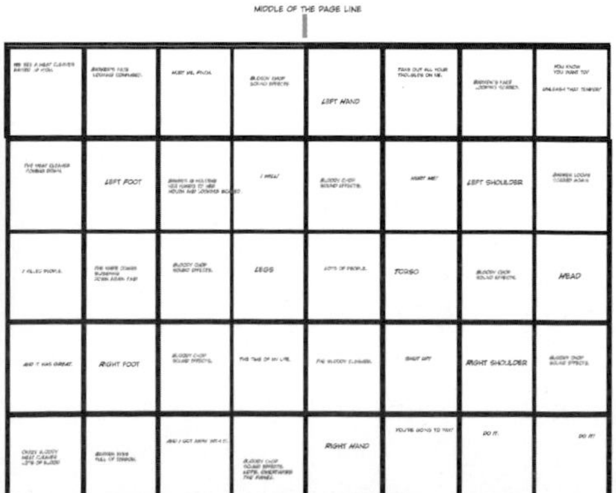
MIDDLE OF THE PAGE LINE

To celebrate the 2nd year of ***Nailbiter*** we had two guest cover artists. Both were showcased in the previous two pages:

PAGE 119: RILEY ROSSMO
PAGE 120: DUSTIN NGUYEN

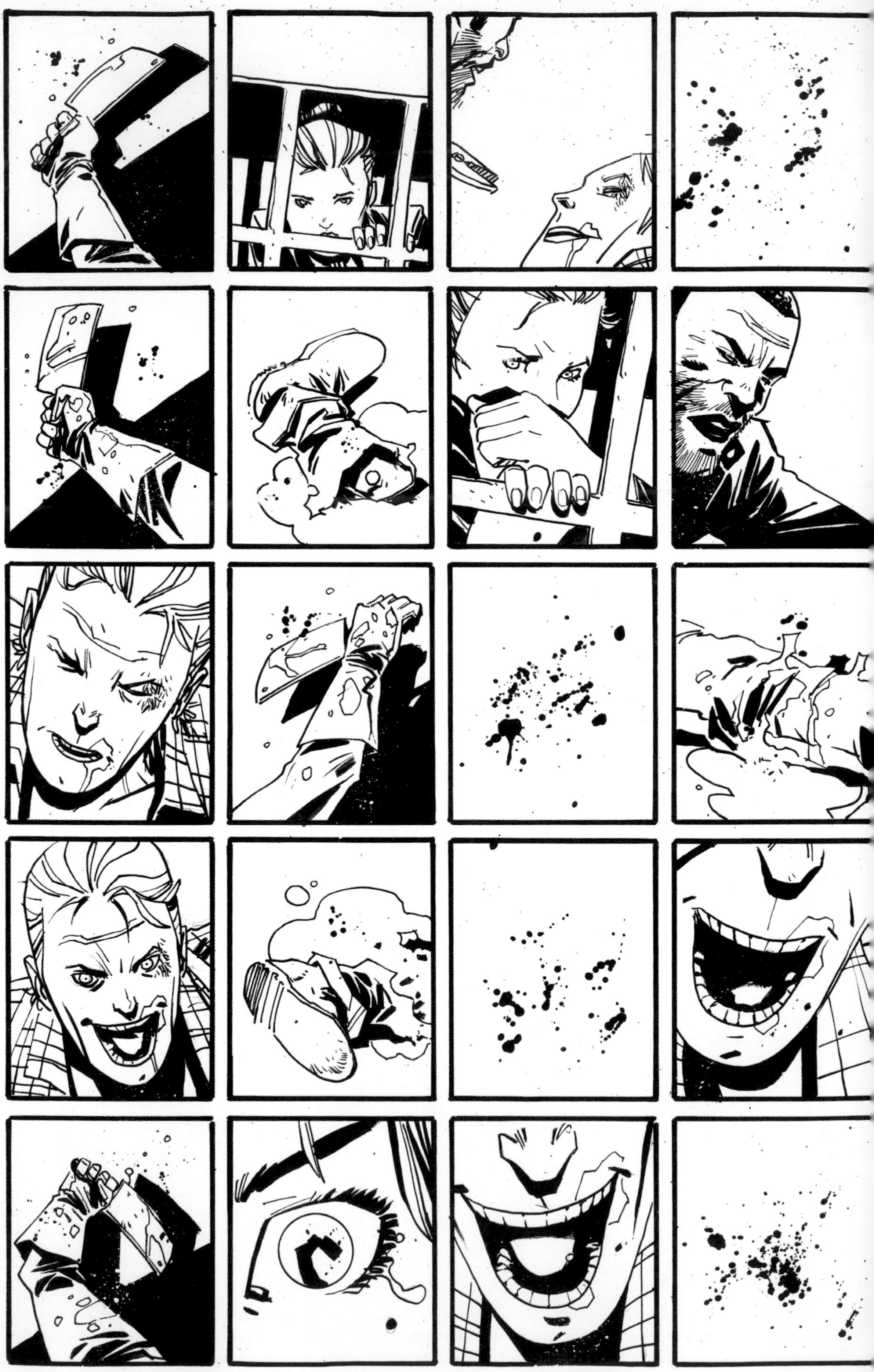

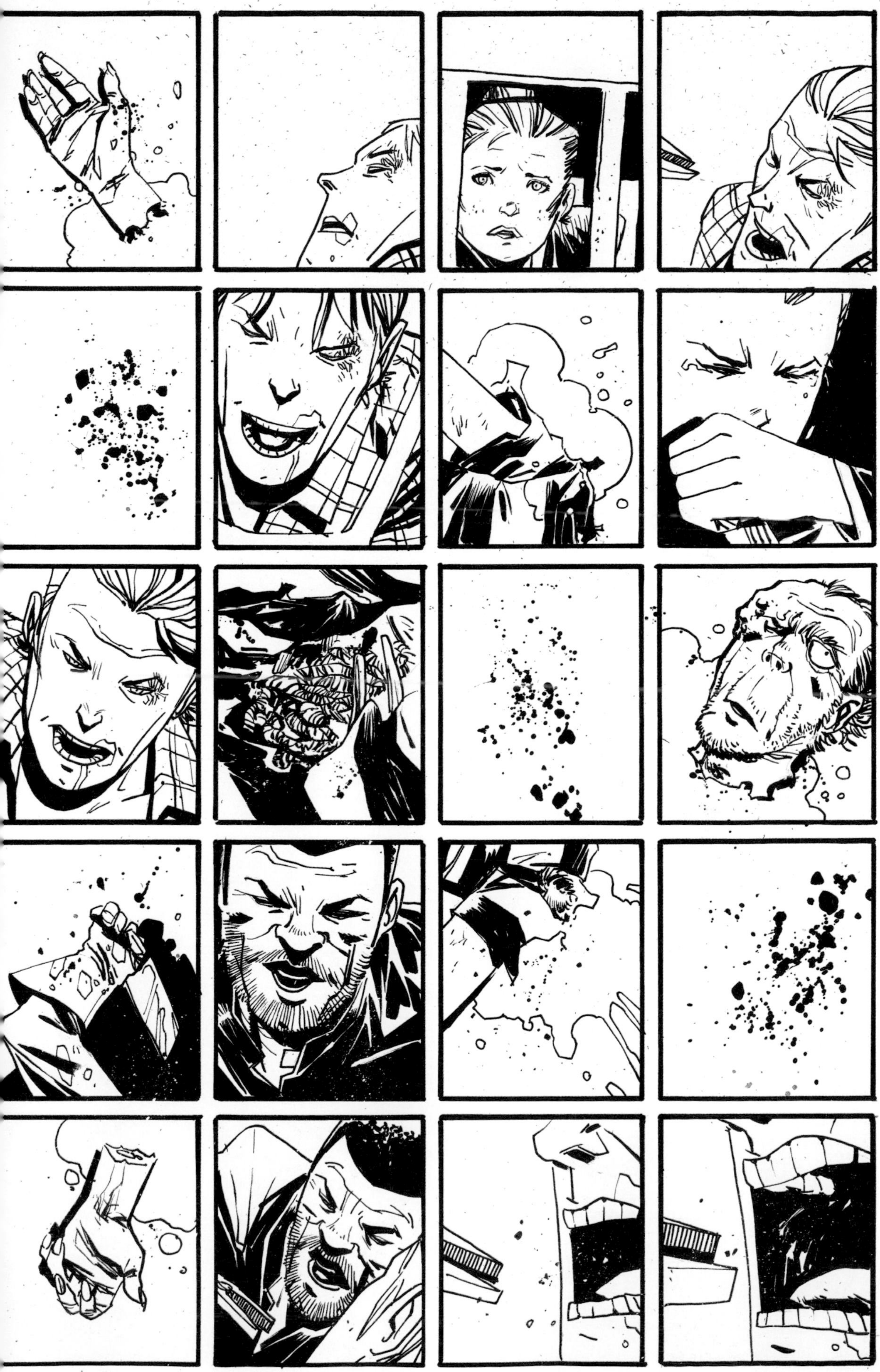

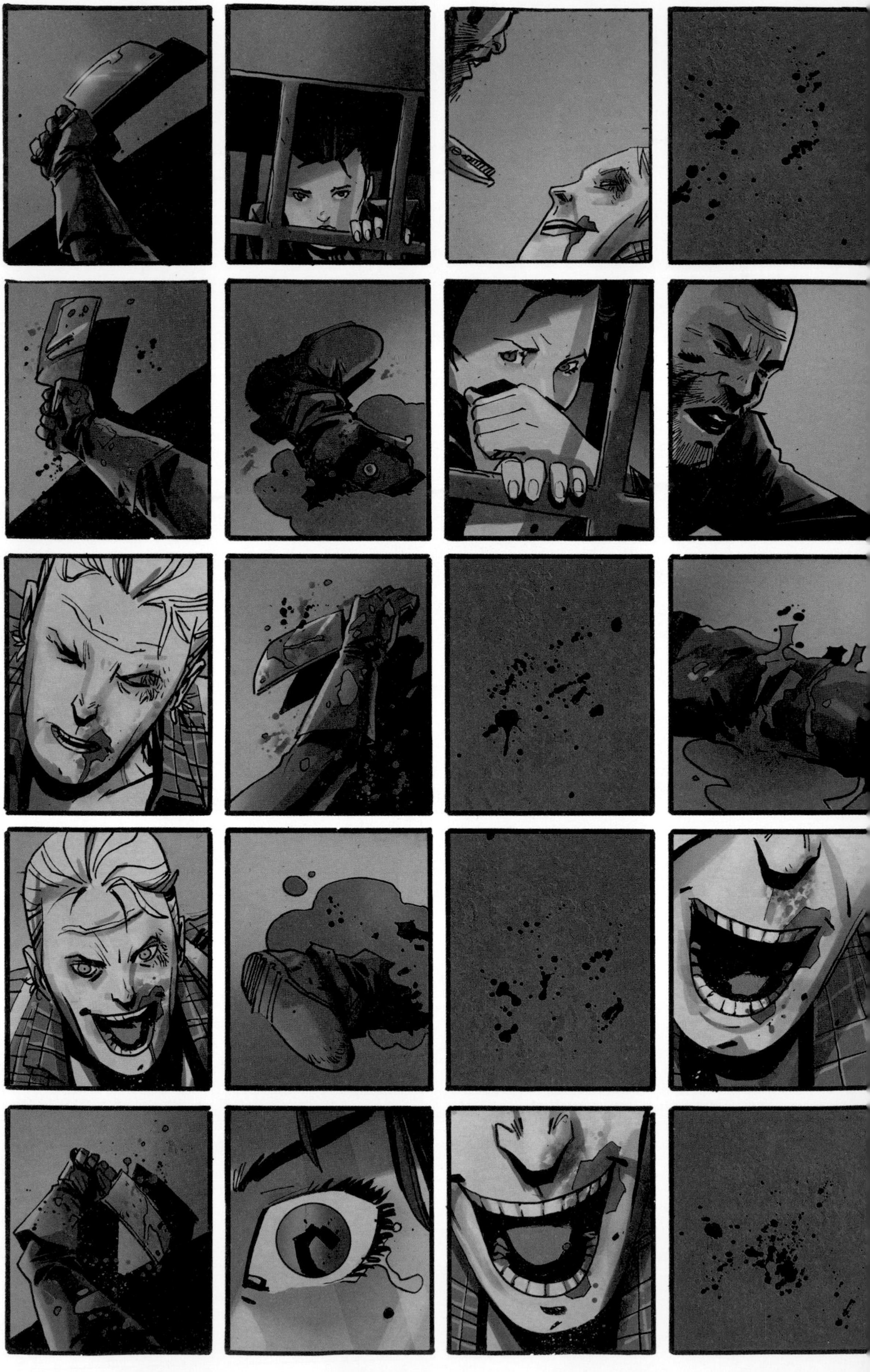

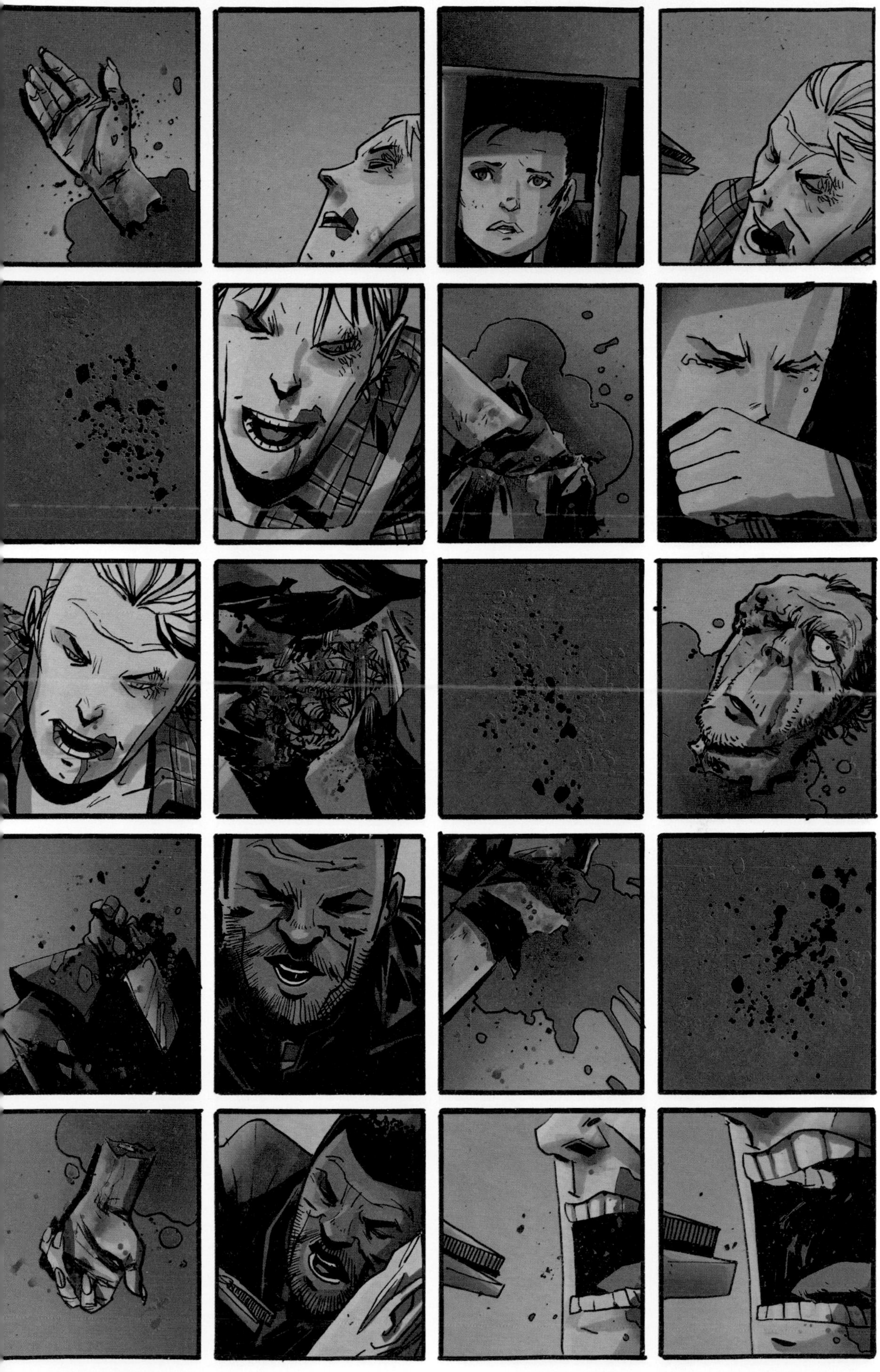

IF YOU LIKED

NAILBITER

TRY THESE OTHER COLLECTIONS:

JOSHUA WILLIAMSON · GORAN SUDZUKA · MIROSLAV MRVA
GHOSTED
VOLUME ONE · HAUNTED HEIST

GHOSTED VOL. 1
Joshua Williamson,
Goran Sudzuka & Miroslav Mrva

144 PAGES SOFTCOVER
ISBN: 978-1607068365

GHOSTED VOL. 2
Joshua Williamson,
Davide Gianfelice & Miroslav Mrva

120 PAGES SOFTCOVER
ISBN: 978-1632150462

JOSHUA WILLIAMSON · DAVIDE GIANFELICE · MIROSLAV MRVA
GHOSTED
VOLUME TWO · BOOKS OF THE DEAD

WILLIAMSON · GIANFELICE · SUDZUKA · MRVA
GHOSTED
VOLUME THREE · DEATH WISH

GHOSTED VOL. 3
Joshua Williamson, Goran Sudzuka,
Davide Gianfelice, Miroslav Mrva

120 PAGES SOFTCOVER
ISBN: 978-1632150516

GHOSTED VOL. 4
Joshua Williamson, Goran Sudzuka,
Vladmir Krstic , Juan Jose Ryp &
Miroslav Mrva

112 PAGES SOFTCOVER
ISBN: 978-1-63215-317-3

WILLIAMSON · LACI · RYP · MRVA
GHOSTED
VOLUME FOUR · GHOST TOWN

BIRTHRIGHT
WILLIAMSON BRESSAN LUCAS
VOLUME ONE
HOMECOMING

BIRTHRIGHT VOL. 1
Joshua Williamson,
Andrei Bressan & Adriano Lucas

128 PAGES SOFTCOVER
ISBN: 978-1-63215-231-2

BIRTHRIGHT VOL. 2
Joshua Williamson,
Andrei Bressan & Adriano Lucas

128 PAGES SOFTCOVER
ISBN: 978-1-63215-446-0

BIRTHRIGHT
WILLIAMSON BRESSAN LUCAS

image

PLEASE VISIT: **IMAGECOMICS.COM** for more information.
To find your local comic shop call **1-888-comicbook** or visit **www.comicshop.us**

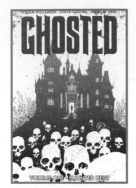